Microsoft

Microsoft
Copilot Pro
Step by Step

Lisa Crosbie

Microsoft Copilot Pro Step by Step
Published with the authorization of Microsoft Corporation by:
Pearson Education, Inc.

ISBN-13: 978-0-13-536942-5
ISBN-10: 0-13-536942-8

Library of Congress Control Number: 2024948518

1 2024

Trademarks

Microsoft and the trademarks listed at *http://www.microsoft.com* on the "Trademarks" webpage are trademarks of the Microsoft group of companies. All other marks are property of their respective owners.

Warning and Disclaimer

Editor-in-Chief
Brett Bartow

Executive Editor
Loretta Yates

Associate Editor
Shourav Bose

Development Editor
Songlin Qiu

Managing Editor
Sandra Schroeder

Senior Project Editor
Tracey Croom

Copy Editor
Dan Foster

Indexer
Valerie Haynes Perry

Proofreader
Kim Wimpsett

Technical Editor
Naga Santhosh Reddy Vootukuri

Editorial Assistant
Cindy Teeters

Cover Designer
Twist Creative, Seattle

Compositor
Danielle Foster

Figure Credits
Page 137: Courtesy of NASA
Page 167: OpenTable, Inc

Contents at a glance

Contents

Part 1: Get started with Copilot Pro

Part 2: Use Copilot Pro on the web and the mobile app

Part 3: Use Copilot Pro in Microsoft 365 applications

8   Copilot in PowerPoint **287**

Acknowledgments

As someone who has had a long career in book publishing, it has been a fascinating experience to be on this side of the publishing process for the first time. Thank you to the huge team of people behind making this book a reality, from the inception of the idea to getting the book in the hands of readers. I appreciate you.

Special thanks to the publishing and editorial team who have kept me on track and made the book better at every stage. Thank you to Loretta Yates for discovering me and inviting me to be part of this series, Shourav Bose for guiding me through the entire process, Songlin Qiu for getting the structure into shape, Dan Foster for making it all read beautifully, and Tracey Croom for bringing everything together so seamlessly, especially through last minute updates. Thank you also to my technical editor, Naga Santhosh Reddy Vootukuri (Sunny), for making sure everything was accurate and up to date, and for additional tips, validation, and positive feedback throughout.

I am grateful to my amazing cheer squad of family, friends, and colleagues who instinctively understood how important this project was to me. Thank you for your enthusiasm and encouragement, which was such an important part of keeping me going through the many months of hard work.

My deepest gratitude and thanks to my husband, David Barnes, for the unwavering support that allows me to pursue my dreams as we navigate life together. I could not have done this without you.

With love to my daughters Steph and Bridget, and to Mum for reminding me how much this means to eight-year-old Lisa.

For Dad, who sparked my interest in tech from the start. You loved a good "how to" book, and you would have been the first person with a copy in your hand, asking me a million questions.

About the author

 **Lisa Crosbie** is a highly respected expert in Microsoft business applications, with a focus on leveraging Copilot and low-code solutions to transform how businesses operate. A five-time Microsoft Most Valuable Professional and Microsoft Certified Trainer, Lisa is known for her ability to break down complex technologies into easy-to-understand concepts, making them accessible and enjoyable for everyone.

Lisa's extensive experience and enthusiasm for technology have made her a sought-after speaker at international conferences and a trusted educator through her popular YouTube channel. She is passionate about empowering beginners to take their first steps with tools like Copilot, helping them build confidence and skills from the ground up. Lisa is also focused on staying at the cutting edge of technology, regularly sharing insights on the latest advancements in Copilot and Power Platform and educating the community on how to leverage these technologies to solve real-world challenges.

Lisa lives in Melbourne, Australia, with her husband, two daughters, one dog, two guinea pigs, and three fish. She is a long-time reader and first-time author.

Introduction

Copilot Pro is a Microsoft Copilot subscription for individuals who want to work with generative AI in Microsoft 365 applications and get access to premium experiences for creating content. Copilot Pro works alongside you as a virtual assistant embedded in Excel, Outlook, Word, PowerPoint, and OneNote, helping you generate a first draft, edit or rewrite for different purposes, summarize, understand, and analyze your content in spreadsheets, emails, documents, presentations, and notes. It also helps you brainstorm and develop new ideas, generate images, kickstart creative projects, and get answers to your questions across web, mobile, and Windows experiences.

Who this book is for

Copilot Pro Step by Step and other books in the Step by Step series are designed for beginning to intermediate computer users. This book introduces you to the fundamentals of generative AI and Microsoft Copilot, providing hands-on skills and techniques to enable you to use these tools effectively. The examples shown in the book cover both home and business scenarios. Copilot Pro is for ideal for power users, small business owners, home office workers, freelancers, creators, consultants, students, researchers, programmers, hobbyists, community leaders, or anyone looking to enhance their productivity and creativity with generative AI. The skills you learn in this book are also applicable to Copilot for Microsoft 365, although this book does not cover the additional apps and features that are exclusive to the Copilot for Microsoft 365 license.

The Step by Step approach

This book is divided into three parts. Part 1 explores core concepts of Microsoft Copilot, generative AI, and effective prompting techniques. Part 2 covers the Copilot Pro experiences for web and mobile. Part 3 demonstrates how to use Copilot Pro inside the Microsoft 365 applications, with a chapter dedicated to each application: Excel, Outlook, Word, PowerPoint, and OneNote. This structure allows readers who are new to generative AI to learn the basic concepts and skills, while readers who are familiar with prompting and other generative AI experiences can focus on material in the specific apps that are of most interest to them.

At the end of each chapter, you will find a series of practice tasks that you can complete on your own by using the skills taught in the chapter. Generative AI is creative by nature, so even as you work through the tasks, you will discover new possibilities depending on your context and prompts.

Features and conventions

This book has been designed to lead you step-by-step through all the tasks you're likely to want to perform with Copilot Pro. The topics are all self-contained, so you can start at the beginning and work your way through all the chapters or reference them independently. The following features of this book will help you locate specific information:

- **Detailed table of contents** Browse the listing of the topics, sections, and sidebars within each chapter.

- **Chapter thumb tabs and running heads** Identify the pages of each chapter by the thumb tabs on the book pages' open fore edge. Find a specific chapter by number or title by looking at the running heads at the top of even-numbered (verso) pages.

- **Topic-specific running heads** Within a chapter, quickly locate the topic you want by looking at the running heads at the top of odd-numbered (recto) pages.

- **Practice tasks page tabs** Easily locate the practice tasks at the end of each chapter by looking for the full-page stripe on the book's fore edge.

- **Detailed index** Look up coverage of specific tasks and features in the index at the back of the book.

You can save time when reading this book by understanding how the Step by Step series provides procedural instructions and auxiliary information and identifies on-screen and physical elements that you interact with. The following table lists content formatting conventions used in this book.

Convention	Meaning
TIP	This reader aid provides a helpful hint or shortcut to simplify a task.
IMPORTANT	This reader aid alerts you to a common problem or provides information necessary to successfully complete a procedure.
SEE ALSO	This reader aid directs you to more information about a topic in this book or elsewhere.
1. Numbered steps 2. 3.	Numbered steps guide you through generic procedures in each topic and hands-on practice tasks at the end of each chapter.
■ Bulleted lists	Bulleted lists indicate single-step procedures and sets of multiple alternative procedures.
Interface objects	In procedures and practice tasks, semibold black text indicates on-screen elements that you should select (click or tap).
User input	Light semibold formatting identifies specific information that you should enter when completing procedures or practice tasks.
Ctrl+P	A plus sign between two keys indicates that you must select those keys at the same time. For example, "press Ctrl+P" directs you to hold down the Ctrl key while you press the P key.
Emphasis and *URLs*	In expository text, italic formatting identifies web addresses and words or phrases we want to emphasize.

Download the practice files

Before you can complete the exercises in this book, you need to download the book's practice files to your computer. For access to these practice files, and other resources, visit *MicrosoftPressStore.com/register*, sign in or create a new account, and register ISBN 9780135369425 by December 31, 2027.

 IMPORTANT Copilot Pro is a paid subscription and is not available from this website. You will need to purchase a Copilot Pro license before using this book.

The following table lists the practice files for this book.

Chapter	File
Chapter 3: Copilot on the Web	Corporate Catering Practice Task.docx
	Contoso Ltd Digital Transformation.pdf
Chapter 5: Copilot in Excel	Packaging Inventory.xlsx
Chapter 9: Copilot in OneNote	Catering Notes.onepkg

Important note about changes to Copilot

Generative AI tools, including Copilot Pro, are evolving at a rapid pace that is unlike anything we have experienced before. As the technology evolves, Microsoft is constantly innovating to take advantage of the latest capabilities, which means that Copilot user interfaces can look and function differently from one week to the next. As a result, there may be some differences between the steps and screenshots in this book, and what's currently deployed, although the core principles and concepts remain the same. Working with this cutting-edge technology is an exciting journey, and I encourage you to embrace the growth mindset that will help you adopt these tools and the nature of constant change that goes with that.

We will do our best to keep this content up to date in subsequent editions of the book. You can also find updates and links to the latest resources on the Microsoft Copilot Pro homepage at *copilot.cloud.microsoft/en-us/copilot-pro* or on Lisa's YouTube channel at *youtube.com/lisacrosbie*.

Get support and give feedback

The following sections provide information about getting help with this book and contacting us to provide feedback or report errors.

Errata

We've made every effort to ensure the accuracy of this book and its companion content. Any errors that have been reported since this book was published are listed at:

MicrosoftPressStore.com/CopilotSBS/errata

If you discover an error that is not already listed, please submit it to us at the same page.

For additional book support and information, please visit *MicrosoftPressStore.com/Support*.

Please note that product support for Microsoft software and hardware is not offered through the previous addresses. For help with Microsoft software or hardware, visit *support.microsoft.com*.

Stay in touch

Let's keep the conversation going! We're on X/Twitter at: *twitter.com/MicrosoftPress*

Part 1

Get started with Copilot Pro

Introduction to Copilot Pro

Generative AI is a type of artificial intelligence that can create new content, such as text, images, or code, based on a user providing a natural language request or instruction, known as a *prompt*. Generative AI is powered by large language models (LLMs), which are trained on a vast amount of data from books, websites, and other sources. It uses this knowledge to provide you with a human-like response based on the request or instruction in your prompt.

Microsoft Copilot brings generative AI into your everyday computing and mobile experiences, at home or at work. Copilot is like your assistant, helping you to be more creative or productive wherever you are working. You can use Copilot to generate new ideas, help you generate or rewrite your draft, help you create to-do lists and plans, analyze your data, summarize long blocks of text or email threads, extract action items from meeting notes, answer questions about your content, search for information on the web, and generate images.

Copilot Pro is a premium Microsoft Copilot subscription for individuals who want to work with generative AI in Microsoft 365 applications and get access to premium experiences for creating content. In this chapter, you will learn all about what Copilot Pro is and what it can do, compare it with other Microsoft Copilot subscriptions, learn how to get started, and learn how to access Copilot Pro on the web, on mobile devices, and in Microsoft 365 applications. You will also understand the core principles of data privacy and responsible AI that apply when using Copilot Pro.

In this chapter

- Get started with Copilot Pro
- Access Copilot Pro on the web, on mobile devices, and in Windows
- Use Copilot Pro in Microsoft 365 applications
- Provide feedback to Microsoft

Practice files

No practice files are necessary to complete the practice tasks in this chapter.

Get started with Copilot Pro

Copilot Pro is a premium Microsoft Copilot subscription for individuals, ideal for power users, small business owners, home office workers, freelancers, creators, consultants, students, researchers, programmers, hobbyists, community leaders, or anyone who wants to boost their productivity and creativity using generative AI.

Copilot Pro offers faster and higher-quality performance when using Microsoft Copilot on web and mobile platforms. It also enables the use of Copilot features in Excel, Outlook, Word, PowerPoint, and OneNote.

Copilot Pro can help you:

- Draft new content for documents, emails, presentations, and notes.
- Get started with a creative writing project.
- Generate, brainstorm, and work through new ideas.
- Compare, understand, and analyze spreadsheet data.
- Rewrite your text in different ways and suggest ways to edit your work.
- Edit and organize notes and presentations and add images to your work.
- Summarize documents, extract key points and dates, and create to-do lists.
- Answer questions about your content or about related ideas.

Compare Copilot Pro with other Microsoft Copilot versions

Microsoft Copilot is available in different versions that you can choose from depending on the features you want to use. In this section, you will learn the differences between Copilot Pro and the other available Copilot versions.

Copilot (Free)

The free version of Microsoft Copilot enables you to use generative AI on Windows, on the web, and on mobile devices. You can chat using text, voice, and images, and work with the context of webpage content or PDFs open in the browser.

You can create images from text descriptions using Designer, which is part of the free version of Copilot. Copilot includes "boosts" that provide faster image creation and editing, and the ability to resize images. With the free version of Copilot, you get 15 boosts per day.

You can sign in to the free version of Copilot to access these features with either your Microsoft account or your work account.

- When you sign in to the free version of Copilot using your Microsoft account, you will experience interactions designed for personal use. You will see a carousel of prompt suggestions, a prompt area, and your recent chat history.

When you sign in to Copilot with your Microsoft account, you see a carousel of suggested prompts, a prompt area, and your chat history.

- If you sign in to the free version of Copilot with your work account using your organization's Entra ID, you will also have commercial data protection, which means Microsoft doesn't retain your prompts or responses, it doesn't see your chat data, and it doesn't use any of your chats to train the underlying AI models.

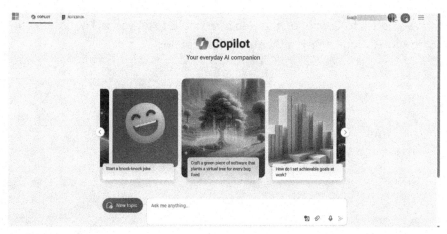

When you sign in to Copilot with your work account using your organization's Entra ID, you have commercial data protection.

When you sign in to Copilot using your work account, you get commercial data protection, indicated by a green security icon.

The free version of Copilot does not include the Copilot features in any Microsoft 365 apps. If you want to use Copilot with Microsoft 365 applications such as Excel, Word, PowerPoint, Outlook, and OneNote, you will need a paid Copilot Pro or Microsoft 365 Copilot license.

Copilot Pro

Copilot Pro is a premium subscription for individuals, for personal or professional use. You must use your Microsoft account (not your work account) to purchase a Copilot Pro license, and you do not need a Microsoft 365 subscription. However, if you add Copilot Pro to your Microsoft 365 Personal or Family subscription, you will unlock some additional features.

 SEE ALSO The next section in this chapter shows you step by step how to sign up for a Copilot Pro trial or license.

When you sign in to Copilot on the web with Copilot Pro, you will notice that the heading shows "Copilot Pro" rather than just "Copilot."

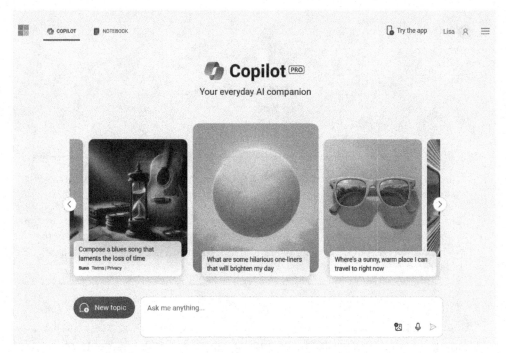

When you sign in to Copilot using your Microsoft account with Copilot Pro, you will see that the heading has changed to Copilot Pro. You will have access to premium features that you don't get with the free version.

When signed in with your Copilot Pro subscription, you get premium features using Copilot on the web and mobile devices, as well as access to Copilot features in some of the Microsoft 365 applications—Excel, Outlook, Word, PowerPoint, and OneNote—as follows:

- **Priority access to GPT-4 Turbo:** With a Copilot Pro subscription, when you use Copilot on the web or mobile devices, you get the option to switch to the best available large language model (known as GPT-4 Turbo), which provides faster and higher quality responses than the GPT-4 large language model. You will also get priority access to this GPT-4 Turbo model at peak usage times.

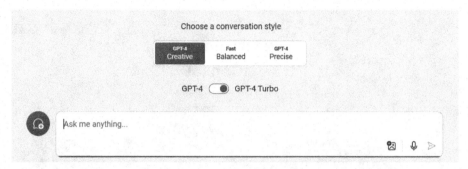

Copilot Pro gives you priority access to the GPT-4 Turbo model. You can use this toggle to switch it on or off.

> ⚠️ **IMPORTANT** The GPT-4 Turbo toggle switch only appears when you have the Creative conversation style selected. It does not add value in the Balanced or Precise style.

- Additional boosts for image generation: Copilot Pro gives you 100 boosts per day for image generation (rather than the 15 you get with the free version). Image generation can often take multiple prompts and refinements, so if you want to generate images regularly, additional boosts will make this process faster and better.

Copilot Pro gives you 100 boosts per day for faster and more flexible image generation. The coin icon at the bottom right of the image generation results shows you how many boosts you have left.

- Copilot features in Microsoft 365 apps: With your Copilot Pro subscription, you can also use Copilot in Excel, Outlook, Word, and PowerPoint on the web. If you also have a Microsoft 365 Personal or Family subscription in addition to Copilot Pro, you can use Copilot in the desktop versions of these apps, and you can use Copilot in OneNote.

1

Microsoft 365 Copilot

Microsoft 365 Copilot is a premium subscription for organizations. You must have a Microsoft 365 business or enterprise subscription and purchase the add-on Copilot for Microsoft 365 license.

Microsoft 365 Copilot provides additional capabilities over Copilot Pro because it works across all your data at work—emails, meetings, chats, documents, and more. This adds some capabilities to Copilot on the web and mobile devices, allowing you to chat with your work data. It enables you to create content in Copilot in Word and PowerPoint using existing documents and unlocks Copilot features in a wider suite of Microsoft 365 applications, including Microsoft Teams, Loop, Whiteboard, Planner, and Stream.

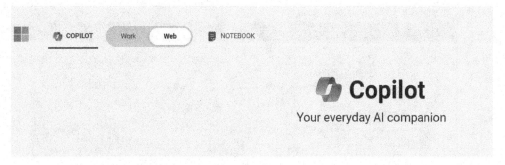

When you use Copilot on the web with a Copilot for Microsoft 365 license, you can toggle between Work and Web content.

⚠️ **IMPORTANT** All the skills you learn in this book about Copilot Pro can also be applied to Copilot for Microsoft 365. However, this book does not cover the additional apps and features that are available only with the Copilot for Microsoft 365 license.

Sign up for a Copilot Pro license

Copilot Pro is a paid subscription that is billed by the month. You can get started by signing up for a free trial.

To sign up for a Copilot Pro license

1. Navigate to the Copilot Pro home page: *https://www.microsoft.com/en-us/store/b/copilotpro*.

> ⚠️ **IMPORTANT** If you are outside the US, you will get a pop-up message asking whether you want to be redirected to the Microsoft store in your country. Choose your home country so that you can enter your payment details in later steps.

You can sign up for a free trial of Copilot Pro from the home page.

2. Scroll down to see the pricing, and then select the **Start your free trial** button.

Scroll down to view the pricing in your local currency, and then select the button to start your free trial.

1

3. You will be taken to the checkout page, where you can review and confirm the price and details of your Copilot Pro subscription.

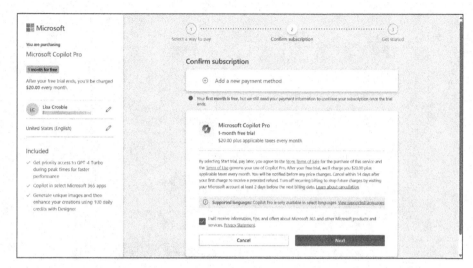

Read and understand the details of the Copilot Pro license, and then select Next to enter payment details.

4. Select the **Next** button, choose a payment method, and enter payment details.

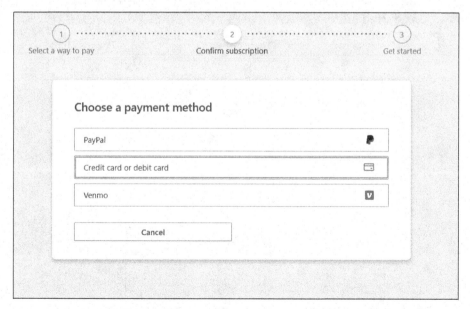

Enter your payment details to continue.

5. Once your payment method has been accepted, you will see a **Start trial, pay later** button appear on the Confirm subscription screen. Select this button.

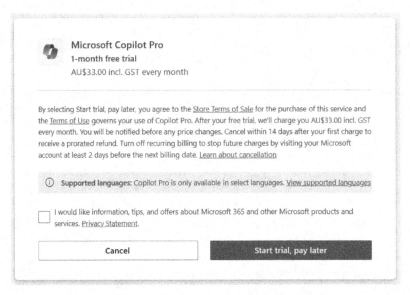

Select the Start trial, pay later button to confirm your trial subscription.

6. Wait for the confirmation message to appear, and then select the **Get started** button.

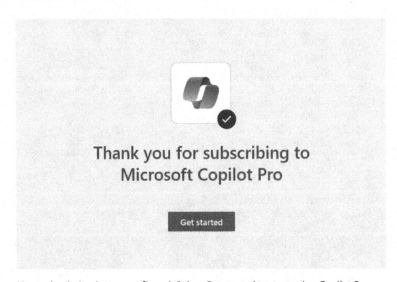

Your subscription is now confirmed. Select Get started to start using Copilot Pro.

7. You will be redirected to Copilot on the web (*https://copilot.microsoft.com*), where you can start chatting with Copilot to generate text, code, or images, get answers to your questions, and more.

8. Add this page to your favorites in your browser.

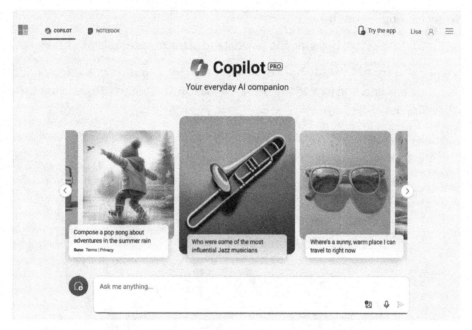

You will be redirected to the main Copilot Pro page on the web where you can start chatting with Copilot to generate content, ask questions, and more.

9. You will receive an email confirming your subscription details, with a link to the Microsoft account Services & subscriptions page where you can manage your subscription (*https://account.microsoft.com/services/copilot*).

Access Copilot Pro on the web, on mobile devices, and in Windows

You can use Copilot across a range of web and mobile devices and in Windows. In this section you will learn about the options available and how to access Copilot Pro through each of these experiences.

Access Copilot Pro on the web

Copilot on the web is the main access point you can use for chatting with Copilot to ask it to generate text, images, or code, or ask it to help you brainstorm an idea or search for an answer to something.

To access Copilot on the web

1. Open the Edge browser and navigate to *https://copilot.microsoft.com*.

2. If you are not already signed in, select the Sign in button at the top right of the screen, and sign in with the personal Microsoft account you used to sign up for Copilot Pro.

3. You will now have the full features of Copilot Pro available using Copilot on the web.

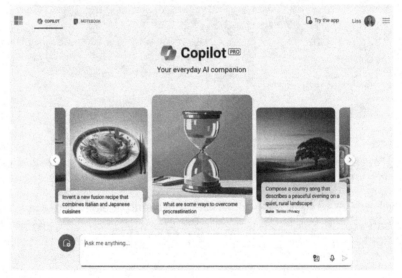

When you have signed in with the Microsoft account you used to sign up for Copilot Pro, you will see your name and icon in the top right corner, and the main heading will show "Copilot Pro."

> **SEE ALSO** You will learn how to write effective prompts for Copilot in Chapter 2, "Writing effective prompts for Copilot." Chapter 3, "Copilot on the web," covers all the features of using Copilot on the web.

> **TIP** You will have a more fully featured experience with Copilot Pro using the Microsoft Edge browser.

Access Copilot Pro in Edge

You can also access Copilot in the Microsoft Edge sidebar, which provides some additional features that are not available with other browsers. Copilot in Edge allows you to ask questions based on the content of the open webpage or a PDF document open in Edge. It also has a feature that allows you to quickly compose paragraphs, emails, ideas, or blog posts in different lengths and tones.

To access Copilot in Edge

1. Select the **Copilot** icon on the upper right side of the Edge browser to open Copilot in the sidebar.

Select the Copilot icon on the side of Edge to open Copilot in the sidebar.

2. Select **Sign in** if you are prompted to do so.

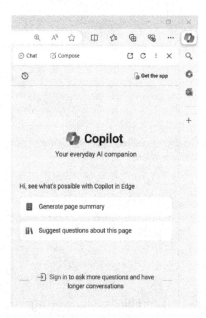

Select Sign in to get the full Copilot Pro experience in the Edge sidebar.

3. You can now use the suggested prompts to summarize or ask questions about the open page or use the main prompt area in the sidebar experience to ask questions with reference to relevant sources.

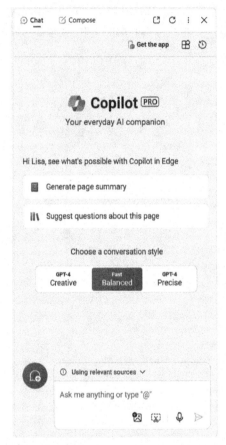

When you have signed in, Copilot will greet you by name. You will also notice that the heading shows you are using the Copilot Pro experience with this license.

 SEE ALSO You will learn more about how to use Copilot in Edge in Chapter 3 of this book.

Access Copilot Pro in Bing

Copilot in Bing provides you with an experience that combines search and generative AI so that with one prompt you get the webpage results you would normally expect from a search engine, as well as an AI-generated response to your search prompt.

To access Copilot on Bing

1. Navigate to bing.com in your browser and enter your search prompt.

Enter your search prompt into Bing to get web search results and an AI-generated answer.

2. Your search results return webpages and an AI-generated Copilot response side-by-side.

Bing returns search results from the web together with a Copilot generated response.

3. You can switch between the Bing search results and the main Copilot page using the options directly under the search area.

You can switch between Search and Copilot experiences in Bing using the options under the search box.

Access Copilot Pro on mobile devices

You can access Copilot Pro on your mobile device and use many of the same features as Copilot Pro on the web to search; generate text, code, or images; and get answers to your questions on the go.

In addition to these features, you can also use the camera and microphone on your mobile device to interact with Copilot. This is useful for dictating prompts and using images from your device or taking photos with your device camera to use in your searches and prompts.

You can also access Copilot Pro on your mobile device to get answers to questions, create text and images, and more.

1

To access Copilot Pro on your iOS or Android device, install and use any of the following apps:

- Microsoft Copilot mobile app. This is a dedicated Copilot experience on mobile devices, and the one recommended by Microsoft.

- Bing mobile app.

- Edge mobile app.

- Microsoft 365 mobile app.

 TIP You can also access Copilot Pro using the browser on your mobile device.

 SEE ALSO You will learn how to use all the features of Copilot Pro using the Microsoft Copilot mobile app in Chapter 4.

Access Copilot Pro in Windows

To access Copilot on Windows devices

1. Select the Copilot icon in your windows taskbar, or open the Copilot app from the Start menu, if the icon is not on your taskbar. If your device has a Copilot key, you can press that to launch Copilot in Windows.

 TIP If you don't find the Copilot icon on your taskbar or via the Start menu, you can download it from the Microsoft store.

Select the Copilot icon at the right end of the taskbar to launch Copilot on Windows.

2. The Copilot Windows app will open, enabling you to chat, search, and generate content without needing to open a web browser.

> **TIP** You can move this app around, resize it, use Alt + Tab to switch to another app, and work with it in the same way as you would with any other Windows app.

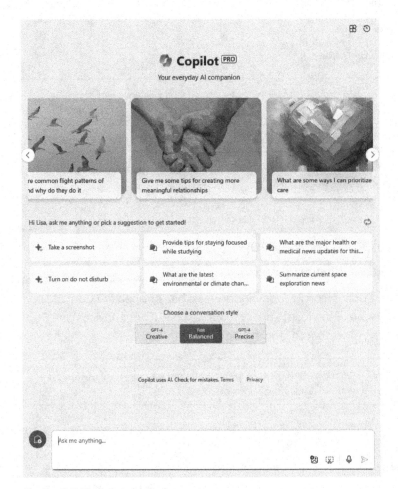

The Copilot Windows app launches on your screen.

The Copilot Windows app includes an additional feature that allows you to take a screenshot to include in your Copilot prompt.

To use a screenshot in you Copilot prompt

1. Open the Copilot Windows app using the icon in your taskbar or via the Start menu.

2. Select the **snip** icon at the bottom right of the Copilot prompt area.

Select the snip icon in the Copilot prompt area to add a screenshot.

3. Select the area of your screen that you want to snip to use in your prompt.

Select the section of the screen you want to snip as a screenshot.

4. Confirm your selection by selecting the blue check mark.

Select the blue check mark to confirm your selection.

5. That screenshot will automatically be added to the Copilot prompt area in the Copilot Windows app. Continue to type your prompt.

The screenshot is added to your prompt.

Use Copilot Pro in Microsoft 365 applications

With your Copilot Pro subscription, you can access Copilot in Excel, Outlook, Word, and PowerPoint on the web.

When working with these apps, make sure you are signed in with the Microsoft account you used to sign up for Copilot Pro. You will find Copilot immediately available in these applications on the web.

 SEE ALSO Refer to the individual chapters for each Microsoft 365 app later in this book for instructions on how to get started with Copilot in each app.

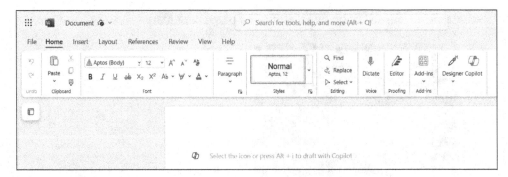

You can launch Copilot in the web apps by selecting the icon at the right end of the Home ribbon.

If you have a Microsoft 365 Personal or Family subscription as well as a Copilot Pro subscription, you can also access Copilot in the desktop versions of Excel, Outlook, Word, and PowerPoint, and use Copilot for OneNote.

> ⚠️ **IMPORTANT** You must be signed into the web or desktop apps using your Microsoft account. You cannot access Copilot Pro features using your work account.

To sign in and use Copilot Pro with the desktop apps

1. Open Microsoft Word and start a new blank document. Make sure you are signed in with the Microsoft account you used to sign up for Copilot Pro.

You must be logged in with the Microsoft account you used to sign up for Copilot Pro.

2. You usually must update your license the first time to see Copilot in the desktop apps. If you don't see the Copilot icon at the right end of the ribbon in the Home menu, follow the steps below.

3. Select the **File** menu, and then select **Account** near the bottom left of the screen.

Select File and then select Account to activate your Copilot Pro license in the desktop apps

4. In the Product Information section, select the **Update License** button.

Select the Update License button in the Product Information section of the Account settings.

5. When prompted, sign in with your Microsoft account.

6. You will see a confirmation message asking you to close and restart all your Microsoft apps.

7. Once you have done that, when you reopen Word (or any of the other desktop apps), you will now find the Copilot icon available on the ribbon.

The Copilot icon is now available on the Home ribbon of the desktop app.

The following sections provide an overview of the features of Copilot Pro in Excel, Outlook, Word, PowerPoint, and OneNote. Each application has a dedicated chapter later in the book, taking you through many different scenarios and use cases, and providing step-by-step instructions on how to use all the features.

Copilot in Excel

With your Copilot Pro license, you can use Copilot in Excel to:

- Generate formula columns by describing a calculation you want to perform with your data. Copilot will suggest the formula, explain the formula, and add it in a new column in your spreadsheet.

1

- Highlight data and exceptions in your data by describing what you want to identify. Copilot will apply conditional formatting to your spreadsheet.

- Sort and filter your data by describing how you want the data sorted.

- Understand the data in your spreadsheet to gain insights. Copilot can analyze your data and identify outliers. It can also help you visualize your data by creating charts and PivotTables.

You can use Copilot in Excel to add formula columns and edit, highlight, sort, and analyze data.

Copilot in Outlook

With your Copilot Pro license, you can use Copilot in Outlook to:

- Write a draft of an email for you, based on your prompt. You can describe the content of what should be in the email, as well as the length and tone.

- Help you with coaching to improve the emails you write before you send them. Copilot can offer suggestions about tone, clarity, and sentiment.

- Summarize the key points in an email thread.

> **IMPORTANT** Copilot Pro features in Outlook apply only to accounts with @outlook.com, @hotmail.com, @live.com, or @msn.com email addresses.

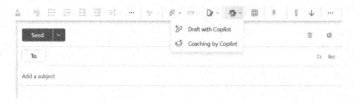

You can use Copilot in Outlook to draft emails and get coaching help to improve your emails.

Copilot in Word

With your Copilot Pro license, you can use Copilot in Word to:

- Draft content for your document based on your description or from content already in your document. Copilot can generate any type of content, including helping you get started with creative writing projects or more formal business documents.

- Rewrite the content in your document so that it is a different length or tone or is suitable for a different audience or purpose.

- Transform content in your document into a table and use generative AI to fill in additional related information in the table.

- Summarize your document and answer questions about the content in the document or related topics.

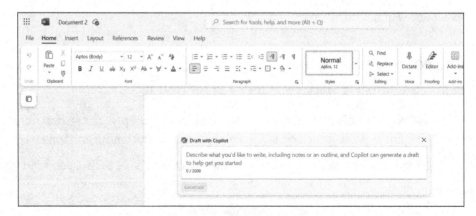

You can use Copilot in Word to draft new content for your document.

1

Copilot in PowerPoint

With your Copilot Pro license, you can use Copilot in PowerPoint to:

- Create a presentation on any topic based on your description.

- Add additional slides, content, and images to your presentation.

- Organize your presentation into sections and add agenda and conclusion slides.

- Summarize the content in your presentation and answer questions about the presentation content and related topics.

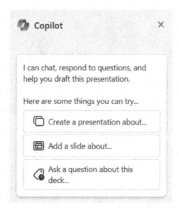

You can use Copilot in PowerPoint to create presentations, add slides, and ask questions about your presentation.

Copilot in OneNote

With your Copilot Pro license, you can use Copilot in OneNote to:

- Draft new content for your notes in a variety of formats. Copilot can draft single paragraphs or whole pages of notes, as well as meeting agendas, tips, and lists of pros and cons.

- Rewrite notes in a different length or tone or for a different purpose.

- Create to-do lists and plans based on general prompts or the content in your notebook.

- Summarize your notes, answer questions, and find information across multiple pages in your notebook.

> ⚠️ **IMPORTANT** Copilot in OneNote is available only in OneNote for Microsoft 365 on Windows. You will need a Microsoft 365 Personal or Family subscription as well as your Copilot Pro license to use Copilot in OneNote.

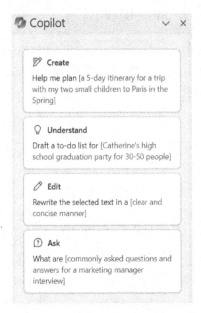

You can use Copilot in OneNote to create, understand, and edit notes, and ask questions about the content in your notebook.

Moving and resizing the Copilot pane in the desktop apps

When you open Copilot from the ribbon in Excel, Word, PowerPoint, and OneNote, the Copilot pane is docked to the right side of the screen. You can use the Task Pane Options to move or resize the Copilot pane as you work.

To move the Copilot pane:

1. Select the **Task Pane Options** dropdown menu.

Select the Task Pane Options dropdown menu.

2. Select **Move**.

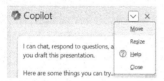

Select Move from the Task Pane
Options dropdown menu.

3. Position your cursor near the top of the Copilot pane. When your cursor changes into the move cursor, drag and move the Copilot pane to where you want it on the screen.

Move the Copilot pane around the screen
to reposition it where you want.

> **TIP** You can dock the Copilot pane on the left side of the app if you prefer.

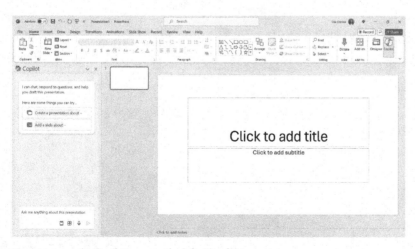

You can move the Copilot pane to the left side of the screen.

In PowerPoint and OneNote, where Copilot often generates a lot of content in the chat, it can be much easier to read the response by making the Copilot pane wider.

To resize the Copilot pane:

1. Select the **Task Pane Options** dropdown menu.

2. Select **Resize**.

3. Position your cursor at the edge of the Copilot pane, and when it changes to the resize cursor, drag the edge of the pane horizontally until you get the width you want to work with.

4. You can change the width at any time.

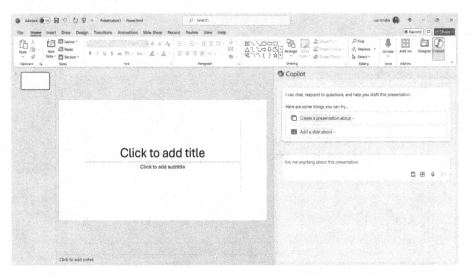

Make the Copilot pane wider to make it easier to read longer responses.

Resizing the Copilot pane in the web apps

You can't move the Copilot pane or set a specific width in the web apps, but you can use the icon at the top right of the pane to toggle between expanding or collapsing the chat, making it wider or narrower.

Select the icon at the top right of the Copilot pane in the Microsoft 365 web apps to expand or collapse the chat.

Provide feedback to Microsoft

In the Copilot experiences in the Microsoft 365 apps, you can provide user feedback to Microsoft on the Copilot experience and results. This is helpful in providing Microsoft with feedback that can help improve Copilot and prioritize feature requests.

Whenever Copilot gives you a response, you have the option to select either a thumbs up or thumbs down icon to provide feedback.

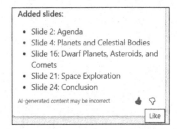

Select the thumbs up or thumbs down icon on the Copilot response to provide feedback to Microsoft.

After you have selected one of these icons, you will be prompted with a feedback pane that asks for more information. You should provide as much detail as you can about what you liked about the response and why, or what didn't work or what went wrong.

When you provide feedback, Microsoft will collect the prompt that you entered and the response that Copilot generated. You have the option to share additional data that might help Microsoft better understand the response. This can include the history of your chat with Copilot, the content from your files, or personal data. You can select the preview in the feedback pane or follow the link to understand what is being shared before you select Submit.

You can provide details to Microsoft about your feedback and select which data to share.

Skills review

In this chapter, you learned how to:

- Understand the difference between Copilot Pro and the other Microsoft Copilot options.

- Get started with Copilot Pro by signing up for a free trial and signing in to Copilot on the web.

- Access Copilot across different web, mobile, and Windows experiences.

- Access Copilot Pro in selected Microsoft 365 applications (Excel, Outlook, Word, PowerPoint, and OneNote).

- Provide feedback to Microsoft about your experience with Copilot.

Practice tasks

No practice files are necessary to complete the practice tasks in this chapter.

Get started with Copilot Pro

Open the Edge browser and then complete the following tasks:

1. Navigate to the Copilot Pro home page: *https://www.microsoft.com/en-us/store/b/copilotpro.*

2. Scroll down to see the pricing, and then select the **Start your free trial** button.

3. You will be taken to the checkout page, where you can review and confirm the price and all the details of your Copilot Pro subscription.

4. Select the **Next** button, choose a payment method, and enter payment details.

5. Once your payment method has been accepted, you will see a **Start trial, pay later** button appear on the Confirm subscription screen. Select this button.

6. Wait for the confirmation message to appear and then select the **Get started** button.

7. You will be redirected to Copilot on the web (*https://copilot.microsoft.com*); where you can start chatting with Copilot to generate text, code, and images; get answers to your questions; and more.

8. Add this page to your favorites in your browser.

Access Copilot Pro on the web, on mobile devices, and in Windows

Open a new tab in Edge and then complete the following tasks:

1. Navigate to the Bing home page at *https://www.bing.com*.

2. Enter the following into the search area: what is Seattle known for.

3. Scroll down below the first search results to see the Copilot-generated part of the response. You will see citations, suggested prompts, and a prompt area where you can continue the conversation.

4. Select one of the suggested prompts (for example, "What are the best neighborhoods?" or "What are some local dishes?"). You may see different suggested prompts because Copilot generates different responses each time.

5. You will be switched to the Copilot experience in your browser, with a response to the prompt you selected.

Use Copilot Pro in Microsoft 365 applications

Open a new tab in Edge and then complete the following tasks:

1. Open PowerPoint in Edge by navigating to *https://www.microsoft365.com/launch/PowerPoint*.

2. Select **Blank presentation** to start a new blank presentation.

3. Select the **Copilot** button on the right end of the Home toolbar to open the Copilot pane on the right side of the screen.

4. Select the suggested prompt, **Create a presentation about....**

5. In the prompt area, complete that prompt by describing what you want the presentation to be about—for example, "Create a presentation about Seattle."

6. Select the arrow to submit your prompt and wait for Copilot to generate the presentation.

Provide feedback to Microsoft

Continue working in PowerPoint where you finished the last task and then complete the following tasks:

1. Select either the **Like** or **Dislike** icon to provide Microsoft with feedback on the presentation just generated by Copilot.

2. Provide some detail about what you liked or disliked in the pop-up window and select the **Submit** button.

Writing effective prompts for Copilot

2

The most important skill to master when working with Copilot is writing effective prompts. Any instruction or request that you give to Copilot is a prompt. Prompts can be simple instructions with a single response, or they can include context, source content, examples, and details of the desired output format. Prompting can also be more than just a single request and response. Understanding how to refine and iterate your prompts will enable you to have a conversation with Copilot that will give you much better results. In this chapter, you will learn how to write prompts to help you work effectively with Copilot with both text and images, using the main elements of prompting. You will understand different prompting techniques and the scenarios in which you can use them. You will also learn how to use Copilot Lab to find suggested prompts to help you get started.

In this chapter

- Understand prompts and responses
- Discover and use suggested prompts with Copilot Lab
- Use the elements of effective prompts
- Write prompts to generate images
- Use more advanced prompting techniques

Practice files

No practice files are necessary to complete the practice tasks in this chapter.

Understand prompts and responses

Prompts and responses are the fundamental components of the interactions you will have with Copilot.

How generative AI works

When you chat with Copilot or ask Copilot to do something for you, it uses a large language model (LLM) to process your prompt and provide a natural language response. A large language model is a type of AI designed to process and generate text. It has been trained on huge datasets to understand how language patterns work and is able to process your request and generate a response by predicting what comes next using these language patterns. Copilot uses the LLM to write text, provide responses, and carry on a conversation in the context of what you've requested. Copilot doesn't actually understand what you are asking, or what it is saying in response, and it doesn't have any thoughts, opinions, or feelings. It is simply using the patterns it has learned from the training data to predict the most likely words or sentences to generate a response.

Generative AI is creative by design, making different predictions each time you provide a prompt. This means it won't always generate the same answers, even when you use the same prompt. The more specific you are with your prompt, the more likely you are to get a similar, or even the same response each time. If you ask Copilot to generate content on a narrow or specialized topic, such as "Explain how to fold a paper crane," you will get almost the same content each time. If you ask Copilot for a well-established fact that doesn't change, such as "What is the capital of France?" you will also get a consistent answer. If you work with more general or creative prompting, such as "Write an outline for a detective story," the generated responses will be very different each time.

Generative AI has a "temperature" control that determines the scale of how predictable or creative the response will be. Lower temperatures mean the response will closely follow predictable, learned patterns, whereas higher temperatures encourage more creativity and innovation in the response. When you use Copilot on the web and mobile experiences, you can choose whether you want Copilot to respond in a way that is more precise, more balanced, or more creative. Using the more precise option will give you more factual and consistent responses, whereas the more creative option can be more likely to fabricate information, known as *hallucinations*. The more creative option, however, will give you better results when you want to use language in a creative way, such as writing a poem or thinking about a question or problem in different ways.

SEE ALSO You will learn how to use these options with Copilot on the web in Chapter 3, "Copilot on the web."

Generative AI is by nature creative, even at a low temperature or using the more precise option. It is therefore important to expect that as you use Copilot to generate drafts or rewrite content, that can yield a different response even if you use the same prompt. If you get an answer you like, make sure to accept or save it, or copy and paste it into a document or notes for future use. This creative aspect also means that if you don't like the response to your prompt, one thing you can try is submitting the same prompt again to regenerate a different version of the response. In most cases, however, learning how to write better prompts and refine your instructions through a conversation with Copilot will be the way to get the best results.

This chapter teaches you the skills you need to write effective prompts in a range of different scenarios with Copilot.

The best use cases for Copilot

One of the biggest challenges with adopting Copilot is learning to think differently and understanding how and where generative AI can provide value to enhance your creativity and productivity. When you first start using Copilot, you are likely to get some disappointing or unexpected results. It is important not to give up. Think about Copilot as your virtual assistant and consider when and how to use Copilot in the same way you would if you were delegating a task to a junior assistant.

The easiest way to get started is to think about how Copilot can free up your time. Think about tasks that take up a lot of your time, or tasks that are tedious, which don't need the full power of your knowledge or creativity to complete. For instance, you could ask Copilot to help you put together a meeting agenda based on your notes.

Copilot can also help you rewrite or repurpose your work, where you have already done the thinking or creative work. This can include turning a document into a presentation, rewriting it for a different audience, or writing an executive summary.

You can go beyond productivity tasks with Copilot, using it to help you solve problems or brainstorm new ideas. You can also reverse the pattern of the conversation, asking Copilot to ask you the questions to help you think differently, or to challenge your assumptions on a topic.

Prompting in the web experience vs. app experience

With Copilot Pro, you can chat with Copilot on the web and in mobile apps, as well as in Microsoft 365 applications. These experiences provide you with different ways to work with Copilot.

When working with Copilot in the web or mobile experiences, you can have a more free-form conversation. This is a great place to start with idea generation, problem solving, or brainstorming. This is also the best place to work if you want to have a conversation with Copilot in which you go back and forth and refine your ideas and requests, or to use more advanced prompting techniques covered later in this chapter, such as the persona pattern. Copilot on the web or mobile is also the best place to generate images.

 SEE ALSO You will learn more about how to use Copilot on the web in Chapter 3.

Think about Copilot in the Microsoft 365 applications as a series of "specialist" assistants that are designed to help you with the kinds of work you do in each application. For instance, Copilot in Word is very good at helping you draft and rewrite documents, whereas Copilot in OneNote is great at identifying action points and creating to-do lists and summaries from your unstructured notes.

When you work with Copilot in the Microsoft 365 applications, the prompts you write will mostly fall into one of these task areas:

- *Create* prompts ask Copilot to create a first draft of something for you, like a document, paragraph, meeting agenda, presentation, column, or email.

- *Edit* prompts ask Copilot to rewrite your content in different ways, changing the length, tone, or purpose, including giving you variations to choose from. Edit prompts can also help with organizing your presentations and applying conditional formatting to your spreadsheets.

- *Ask* prompts help you find specific information, coach you to create better content, or answer questions about your content or related topics.

- *Understand* prompts help you summarize your content, find insights, and extract to-do lists or key points.

SEE ALSO You will learn how to use each of these types of task prompts in Excel, Outlook, Word, PowerPoint, and OneNote in Chapters 5–9 of this book.

You can get the most out of Copilot Pro by using the web and application experiences together. For instance, you can start by brainstorming and working through a new idea in Copilot on the web, and then use the output of that as a prompt to draft a new document in Word. You can even ask Copilot on the web to help you write or improve your prompts.

Discover and use suggested prompts with Copilot Lab

The best way to get started with learning how to write effective prompts for Copilot is to use Copilot Lab. Copilot Lab provides suggested prompts for all the Copilot experiences, arranged in categories, making it easy to browse through the options to discover new ideas and save prompts to use later. Copilot Lab is available on the web, where you will find prompts for all the apps in a single place. You can also get to Copilot Lab from the menu in each of the Microsoft 365 applications, which is the best way to discover suggested prompts in the context of the app you are using.

Copilot Lab on the web

The full Copilot Lab experience on the web provides you with suggested prompts to use, as well as other advice, tips, and learning resources for prompting with Copilot. This is a great resource to explore further.

To use Copilot Lab on the web

1. Navigate to the Copilot Lab home page: *https://copilot.cloud.microsoft/ en-US/prompts*.

2. Select the **Sign in** icon at the top right of the window, and sign in using the Microsoft account you used to sign up for Copilot Pro.

Sign in to Copilot Lab using your Microsoft account.

3. Scroll down to the suggested prompts.

4. Select **View all prompts.**

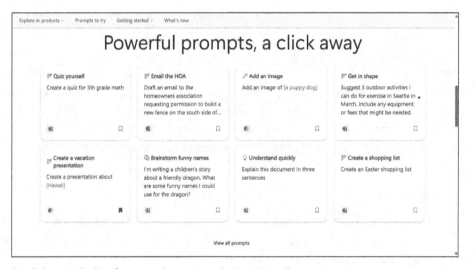

Scroll down to the list of suggested prompts and select View all prompts.

You can browse prompts by app, task, job type, or a combination of these by using the dropdown menus near the top of the page.

Start by selecting the **App** menu to view the options. You will see the apps for which Copilot is available with your Copilot Pro License: Outlook, Word, Excel, PowerPoint, and OneNote.

Use the dropdown menu to browse prompts by app.

Select the app or apps you want to explore.

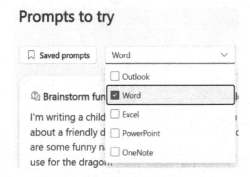

Check the box for the app for which you want to explore Copilot prompts.

When you find a prompt that looks interesting, select it to open it and view more information. You will find information about how to make changes to make it work for your context, as well as other suggested prompts that are similar to the one you've chosen.

The suggested prompt also includes suggestions for how to make the prompt your own and other similar prompts you can explore.

To save a prompt to use later

1. Select the **ribbon** icon on your open prompt.

2. Wait for the **Prompt saved** message to appear.

3. Close the selected prompt.

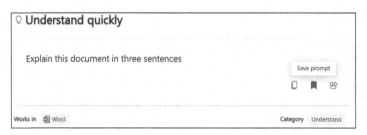

Select the ribbon icon to save the prompt.

You will see a message confirming that your prompt has been saved.

You will see that your prompt now has the ribbon icon highlighted in the main dashboard.

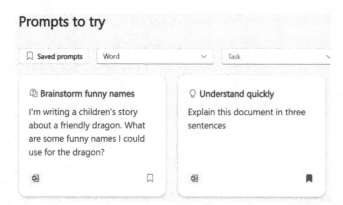

You can see which prompts you've saved by the ribbon icon status on the card.

 TIP You can also select the ribbon icon in the main dashboard of prompts without needing to open it.

 TIP To remove a prompt from your Saved prompts list, select the ribbon icon again to deselect it.

You can also browse Copilot Lab to find prompts that fit into each of the five main task categories you learned about earlier: Create, Edit, Ask, Catch up, and Understand.

To browse prompts by tasks and job type

1. Clear your selection from the **App** menu from the previous steps.

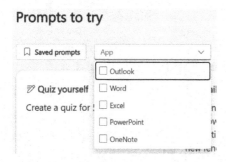

Clear your selection in the App menu to view prompts for all apps.

2. Open the **Task** menu and select **Edit**.

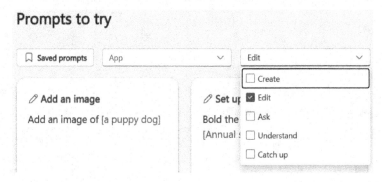

Expand the Task menu and select Edit.

3. You will **see** the list of **Edit** prompts. Save some of them as favorites.

Save some of the suggested prompts by selecting the ribbon icon on each card.

4. Repeat the previous steps to browse prompts by job type.

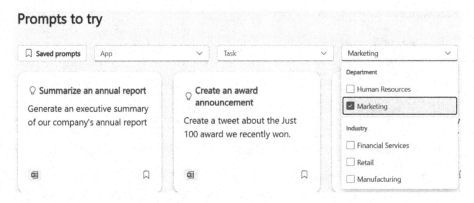

Expand the Job type menu and select the Marketing option.

5. Browse and save some more prompts from this selection.

> ✅ **TIP** You can use these menus together to narrow your selection by multiple fac-
> tors—for instance, all Marketing ideas in PowerPoint. You can also choose more
> than one option from each list.

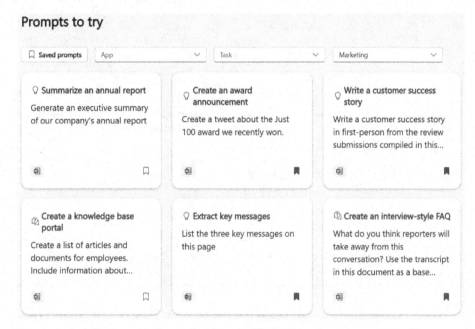

Browse the suggested prompts for marketing and select the ribbon icons to save some of them.

To view your saved prompts in Copilot Lab, select the **Saved prompts** button at the top left of the dashboard.

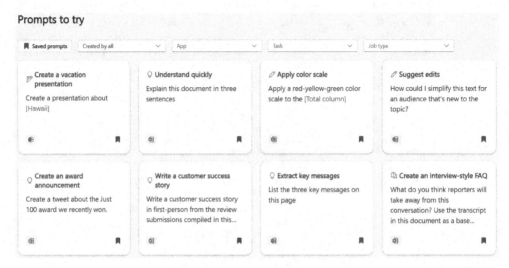

Select the Saved prompts button to view all your saved prompts.

 TIP You can use the dropdown menus on your saved prompts to filter by app, task, or job type.

Scroll down below the main suggested prompts area in Copilot Lab to find some quick tips for better prompts.

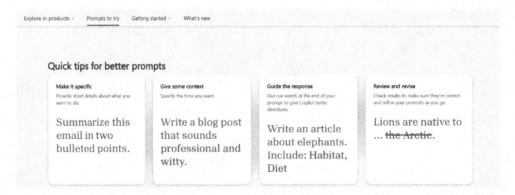

You will find more tips for prompting further down the Copilot Lab page.

Copilot Lab from the app experiences

You can also access Copilot Lab in each of the Microsoft 365 app experiences, to quickly get suggested prompts for that app. Any prompts you have saved in the main Copilot Lab experience will also show up as saved prompts in these apps, making them quick and easy for you to find and use.

To use Copilot Lab inside the Microsoft 365 apps

1. Open the Copilot pane from the right end of the Home ribbon in the app.

2. Select the **book** icon in the prompt area at the bottom of the Copilot pane.

3. Select **View more prompts**.

4. This will launch Copilot Lab as a window.

> **TIP** The images here show the experience in PowerPoint, but you will find that the experience of navigating to Copilot Lab is the same in each app.

Open the Copilot pane in PowerPoint by selecting the icon at the right end of the Home ribbon.

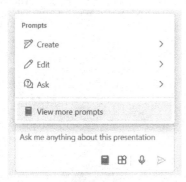

Select the book icon in the prompt area and then select View more prompts to open Copilot Lab.

To use a prompt from Copilot Lab

1. Select the **Saved prompts** button to view your saved prompts or use the **Task** or **Job type** menus as shown in the previous section to browse prompts for the app you are using.

2. Select the prompt you want to use.

3. This will close the Copilot Lab window.

4. Your prompt will appear in the prompt area.

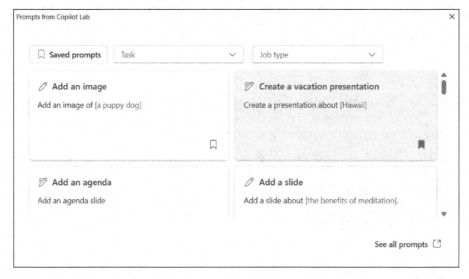

Select the prompt you want to use.

Any part of the prompt that was in square brackets will be removed. You should complete the prompt with your own instruction.

Complete the prompt with your own request.

In this example, this prompt in PowerPoint creates a presentation with images, content, and speaker notes.

 SEE ALSO You will find detailed step-by-step instructions for using Copilot Lab in OneNote in Chapter 9, "Copilot in OneNote."

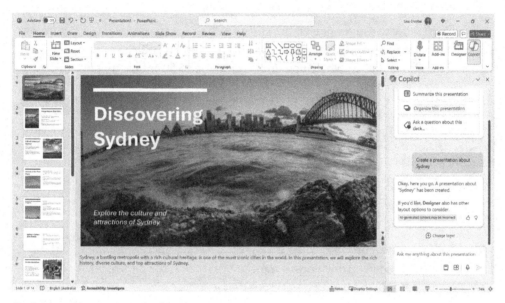

Copilot generates a presentation based on your prompt.

Use the elements of effective prompts

A prompt can be a very simple instruction, such as "Write a blog post about the benefits of remote work," or it can be a much longer prompt including specific detail about the context and desired output, along with examples of what you want to include or create. Sometimes a simple instruction will be enough to generate what you need, but other times you will find that providing Copilot with more detail and more information will give you a better result.

In this section, you will learn the four main elements you can use to write effective prompts and how each element affects the response you get from Copilot.

The elements of effective prompting for Copilot are:

- Goal

- Context

- Source

- Expectations

You will learn how to use these elements through a series of examples using different Copilot Pro experiences. This section shows prompts and responses in Copilot on the web and Copilot in Word, to help you understand the different prompting scenarios and examples in context.

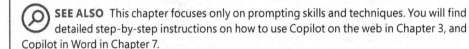

SEE ALSO This chapter focuses only on prompting skills and techniques. You will find detailed step-by-step instructions on how to use Copilot on the web in Chapter 3, and Copilot in Word in Chapter 7.

Goal

When you first write a prompt, you are likely to provide Copilot with a simple statement or instruction telling it what you want to do. Usually, this simple instruction is a goal. For example, "Write a blog post about the benefits of remote work."

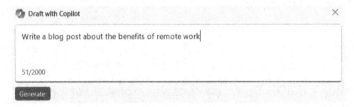

You can provide a simple prompt with a goal.

This type of prompt will produce a very general response. This can work well if you don't have something specific in mind or if you are using Copilot to help you brainstorm ideas or understand more about a topic to help you get started, but you are not likely to get what you want from Copilot with a simple general prompt like this. The results will usually feel very generic and not likely aligned with what you had in mind.

Return to the idea that prompting Copilot is like delegating a task to an assistant. If you gave this instruction to an assistant exactly as it is typed here, what might you expect? Most likely you'd get a very general blog post on the topic, covering the most widely acknowledged benefits. If you were in a workplace where the assistant also had additional context, they might apply that; but in this case, Copilot doesn't have anything else to work with. It only has this very general instruction with no context.

The result is a well-structured, easy-to-read, but very generic blog post.

Why Remote Work Rocks: The Ultimate Guide to Working from Anywhere

Discover the benefits of remote work for yourself, your team, and your business.

Introduction

Remote work is not a new concept, but it has gained popularity in recent years due to the advances in technology, the changing expectations of employees, and the global pandemic. Remote work is the ability to work from anywhere, whether it's your home, a coworking space, a coffee shop, or a different country. Remote work offers many benefits for both workers and employers, such as increased productivity, flexibility, diversity, and cost savings. In this blog post, we will explore some of the main benefits of remote work and how you can make the most of it.

Benefit #1: Productivity

Copilot responds by writing a blog post on the topic as requested.

If your request is very specific, you may get a satisfactory result from a simple prompt like this, whereas if it is a request that can be broadly interpreted in different ways, the result will be less predictable. Compare the following two examples:

Example 1: A simple prompt with a broad goal.

The prompt "Create a workout plan" is very broad. Imagine approaching your assistant and asking them to do this. There is no information here about who the plan is for or what you want to achieve. You would be unlikely to get a great result from asking them to do this with no context or expertise.

Create a workout plan

A simple prompt with a broad goal and no detail.

As expected, Copilot returns a very general response to the prompt. It starts by saying "it depends" and then proceeds to offer some general advice and links to resources. This is not likely to be particularly useful.

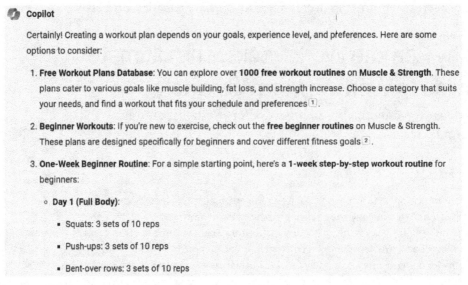

Copilot

Certainly! Creating a workout plan depends on your goals, experience level, and preferences. Here are some options to consider:

1. **Free Workout Plans Database**: You can explore over **1000 free workout routines** on **Muscle & Strength**. These plans cater to various goals like muscle building, fat loss, and strength increase. Choose a category that suits your needs, and find a workout that fits your schedule and preferences [1].

2. **Beginner Workouts**: If you're new to exercise, check out the **free beginner routines** on Muscle & Strength. These plans are designed specifically for beginners and cover different fitness goals [2].

3. **One-Week Beginner Routine**: For a simple starting point, here's a **1-week step-by-step workout routine** for beginners:

   ○ **Day 1 (Full Body)**:
     ■ Squats: 3 sets of 10 reps
     ■ Push-ups: 3 sets of 10 reps
     ■ Bent-over rows: 3 sets of 10 reps

Copilot responds with a general workout plan.

Example 2: A simple prompt with a specific goal

In this example, the prompt is also very simple, "Create a recipe for vegan gingerbread," but the request is very specific. Gingerbread is made up of largely the same ingredients, and there are a limited number of ways to make it vegan.

Create a recipe for vegan gingerbread

A simple prompt with a specific goal.

In this case, the Copilot response is specific and well aligned to the instruction. This is likely to be a satisfactory output without needing any additional context or information in the prompt.

> 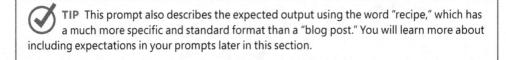 **TIP** This prompt also describes the expected output using the word "recipe," which has a much more specific and standard format than a "blog post." You will learn more about including expectations in your prompts later in this section.

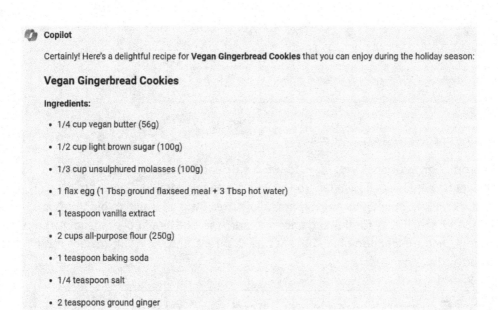

Copilot provides a recipe in response to the prompt.

Context

One of the most impactful things you can do to improve the responses you get from Copilot is to add context to your prompt. This helps Copilot understand the "why" behind your instruction and any other detail about what else you had in mind when you came up with the task. Think about how you would delegate this task to an assistant. You would likely start by positioning the request with information about why you wanted it done and what it will be used for.

You can add context to your prompt by describing the purpose, the intended audience, or how it will be used. Providing context completely changes the result you will get from Copilot from something generic to something that more specifically aligns with your goal.

Compare the following prompt with the simple instruction used in the previous step, where you asked Copilot to write a blog post about the benefits of remote work. This prompt now describes the intended audience ("small business owners") and goes a step further to provide even more specific detail about the mindset of the audience ("who are considering allowing their employees to work remotely"). It also describes the "why" behind the goal – "to highlight the advantages and persuade them to adopt remote work policies."

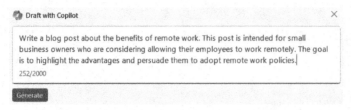

A prompt that includes both a goal and context.

This prompt gives Copilot a lot more to work with, and the result is very different from what you get with a general prompt without all this context. Context matters because it helps Copilot give much more tailored results. The resulting blog post is now written specifically for this audience and purpose. The heading, subheading, content, tone, and explanation of the benefits are different, and the result is much more tailored and less generic.

Why Remote Work is Good for Your Business

Discover the benefits of allowing your employees to work from anywhere

Introduction

Remote work is a trend that is reshaping the way businesses operate. More and more companies are allowing their employees to work from anywhere, whether it's from home, a coworking space, or a coffee shop. But what are the benefits of remote work for your business? How can you make it work for your team and your customers? In this blog post, we will explore the advantages of remote work and give you some tips on how to implement it successfully.

Benefits of Remote Work

Remote work can offer many benefits for your business, such as:

- Increased productivity: Studies have shown that remote workers are more

Copilot responds with a blog post that is aligned to the context in the prompt.

You can provide a lot of detail in your context or use a simple statement. In the example where we asked Copilot to create a workout plan, adding the context about who the plan is for makes a huge difference to the relevance and usefulness of the response.

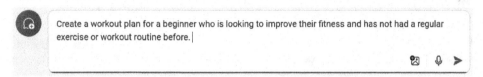

A prompt that provides a goal and the context.

Now that Copilot knows the workout plan is for a beginner looking to improve their fitness, the result is much more specific, and likely something that you could put into action, rather than the generic advice it provided from the broad prompt.

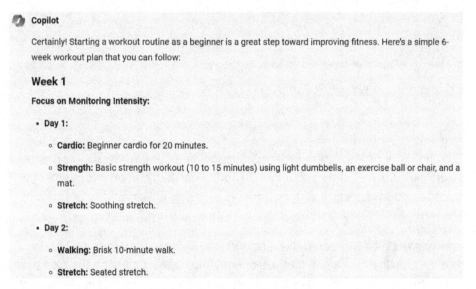

Copilot responds with a tailored workout plan based on the context.

Compare the following result when you give Copilot the same basic instruction with a completely different context.

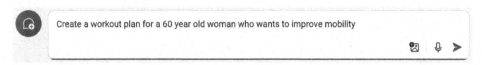

A prompt that provides a goal and a different context.

As you would expect, the response is different and aligned to the context provided.

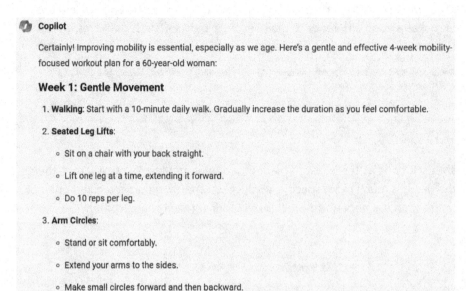

Copilot

Certainly! Improving mobility is essential, especially as we age. Here's a gentle and effective 4-week mobility-focused workout plan for a 60-year-old woman:

Week 1: Gentle Movement

1. **Walking**: Start with a 10-minute daily walk. Gradually increase the duration as you feel comfortable.

2. **Seated Leg Lifts**:
   - Sit on a chair with your back straight.
   - Lift one leg at a time, extending it forward.
   - Do 10 reps per leg.

3. **Arm Circles**:
   - Stand or sit comfortably.
   - Extend your arms to the sides.
   - Make small circles forward and then backward.

Copilot responds with a tailored workout plan based on the context.

Source

You can refine your prompt and the output by providing Copilot with source material to work with. Source material can include additional information or examples in the prompt; content already in your documents, notes, or presentations; or content from the web.

Let's return to the blog post about remote work and develop the prompt further to include examples. Imagine again that you are briefing your assistant on the blog post you want. You have provided the goal and the context of the intended audience, but you also have in mind some specific facts or examples that you want to make sure are included. When you delegate that task, you provide that information at the same time. The prompt now includes details of two example scenarios that illustrate the benefits of remote work for small businesses.

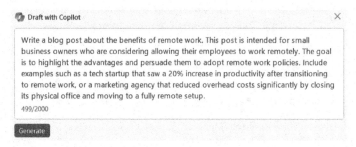

A prompt that includes a goal, context, and examples

The response from Copilot includes the requested examples in the text.

Benefits of Remote Work

Remote work can offer many benefits for your business, such as:

- Increased productivity: Remote workers tend to be more focused, motivated, and self-directed than office workers. They can also avoid distractions, interruptions, and commuting stress that can affect their performance. A study by Stanford University found that remote workers were 13% more productive than their office counterparts. Another example is a tech startup that saw a 20% increase in productivity after transitioning to remote work.
- Reduced costs: Remote work can help you save money on office rent, utilities, equipment, travel, and other expenses associated with maintaining a physical workspace. You can also access a wider pool of talent and hire workers from different locations and time zones, which can lower your labor costs and increase your diversity. A marketing agency that reduced overhead costs significantly by closing its physical office and moving to a fully remote setup is an example of how remote work can help you cut costs.
- Improved employee satisfaction and retention: Remote work can improve your employees' work-life balance, flexibility, autonomy, and well-being. Remote workers can choose their preferred work environment, schedule, and pace, and have more time for their personal and family needs. Remote work can also

Copilot responds with a blog post that includes the requested examples from the prompt.

Copilot uses a large language model to generate the response, as described earlier in this chapter, which means it doesn't understand what it is generating. Copilot is using the large language model and the training data to create content by predicting likely words and sentences. That means sometimes the response includes content that looks true but isn't. This is known as "hallucination." In this response, the cited Stanford University study sounds plausible, but it doesn't actually exist. Copilot is a very effective assistant, but like working with any assistant, you should always check the work it does before relying on it. The more you use web plug-ins or other content in your prompt, the less likely you will find hallucinations in the response.

> ⚠️ **IMPORTANT** Always make sure to fact check the output from Copilot. Generative AI can sometimes "hallucinate," generating content that reads as if it is true when it may not be.

Copilot Pro allows you to use the content of your documents as a source to create new content in some of the Microsoft 365 app experiences.

When you use Copilot in Word, PowerPoint, and OneNote, you can use a simple prompt to summarize the content. In the prompt "Summarize this doc" in Copilot in Word, the phrase "this doc" instructs Copilot that the document is the source you want it to use.

The prompt "Summarize this doc" refers to the document as the source.

Copilot works with the source provided and responds with a summary of the content in your document.

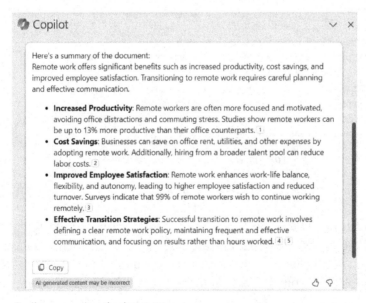

Copilot summarizes the document.

You can also write prompts to ask Copilot to rewrite or draft new content using the content in your document or notes as a source by using a phrase such as "based on this doc" in your prompt.

You can ask Copilot to generate new content based on the content in your document.

Copilot generates a social media post suitable for LinkedIn, using the content of your document as the source.

LinkedIn Post:

Are you thinking about transitioning to remote work? Or have you already made the switch and want to improve your remote work experience? If so, you might find this article helpful. It covers some of the key benefits and challenges of remote work, and offers some practical tips and best practices to make it work for your business. Whether you are a remote worker, a manager, or an employer, you will learn how to define your remote work policy, communicate effectively, and measure results, not hours. Read on and share your thoughts in the comments below!

#remotework #workfromanywhere #productivity #communication #results

Copilot responds with a LinkedIn style post on the topic of remote work.

You can use a Word document as a source to create a presentation using Copilot for PowerPoint by including a link to the document in the prompt.

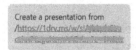

Add a link to a Word document to a prompt in Copilot in PowerPoint to generate a presentation based on that document.

Copilot creates a presentation outline based on the source document and uses the content in the document to create the presentation content, speaker notes, and images.

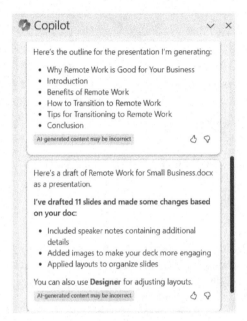

Copilot creates the presentation from your document, outlining the main sections, creating content, speaker notes, and images.

Copilot creates a presentation using your document as the source.

 SEE ALSO You will learn how to create a presentation from a document step by step in Chapter 8, "Copilot in PowerPoint."

> ⚠ **IMPORTANT** Copilot Pro has limited capabilities to use full documents as the source for prompts in the Microsoft 365 applications. To unlock the full capabilities of using your files as source content, you need a Microsoft 365 Copilot license.

You can also add source content to your prompt by copying and pasting it from the source directly into the prompt area. In this example, you have a vegan ginger-bread recipe as your source, and you want to rewrite it to make it easy for children to understand.

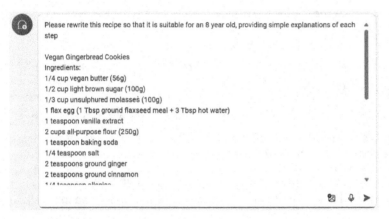

Please rewrite this recipe so that it is suitable for an 8 year old, providing simple explanations of each step

Vegan Gingerbread Cookies
Ingredients:
1/4 cup vegan butter (56g)
1/2 cup light brown sugar (100g)
1/3 cup unsulphured molasses (100g)
1 flax egg (1 Tbsp ground flaxseed meal + 3 Tbsp hot water)
1 teaspoon vanilla extract
2 cups all-purpose flour (250g)
1 teaspoon baking soda
1/4 teaspoon salt
2 teaspoons ground ginger
2 teaspoons ground cinnamon
1/4 teaspoon allspice

Ask Copilot to rewrite the recipe so that it is suitable for an 8-year-old.

Copilot responds with a new version of the recipe written in a different style.

Let's Bake!

1. **Preheat the Oven:**

   ○ Ask an adult to help you set the oven to 350°F (180°C). It's like warming up your gingerbread house!

2. **Mix the Wet Ingredients:**

   ○ In a big bowl, put the vegan butter (it's like magic butter that doesn't come from cows!), brown sugar, and molasses. Mix them together until they're all friends. ☀

3. **Make Your Flax Egg:**

   ○ Flax egg? Sounds fancy! But it's just flaxseed mixed with hot water. Stir it well and add it to your bowl. It helps our cookies stick together.

Copilot rewrites the recipe using language and concepts suitable for an 8-year-old.

> **SEE ALSO** You will learn how to use web content as a source in Chapter 3.

Expectations

Expectations define the length, tone, or format of the output you have in mind. You can ask Copilot to write to a specified word count or to respond in a different format, such as bullet points. You can describe the intended audience or type of language used.

Just like delegating a task to an assistant, you will find that you get better results if you explain the output style and format you have in mind. Compare the following prompts:

- Summarize this doc
- Summarize this doc in three bullet points
- Write an executive summary for this doc

Each of these prompts asks Copilot to summarize the content of the document, but the intended output is different each time.

- When you ask Copilot to summarize this doc with no other explanation of the desired output, you will get a comprehensive summary, which may be written in bullet points or paragraphs, as you saw in the previous section.

- Adding the expectation that you want the output written "in three bullet points" will provide you with a much more concise summary, written in a bullet point format.

Summarize this doc in 3 bullet points

Here's a summary of the document:
Main ideas:

- **Increased Productivity**: Remote work enhances productivity as remote workers are more focused, motivated, and self-directed, free from office distractions and commuting stress. Studies show remote workers are up to 13% more productive than office counterparts. [1]
- **Cost Reduction**: Businesses can save on office rent, utilities, and other expenses by adopting remote work. Additionally, they can hire from a global talent pool, which can reduce labor costs. [2]
- **Improved Employee Satisfaction**: Remote work promotes better work-life balance, flexibility, and autonomy, leading to higher employee satisfaction and retention. Surveys indicate that 99% of remote workers wish to continue working remotely. [3]

Providing expectations in your prompt will change the output of the response.

- You can express the desired output as a style, such as asking for an "executive summary." In this case, Copilot will summarize the key points of the document focusing on the main conclusions and recommendations for a business decision-maker.

> ## Executive Summary
>
> Remote work is not only a convenient option for employees, but also a strategic advantage for businesses. By allowing workers to choose their preferred location and schedule, remote work can boost productivity, efficiency, profitability, and employee satisfaction. Remote work can also help businesses save costs, reduce environmental impact, access a wider talent pool, and increase diversity and innovation. However, remote work also poses some challenges, such as communication, coordination, security, and culture. Therefore, businesses need to adopt remote work policies that suit their specific needs and goals, and provide adequate support and guidance to their remote workers. This blog post will explore the benefits and challenges of remote work, and offer some examples and tips on how to implement remote work successfully.

Copilot can generate an executive summary of your document.

You can describe in detail your expectations from the output, including structure, content, and tone. Here is an example of a prompt that now includes the desired length (1000 words) and specific subheadings (Increased Productivity, Cost Savings, Employee Satisfaction) and asks for a concluding paragraph. It also specifies the tone that should be used (professional yet friendly).

Write a 1,000-word blog post about the benefits of remote work. This post is intended for small business owners who are considering allowing their employees to work remotely. The goal is to highlight the advantages and persuade them to adopt remote work policies. Include examples such as a tech startup that saw a 20% increase in productivity after transitioning to remote work, or a marketing agency that reduced overhead costs significantly by closing its physical office and moving to a fully remote setup. The post should have at least three subheadings (e.g., Increased Productivity, Cost Savings, and Employee Satisfaction) and a concluding paragraph that summarizes the key points. Maintain a professional yet friendly tone throughout.

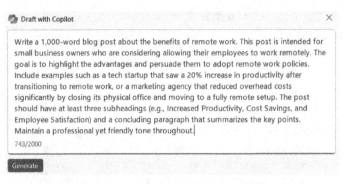

A prompt that uses a goal, context, examples, and a description of the expected output.

The response follows the expected output requested in the prompt.

Increased Productivity

One of the main benefits of remote work is that it can boost the productivity of your employees. According to a study by Stanford University, remote workers are 13% more productive than their office counterparts. They also take fewer breaks, sick days, and time off. This is because remote workers have more control over their work environment, schedule, and distractions. They can choose the best time and place to work, according to their preferences and needs. They can also avoid the stress and hassle of commuting, which can save them time and money. Remote workers also tend to be more engaged and motivated, as they have more autonomy and flexibility in their work. They can balance their personal and professional lives better, and achieve higher levels of satisfaction and well-being.

Cost Savings

Another benefit of remote work is that it can save you money. By allowing your employees to work remotely, you can reduce the expenses associated with maintaining a physical office, such as rent, utilities, equipment, furniture, and supplies. You can also save on travel costs, such as flights, hotels, and meals. According to a report by Global Workplace Analytics, a typical employer can save an average of $11,000 per year for each employee who works remotely half of the time. Remote work can also help you lower your turnover rate, as you can retain your employees longer and reduce the costs

Copilot responds with a blog post that takes in the instructions from the prompt.

Compare the output with a prompt on the same topic that sets a very different expectation.

Write a 150 word elevator pitch about the benefits of remote work. This is intended to help me explain to small business owners that they should consider allowing their employees to work remotely. Use a conversational, friendly, but persuasive tone.

A prompt requesting a different style of output on the benefits of remote work.

From this prompt, Copilot produces a very different response.

Unlocking Success with Remote Work: A Smart Choice for Your Business

Hey there, savvy business owner! Ready to level up your company? Remote work isn't just a trend—it's a game-changer. Here's why:

1. **Boosted Morale**: Happy employees are productive employees. Remote work gives them flexibility and trust.

2. **Crisis-Mode Superpower**: When chaos strikes (hello, pandemic!), remote work keeps your business humming.

3. **Retain Aces**: Top talent wants freedom. Embrace remote work, keep your stars.

4. **Productivity Surge**: Fewer distractions, focused work. Your team becomes productivity ninjas.

5. **Cost Savings**: Say goodbye to pricey office space. Hello, profits!

6. **Global Talent**: Cast your net worldwide. Skills from New Zealand to Brazil.

Ready to make the leap? Your business will thank you!

Copilot responds with a series of quick points using emojis for emphasis.

> ✓ **TIP** The results from your prompt will be different using Copilot on the web than from Copilot in Microsoft 365 applications. In the applications, Copilot expects to work in a certain style—for instance, in Word, it expects to draft a document. For more free-form types of content like this, you are likely to get a better result using Copilot on the web.

Iterate and refine

In this section, you have learned the main components that make up a prompt—goals, context, source, and expectation—and how to use them to get better results. However, it is unlikely that you will ever get a perfect result the first time from a single prompt. It is important to understand that generative AI will not always correctly understand your intent the first time.

Think again about delegating a task to an assistant. You may need to go back and provide additional information, context, source material, or expectations to get the results you were hoping for. More likely, you would engage in a conversation either at the start or throughout the process with the assistant to clarify, refine, and provide additional detail.

When working with Copilot, think about the interaction as a conversation, as you might have with an assistant, rather than only as a single prompt and response. Developing your skills in this area and learning how to iterate and refine your prompts to get better responses is the most important factor in your success using Copilot.

Returning to the example of using Copilot to create a workout plan, when we first asked Copilot to "create a workout plan for a beginner who is looking to improve their fitness and has not had a regular exercise or workout routine before," we got a response that suggested a simple six-week workout plan.

However, it was a general response with very little detail. Perhaps you had in mind that you wanted a four-week program to start with, or you need to provide more details about the exercises to help beginners get started. You can refine the results by responding with another prompt.

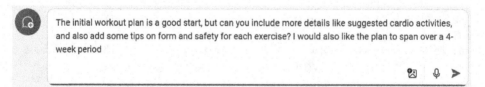

The initial workout plan is a good start, but can you include more details like suggested cardio activities, and also add some tips on form and safety for each exercise? I would also like the plan to span over a 4-week period

Provide Copilot with feedback and ask for changes with another prompt.

 TIP Being polite to Copilot and providing feedback on what you liked or didn't like in the response can also help you get better results.

Copilot takes your feedback and refines the initial response to provide the changes and additional details you requested.

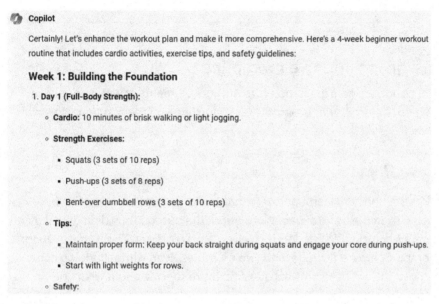

Copilot adjusts the response based on the changes you requested in your prompt.

You can continue the conversation in this style until you get the result you want, iterating to ask for more changes or for additional information to be added.

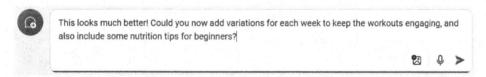

Provide Copilot with feedback and ask it to make changes and additions with another prompt.

Nutrition Tips for Beginners:

- **Hydrate:** Drink water before, during, and after workouts.
- **Balanced Diet:** Include whole grains, lean proteins, fruits, and vegetables.
- **Pre-Workout Snack:** Have a small meal 1-2 hours before exercising.
- **Post-Workout Fuel:** Consume protein and carbs within 30 minutes after workouts.
- **Listen to Your Body:** If something feels uncomfortable or painful, stop and consult a professional.

Enjoy your fitness journey! 🏃 🏋️ : Muscle & Strength: Beginner Workouts

Copilot responds based on your prompt. The response now includes nutrition tips for beginners.

TIP Don't forget to use the elements of prompting you learned earlier as you iterate and refine. You can continue to provide additional context, examples, sources, and descriptions of your expected output.

Additional tips to improve prompting

Goals, context, source, and expectations are the core elements of writing effective prompts. You can improve your prompting even further with the additional tips covered in this section.

Be specific

In the previous section, you learned how to make your prompt more specific by adding context, examples, and expectations about the output. Providing detailed and clear instructions helps guide Copilot to give you a better result. This is true even for a simple prompt. Compare the following two examples. Even without adding context or examples, you will get better results by being more specific about what you want Copilot to do.

- Tell me about cats

- Describe the different breeds of domestic cats and their unique characteristics

Tell Copilot when you are starting a new conversation

Copilot expects you to have an ongoing conversation where you iterate and refine your prompts, so when you are ready to start a new topic or conversation, you should tell Copilot. That effectively resets the conversation and avoids confusion.

In the Copilot experiences on web, mobile, and Windows, there is a button you can select next to the prompt area that restarts the conversation.

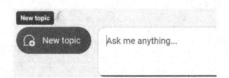

Select the icon next to the prompt area in Copilot on the web to start a new topic.

When you select the icon, it will expand to show the words "New topic," and Copilot will be ready to start a new conversation.

In the Copilot experiences in the Microsoft 365 applications, look for the option to click a button to change topic, just above the prompt area.

Select the "Change topic" option above the prompt area to start a new topic with Copilot in the Microsoft 365 apps.

Use quotation marks

You can use quotation marks in your prompt to provide greater clarity and precision. For example, if you ask Copilot to describe "machine learning," providing quotation marks around the term will focus the output precisely on defining this term.

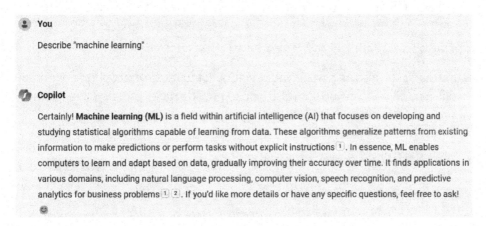

Using quotation marks helps Copilot focus on a specific part of your prompt.

The same prompt without quotation marks will vary in the focus of the response, giving you a more general answer.

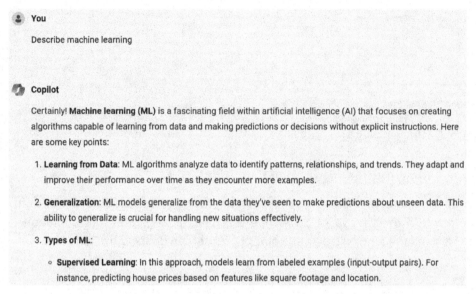

Without quotation marks, Copilot will provide a less focused answer to the same prompt.

Quotation marks can also help when you want Copilot to use an exact phrase or quote rather than paraphrasing it. They can also help to provide clarity on where the quote is in your prompt, rather than the words running together in an ambiguous way.

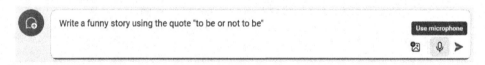

Use quotation marks in your prompt to ask it to use a specific quote.

Quotation marks are also useful when you want to refer to a title in your prompt:

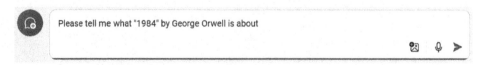

Use quotation marks to indicate a title of a book, movie, or other proper title.

Use tags or labels

You can help make your prompt clearer by using tags to identify different parts of your prompt or describe the desired output. In this example, the prompt asking Copilot to write about the benefits of remote work also includes tags describing the structure and what to include in each section.

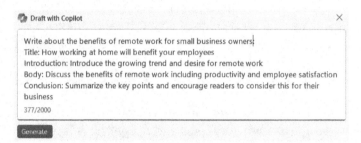

Use tags in your prompt to guide Copilot on the content and structure of the response you're looking for.

The response follows the requested structure and description of the content.

How working at home will benefit your employees

A guide for small business owners who want to embrace remote work

Introduction

Remote work is not a new concept, but it has become more popular and feasible in recent years, thanks to the advances in technology and communication. More and more workers are seeking flexibility and autonomy in their work arrangements, and more and more employers are recognizing the benefits of allowing their staff to work from home or anywhere they choose.

As a small business owner, you might be wondering if remote work is suitable for your business and your employees. You might have some concerns about the challenges and risks of managing a remote team, such as communication, collaboration, accountability, and security. However, you might also be curious about the potential advantages of remote work, such as cost savings, productivity, and employee satisfaction.

Copilot responds with a blog post in the structure requested.

Write prompts to generate images

Copilot can also generate images for you, using the DALL-E 3 model, which is a type of AI model that specializes in creating unique, high-quality, detailed images based on the text description you put in your prompt.

Effective prompting for image generation in Copilot requires some different knowledge and skills than prompting to generate text content. When you are writing prompts to generate images, you should think about fine details, as well as the mood or aesthetic of the image you want to create, and understand the different kinds of art, digital, photography, and other mediums you can use to describe images.

As you learned with prompting for text, using a very broad general prompt to generate an image is unlikely to give you a satisfactory result and can generate vastly different results each time. In this example, the very simple prompt "create an image of a tree" creates two very different styles each time the prompt is used and adds a lot of additional detail that may not be what you had in mind.

A very broad general prompt is unlikely to give you a good response when generating an image.

2

"A tree"

Copilot generates an image of a tree with squirrels, flowers, and butterflies.

"A tree"

Using the same broad general prompt a second time generates a very different looking set of images.

Write a caption to generate an image

One way to write an effective prompt to generate an image is to picture the image in your mind and then write a caption for it. Imagine describing the image to someone else to help them picture the same thing. In this example, the prompt is still relatively simple, but the output is a good match to the description in the prompt, featuring the key elements that were requested.

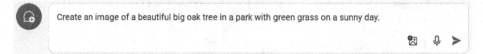

Create an image of a beautiful big oak tree in a park with green grass on a sunny day.

Using a prompt that describes the image in the style of a caption helps Copilot generate something more like what you have in mind.

"A beautiful big oak tree in a park with green grass on a sunny day"

The generated images are well aligned with the description in the prompt.

Describe the background of your image

When you write your prompt, think about what you want in the background of your image and describe that as well as the main part of the image you want to generate. If you don't specify the details of the background, the AI will fill in something for you or even leave it blank. In this example, asking for a 3D cartoon-style image, the background is blank in most options.

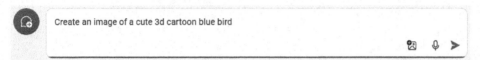

If you don't describe the background of the image in your prompt, Copilot will generate the background or leave it blank.

"A cute 3d cartoon blue bird"

With this prompt, the background is blank in most of the generated images.

Compare this to the following version of the prompt that includes a description of both the cartoon-style bird and the details of the desired background.

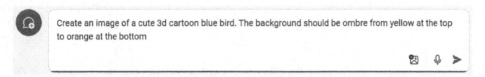

You can write a prompt to describe the background you want as well as the main image.

Copilot adds some background options as described.

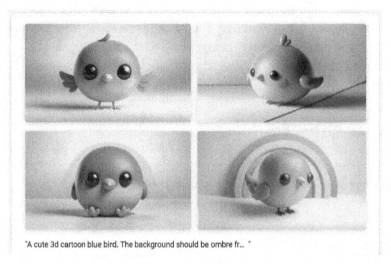

"A cute 3d cartoon blue bird. The background should be ombre fr... "

Copilot generates the image with the background as requested in the prompt.

Refining and iterating your prompt

As you learned earlier in this chapter, think about prompting Copilot as a conversation in which you can continue to refine and iterate your prompts to get what you requested. This is a particularly important skill when you are prompting for image generation, where communicating in words an image you have in your mind can take multiple attempts or iterations, especially when you are starting out.

In this example, the previous prompt asking Copilot to generate an image of an oak tree is refined to describe that the background should be a clear blue sky.

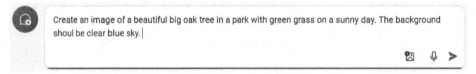

Rewrite the prompt asking for an image of an oak tree, this time describing the background.

This changes the image results and opens up the image to bring the tree into the foreground and adds sky to the background.

"A beautiful big oak tree in a park with green grass on a sunny day..."

Copilot generates images with sky in the background, but it is not clear sky as requested in the prompt.

However, the results here don't match what was requested, which was a "clear blue sky." Copilot has not understood that the phrase was intended to mean that there should be no clouds. You can continue the conversation with Copilot to ask it to try again, providing more details or different wording.

> ✓ **TIP** Remember to be polite and reinforce the things you like to help get better results as you refine your prompt.

 I love this but I want the background to be clear blue sky with no clouds

Give Copilot feedback and use different language to request what you want changed.

The refined results are much better and represent what was requested.

"A beautiful big oak tree in a park with green grass on a sunny day..."

Copilot generates a new set of images that are a better match to the request.

Use adjectives to describe the emotion or aesthetic

When you are writing prompts to generate images, using adjectives to describe the mood, tone, emotion, or aesthetic of the image can help generate the kind of image you have in mind. In the following examples, both prompts ask for an image of a coffee cup, but the description of the aesthetic, even without any specific detail about the scene, produces vastly different results.

In this first example, the aesthetic is described as warm, comfortable, and minimalistic.

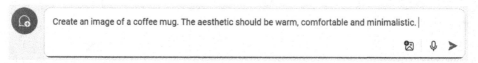

Describing the aesthetic of the image, even without any other detail, can be an effective way to write a prompt.

2

"A warm, comfortable and minimalistic coffee mug"

Copilot generates images based on the aesthetic described.

The same basic prompt with a different aesthetic description (colorful and happy) creates a completely different set of images.

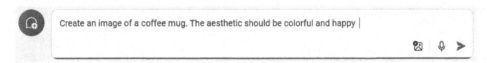

Create an image of a coffee mug. The aesthetic should be colorful and happy |

Using the same prompt with a different aesthetic will create an entirely different image.

"A colorful and happy coffee mug"

Copilot produces images that fit the colorful and happy aesthetic requested in the prompt.

Describe specific artistic or photographic styles

One of the best ways to get an image in the style you have in mind is to describe a specific artistic, digital, or photographic style. Copilot can create images in all sorts of styles and mediums. Think about styles of drawings or paintings, such as "impressionist" or "watercolor." You can ask for realistic photographs and describe photographic techniques or styles or ask for cartoon-style images as shown in the previous example. You can also ask for images in the style of different mediums, such as clay or embroidery.

> **SEE ALSO** Your ability to use these kinds of prompts effectively to generate images will depend on the kinds of styles you can think of and describe. Later in this section, you will learn how to use Copilot to help you better describe image styles.

Let's return to the example of asking Copilot to generate an image of an oak tree, this time using different artistic styles. The first prompt asks for a black and white charcoal etching.

create an image of a large oak tree in a park on a sunny day in the style of a black and white charcoal etching

Describe a specific artistic style as part of your prompt when generating images.

"A large oak tree in a park on a sunny day in the style of a black a… "

Copilot generates images in the style described.

Compare the results using the same basic request with a different art style—this time, a "retro pop-art style."

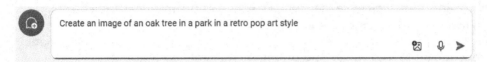

You can use the same prompt with a different artistic style to create different images.

"Oak tree in a park retro pop art"

Copilot generates the images again using the new style.

🔍 **SEE ALSO** When you generate images using Copilot, you will get a series of artistic style suggestions you can use to change your image into different styles. You will learn about this in Chapter 3.

✓ **TIP** You can ask for very specific artistic styles, naming a particular artist, painting, or era.

Ask Copilot to help you with image prompting

One of the most effective ways to learn how to write great prompts for images is to ask Copilot to help you write the prompt. This is particularly useful if you don't know how to describe a particular style in detail.

To ask Copilot to help you write a prompt to generate an image

1. Write a prompt asking Copilot how to write a good prompt for the outcome you are trying to achieve, describing the subject and the style.

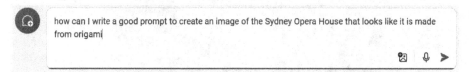

how can I write a good prompt to create an image of the Sydney Opera House that looks like it is made from origami

Ask Copilot to help you write effective prompts to describe the image style you want.

2. Copilot responds with a suggested prompt you can use. It may also explain the thought process behind how it constructed the prompt, helping you with other ideas you can use.

   Putting it all together, your prompt could be:

   "Generate an image featuring an origami-style Sydney Opera House. The folds should be precise, capturing the architectural details. Use a soft color palette reminiscent of paper, and set it against an abstract background with subtle geometric shapes. Illuminate the folds with natural light and create gentle shadows."

   Copilot suggests a prompt you can use to describe the image style you want to create.

3. Copy the text of the suggested prompt.

4. Select the **New topic** button to start a new conversation before generating the image.

5. Paste that prompt into the prompt area.

Copilot generates an image as described, with refined details you may not have known how to request.

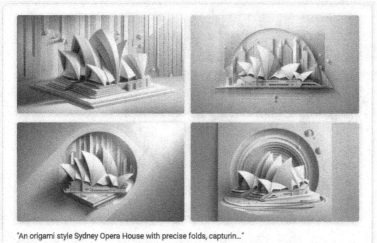

"An origami style Sydney Opera House with precise folds, capturin..."

Copilot generates a set of images based on the prompt.

You can also ask Copilot to help refine your prompt to get more subtle and detailed changes to the results.

In this example, you started by asking for an image in the style of an autochrome photograph.

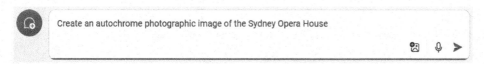

Create an autochrome photographic image of the Sydney Opera House

Describe a photographic style for Copilot to create an image.

"Autochrome photographic image of the Sydney Opera House"

Copilot generates a series of images using the style described in the prompt.

Let's say you want to make some changes to this, but you don't have the knowledge or terminology to describe the way you want to refine or change it to be truer to the style.

You can ask Copilot for help in how to refine your prompt.

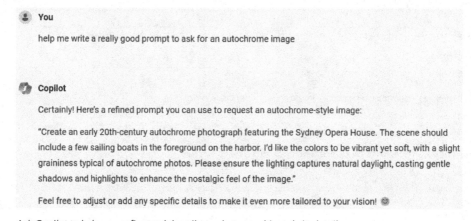

You

help me write a really good prompt to ask for an autochrome image

Copilot

Certainly! Here's a refined prompt you can use to request an autochrome-style image:

"Create an early 20th-century autochrome photograph featuring the Sydney Opera House. The scene should include a few sailing boats in the foreground on the harbor. I'd like the colors to be vibrant yet soft, with a slight graininess typical of autochrome photos. Please ensure the lighting captures natural daylight, casting gentle shadows and highlights to enhance the nostalgic feel of the image."

Feel free to adjust or add any specific details to make it even more tailored to your vision! 😊

Ask Copilot to help you refine and describe a photographic style in detail.

Using this prompt changes the image in subtle ways as described. In particular, notice the change to the lighting in these images compared with the first set of images.

"An early 20th century autochrome photograph featuring the Sydn..."

Copilot generates another four images, making the changes requested in the prompt.

Use more advanced prompting techniques

In addition to the main elements of effective prompting you learned earlier in this chapter, you can use these additional prompting techniques to get more out of your Copilot Pro experience.

Personas

Asking Copilot to take on the role of a persona is a very effective way to use generative AI to take on the point of view and expertise of another person. While this doesn't substitute for actual expertise, it can help you empathize with or anticipate another person's point of view or learn about a problem or topic from a different perspective. You can use the persona pattern of prompting in two ways.

Act as a persona

You can use this type of prompt by starting with the phrase "act as" or "you are a" and then filling in a description of a person or organization before outlining the task.

This type of prompting can help you write in a different style or take a different perspective you don't have, as shown in this example that provides a different angle on the conversation about remote work.

Act as a stand up comedian experienced in doing gigs for corporate events. Write a short funny speech about remote work for an organization that works fully remote using Microsoft Teams. The language and content should be appropriate for the workplace.

Ask Copilot to act as a stand-up comedian persona.

Copilot responds to the topic with a series of jokes.

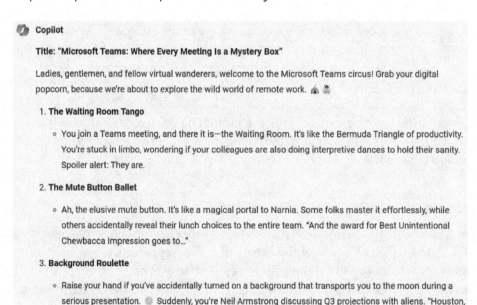

Copilot

Title: "Microsoft Teams: Where Every Meeting Is a Mystery Box"

Ladies, gentlemen, and fellow virtual wanderers, welcome to the Microsoft Teams circus! Grab your digital popcorn, because we're about to explore the wild world of remote work.

1. **The Waiting Room Tango**

   - You join a Teams meeting, and there it is—the Waiting Room. It's like the Bermuda Triangle of productivity. You're stuck in limbo, wondering if your colleagues are also doing interpretive dances to hold their sanity. Spoiler alert: They are.

2. **The Mute Button Ballet**

   - Ah, the elusive mute button. It's like a magical portal to Narnia. Some folks master it effortlessly, while others accidentally reveal their lunch choices to the entire team. "And the award for Best Unintentional Chewbacca Impression goes to..."

3. **Background Roulette**

   - Raise your hand if you've accidentally turned on a background that transports you to the moon during a serious presentation. Suddenly, you're Neil Armstrong discussing Q3 projections with aliens. "Houston, we have a PowerPoint glitch."

Copilot responds with a series of jokes.

You can also use this prompting pattern to generate answers using expertise you don't have, such as in this example, where you are a manager recruiting for a new role, but you don't have much experience as an interviewer. You can ask Copilot to take on the persona of an experienced recruiter to help you with the task.

You are an experienced recruiter interviewing a candidate for a role as a marketing manager. You are looking for someone who can develop a comprehensive marketing plan aligned with your business goals. You want someone who will be a creative thinker, with strong leadership skills. Prepare a list of questions to ask at the interview will help identify whether this person is the right candidate for the job

Ask Copilot to take on the role of an experienced recruiter to help you come up with suggested interview questions.

Copilot

Certainly! Here's a list of questions you can ask during the interview to assess whether the candidate is a good fit for the marketing manager role:

1. **Strategic Thinking:**

   - How do you approach developing a marketing strategy that aligns with overall business goals?

   - Can you share an example of a successful marketing campaign you've led in the past?

2. **Leadership and Collaboration:**

   - Describe a situation where you had to lead a cross-functional team to achieve a marketing objective.

   - How do you foster collaboration between marketing, sales, and other departments?

3. **Creativity and Innovation:**

   - How do you encourage creative thinking within your team?

   - Tell me about a time when you came up with an innovative solution to a marketing challenge.

4. **Data-Driven Decision-Making:**

Copilot responds with a list of suggested interview questions.

The persona pattern can also be helpful in your creative work or to learn about topics in different ways. In this example, we ask Copilot to act as a time-traveling historian, to learn more about life in Ancient Rome.

You are an historian and archaeologist specializing in ancient civilizations. You have just traveled back in time to Ancient Rome during the height of the Roman Empire. Write a detailed account of your first day in Rome, describing the sights, sounds, and interactions you have with the locals. Include observations about the architecture, daily life, and any notable events or figures you encounter.

You can use the persona pattern to get creative and different perspectives on a topic.

The response is presented in an interesting storytelling format as requested.

 Copilot

Title: "A Day in Ancient Rome: A Time Traveler's Tale"

As the sun rose over the Tiber River, I stepped onto the cobblestone streets of Ancient Rome, my heart racing with anticipation. The year was 117 AD, and I found myself surrounded by a bustling metropolis that would shape the course of history.

The Sights: The architecture was awe-inspiring. Marble columns adorned grand temples dedicated to Jupiter, Venus, and countless other gods. The Colosseum loomed in the distance, its massive amphitheater promising gladiatorial spectacles and chariot races. Statues of emperors and heroes stood proudly in every square, their stern gazes following me as I wandered.

The Sounds: The air hummed with activity. Vendors hawked their wares—olives, figs, and amphorae of wine. The clatter of horse-drawn carriages mixed with the chatter of merchants negotiating deals. Children played games, their laughter echoing off the stone walls. And above it all, the distant roar of the crowd from the Circus Maximus carried on the wind.

Interactions with Locals: I approached a woman weaving fabric outside her modest domus. She smiled, her hands deftly working the loom. We exchanged pleasantries in Latin, and she offered me a cup of spiced wine. Her eyes held a mix of curiosity and suspicion—perhaps wondering why a stranger wore such peculiar clothing.

Copilot responds from the perspective of the fictional time traveler.

You can continue the conversation using iterative prompting as you learned earlier in this chapter, such as asking for more information about any of the scenes and experiences in the response.

 TIP You can also use persona prompting to name specific people, such as your favorite author or entrepreneur, to discuss a problem or explain something to you.

Write for a persona

The persona prompting pattern is also useful to create content for a particular audience. In this case, you describe the persona you are writing for, rather than the persona creating the content. This is a useful way to use the "rewrite" capabilities of Copilot in Word. In this example, you ask Copilot to write a message about remote work for the employees of the business, using the original blog post as the source.

2

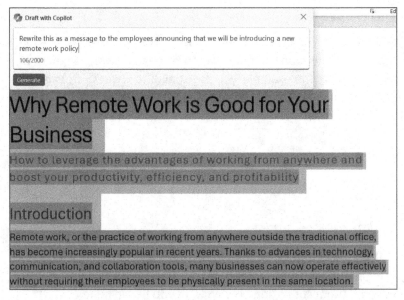

You can use the persona pattern to ask Copilot to write content for a different audience.

Copilot responds with a message written with the employees in mind.

We are excited to announce that we will be introducing a new remote work policy for our company. This policy will allow you to work from anywhere outside the traditional office, as long as you meet your goals and expectations.

We believe that remote work can offer many benefits for our company and for you, such as:

- Increased productivity: You will be able to work in your preferred environment, avoid distractions and interruptions, and manage your own schedule and pace. Research shows that remote workers are more focused, motivated, and self-directed than office workers.
- Reduced costs: We will be able to save money on office rent, utilities, equipment, travel, and other expenses associated with maintaining a physical workspace. We will also be able to hire and retain the best talent from different locations and time zones, which will enhance our diversity and competitiveness.
- Improved employee satisfaction and retention: You will be able to improve your work-life balance, flexibility, autonomy, and well-being. You will have more time for your personal and family needs, and less stress from commuting and office politics. Studies show that remote workers are happier, more loyal, and more

Copilot responds by providing text with the employees in mind first.

 SEE ALSO You will learn how to use the rewrite capability of Copilot in Word in Chapter 7, "Copilot in Word."

Ask for multiple options

If you are using Copilot to help you generate new ideas, you can ask it to provide multiple options or suggestions. This is an example of another way to use the element of expectations in your prompt. In this example, you ask Copilot to suggest more engaging titles for the blog post on remote work, using that as the source.

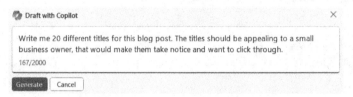

Ask Copilot to generate multiple options or suggestions.

Copilot responds with a list of suggestions to choose from. This can be more effective than just getting a single response and iterating, although you can still refine your prompt at this point if the suggestions don't match what you had in mind.

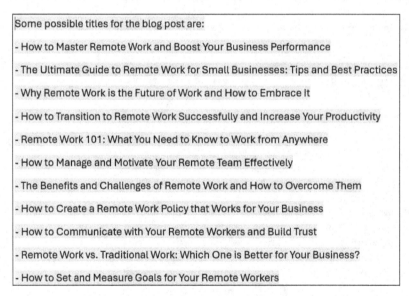

Ask Copilot to provide you with more than one option to use in your content.

Providing examples

Another way to prompt Copilot with expectations is to provide examples of the output you are seeking. This type of prompting is called "in-context learning." You are effectively training the model in the context of the conversation.

2

In this example, you are asking Copilot to create a job description for a marketing manager. You have a particular kind of output in mind, so you provide an example from another job description you already have.

> **TIP** Notice the use of quotation marks here to separate the example from the rest of the prompt.

 You are a recruitment specialist. Here is an example of a job description for a software developer:
Example:
'Job Title: Software Developer
Responsibilities: Develop and maintain software applications, collaborate with cross-functional teams, and participate in code reviews. Requirements: Bachelor's degree in Computer Science, 3+ years of experience in software development, proficiency in Java and Python. Preferred: Experience with cloud technologies and Agile methodologies.'
Now, write a job description for a marketing manager.

Provide Copilot with examples to show how you want the response to be presented.

Copilot responds by following the example provided, generating the job description with a title, list of responsibilities, and list of requirements.

Job Title: Marketing Manager

Responsibilities:

- Develop and execute marketing strategies to drive brand awareness, customer acquisition, and revenue growth.
- Collaborate with cross-functional teams (including sales, product, and creative) to create integrated marketing campaigns.
- Analyze market trends, customer insights, and competitive landscapes to inform marketing decisions.
- Manage digital marketing channels (such as social media, email, and SEO) and track performance metrics.
- Oversee marketing budgets, allocate resources effectively, and optimize ROI.
- Lead a team of marketing professionals, providing guidance, coaching, and performance evaluations.

Requirements:

- Bachelor's degree in Marketing, Business, or a related field.
- 5+ years of experience in marketing, with a focus on strategy, campaign management, and team leadership.
- Proficiency in digital marketing tools and analytics platforms.

Copilot generates a job description following the example format.

Compare this with the response you get from the more general prompt, "write a job description for a marketing manager," where there is no example output format specified.

Without an example, Copilot gives general suggestions about the role of a marketing manager.

Brainstorming and problem solving

You can also change the question-and-answer pattern so that Copilot asks you questions. This is useful if you want Copilot to help you with brainstorming or thinking through or solving a problem. This is known as the "flipped interaction pattern."

Rather than asking Copilot to come up with a workout schedule, you can ask it to ask you questions about your needs first.

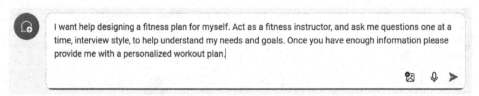

Ask Copilot to ask you a series of questions rather than providing an answer.

Copilot responds with a question instead of an answer and then works through a series of questions with you before generating a final response.

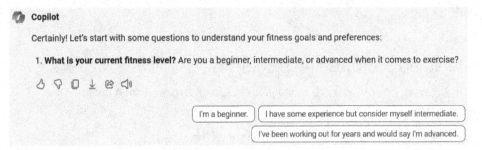

Copilot responds by asking you a question.

Skills review

In this chapter, you learned how to:

- Understand how generative AI works with prompts and responses.

- Discover and use suggested prompts with Copilot Lab for different apps, tasks, and job roles.

- Write effective prompts for Copilot using the main elements of a prompt: goal, context, source, and expectations.

- Write prompts to generate images and use Copilot to help you describe different image styles.

- Use more advanced prompting techniques including the persona pattern, asking for multiple options, using examples, and brainstorming.

Practice tasks

No practice files are necessary to complete the practice tasks in this chapter.

Understand prompts and responses

In your browser, navigate to *https://copilot.microsoft.com*, and then perform the following tasks:

1. Select the **Sign in** button at the top right of the screen.

2. Sign in with the Microsoft account you used to sign up for Copilot Pro.

3. In the prompt area, enter the following prompt: Mary had a

4. Select the arrow icon to submit the prompt.

5. Notice that Copilot completes the first line of the nursery rhyme, "Mary had a little lamb," based on predicting what is most likely to come next from the prompt you entered.

Discover and use suggested prompts with Copilot Lab

Open your browser, navigate to Copilot Lab, and then perform the following tasks:

1. Navigate to the Copilot Lab home page: *https://copilot.cloud.microsoft/en-US/prompts*.

2. Select the **Sign in** icon at the top right of the screen, and sign in using the Microsoft account you used to sign up for Copilot Pro.

3. Scroll down to the suggested prompts.

4. Select **View all prompts**.

5. Select the **App** menu, and then select **PowerPoint**.

6. Select the **Job** menu, and then select **Create**.

7. Scroll through the suggested prompts on the screen, select the suggested prompt to **Develop training materials**, and open it.

8. Read the details of the prompt, and then select the **ribbon** icon to save it. Close the card window.

9. Browse through the other suggested prompts and select the **ribbon** icon for any other prompts you think would be useful.

10. Select the **Saved prompts** button to view your saved prompts.

11. Select the **ribbon** icon to deselect any prompts you don't want to keep after this practice task.

12. Select the **Saved prompts** button again to return to the full list of prompts.

Use the elements of effective prompts

In your browser, navigate to *https://copilot.microsoft.com*, and then perform the following tasks:

1. In the prompt area, enter the following prompt: Help me plan for a holiday to Slovenia

2. Refine this prompt by adding context. In the prompt area, type I will be traveling with my partner and two children aged 8 and 10. We are looking for a mixture of fun activities, beaches, and places to relax.

3. Refine the prompt again by adding expectations about the output. In the prompt area, type This sounds great. Please suggest an itinerary to visit these places for a two-week trip.

4. Select any of the suggested prompts to continue the conversation.

Write prompts to generate images

Remain in the browser with *https://copilot.microsoft.com* open, and then perform the following tasks:

1. Select the **New topic** button to start a new conversation.

2. Enter the following prompt: Create an image of sunset over the beach in a bold impressionist style.

3. After Copilot has generated the images, add a new prompt: Change it to a realistic polaroid photo style.

4. Select the **New topic** button.

5. In the prompt area, ask Copilot for help with your next prompt by typing: How can I write a prompt to generate an image of the New York skyline as a pop-up book.

6. Copy the suggested prompt Copilot provides in the response.

7. Select the **New topic** button.

8. Paste in the suggested response from Copilot or use this one: Design a vibrant pop-up book scene featuring the iconic New York City skyline. Capture the towering skyscrapers, the Statue of Liberty, and the Brooklyn Bridge. Imagine the cityscape coming to life as the pages unfold, revealing intricate paper structures and colorful details.

Use more advanced prompting techniques

Remain in the browser with *https://copilot.microsoft.com* open, and then perform the following tasks:

1. Select the **New topic** button to start a new conversation.

2. Enter the following prompt: Act as an entrepreneur who is investing in new food businesses. You are having a meeting with a young pastry chef who has an idea for a food truck that specializes in desserts. What questions would you ask?

3. Enter the following prompt: Act as the pastry chef. Please suggest 10 ideas for signature desserts you could offer.

4. Select one of the options and write a new prompt asking Copilot to expand on that idea. Your prompt will be I love the sound of [insert dessert name here]. Please help me write a description for the menu and suggest three more ideas for the name of that dessert.

Part 2

Use Copilot Pro on the web and the mobile app

Copilot on the Web

3

You can use Copilot on the web to generate text, images, code, songs, and more. Copilot on the web is the place to have free-form conversations to generate new content outside of a specific application or to learn, brainstorm, solve problems, or explore new ideas. When you chat with Copilot on the web, the conversation is connected to the web via Bing search, so the responses will often include citations and links to webpages. There are also plug-ins you can enable to connect your chat to specific sites and services for restaurant bookings, shopping, travel, and more. Copilot on the web is the Copilot equivalent of ChatGPT. Your Copilot Pro license gives you access to some premium features beyond the free Copilot on the web experience, including priority access to the fastest and most effective language models, and additional boosts for creating images.

In this chapter, you will learn how to chat with Copilot on the web and use all the features available in this interface to generate text, images, and even songs. You will learn how to use different conversation styles, enable plug-ins, and iterate your prompts with the Notebook features. You will also learn how to use Copilot in Microsoft Edge to chat with the content on your webpage or a PDF document open in the web browser.

In this chapter

- Get started with Copilot Pro on the web
- Chat with Copilot
- Choose a conversation style
- Generate images
- Use plug-ins
- Use the Notebook
- Use the Copilot in Edge sidebar

Practice files

You will need to use the practice files provided with this chapter to complete the practice tasks.

Get started with Copilot Pro on the web

You can access Copilot on the web for free without signing in, but to use all the features included in your Copilot Pro license, including access to premium large language models (LLMs) and extra boosts for image generation, you must sign in.

> **TIP** You can access Copilot on the web from any browser, but Edge is highly recommended. Using Edge will provide you with more features, which will be covered later in this chapter.

To use Copilot Pro on the web

1. Navigate to the Copilot home page: *https://copilot.microsoft.com.*

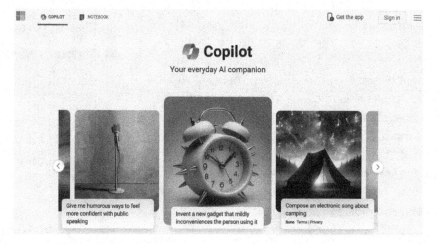

You must sign in to the Copilot home page to access Copilot Pro features.

2. Select the **Sign in** button near the top right of the screen and choose **Sign in with a personal account**.

Sign in with the personal Microsoft account you used to sign up for Copilot Pro.

3. Sign in with the Microsoft account you used to sign up for Copilot Pro.

4. When you have successfully signed in, your name and profile icon will appear in place of the sign-in box, and the main heading will now show "Copilot Pro" rather than just "Copilot."

When you have signed in, you will see the heading change to Copilot Pro.

Copilot provides a carousel of suggested prompts to give you ideas and inspiration to get started. These suggestions offer different ways you can use Copilot, including learning about or getting tips or fun facts on a topic, inventing new recipes, creating plans, composing songs, generating images, writing poems and jokes, solving problems, or getting advice.

 TIP The suggestions will be different each time you visit Copilot on the web. To see more suggestions, you can refresh your browser.

To use a suggested prompt from the carousel

1. Use the **left** and **right arrows** at either end of the carousel to browse through the prompt suggestions.

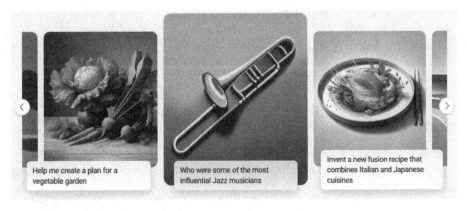

Browse the carousel for prompt ideas and inspiration.

2. When you find a prompt that you'd like to try, select it.

> ⚠️ **IMPORTANT** Do not select a prompt to compose a song at this stage. Composing songs requires enabling a plug-in, which will be covered later in the chapter.

3. Copilot will receive the prompt and immediately start generating a response.

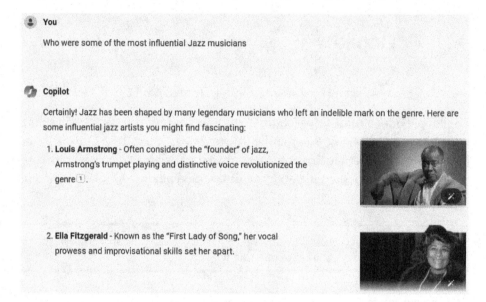

Copilot uses the selected prompt and generates a response.

Chat with Copilot

You will use the main prompt area to chat with Copilot to ask questions and generate content. In this section, you will learn how to use all the features of the prompt area and work with the responses.

Prompts and responses

You should always tell Copilot when you are about to start a new topic of conversation, to clear the context of the previous conversation and avoid any confusion between topics.

To start a new conversation topic

1. Select the **New topic** button to the left of the prompt area.

Select the New topic button to tell Copilot you want to start a new conversation.

2. Copilot responds by clearing the previous responses and letting you know it is ready for a new conversation.

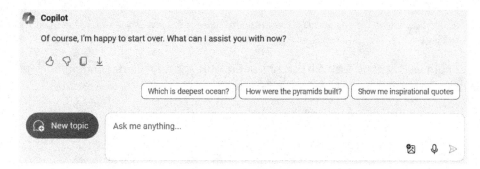

Copilot confirms it is ready to start a new conversation.

3. You can now enter any prompt into the prompt area to begin a new conversation. Enter a prompt and press Enter or select the arrow icon.

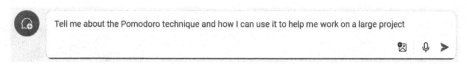

Enter your prompt into the prompt area and press Enter.

> **TIP** You can select the **microphone** icon in the prompt area to dictate your prompt with your voice.

As soon as you have entered your prompt, you will see Copilot start to generate a response. You will also see a Stop Responding button appear above the prompt area. If you realize that you made a mistake in your prompt or notice that the response isn't what you had in mind, select this button to stop Copilot from generating any more content. You can then type in a new prompt.

The Stop Responding button appears above the prompt area as soon as Copilot starts generating a response.

Copilot will respond with paragraphs or bullet points of text, depending on your prompt. It may also include images or emojis.

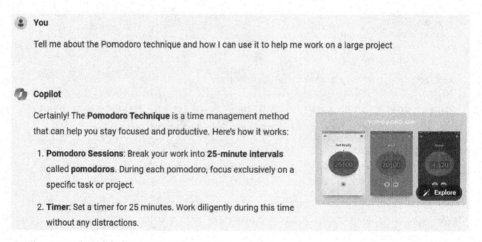

Copilot responds with bullet points and an image.

If Copilot has used web sources to generate the response, you will see citations against those parts of the response, and a list of websites at the end of the response. You can hover over the citations and websites to view more information or follow the links to view the original source.

History: The technique was invented by Francesco Cirillo in the late 1980s. He used a tomato-shaped kitchen timer (hence the name "Pomodoro") to stay focused during short study sessions [1] [2].

Give it a try! Adapt the intervals to suit your prefe

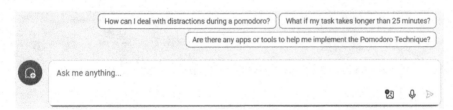

The Pomodoro Technique — Why it works & how to d...
https://todoist.com/productivity-methods/pomodoro-techniq...

Learn more 1 todoist.com 2 w en.wikipedia.org 3 microsoftstart.msn.com +4 more

Copilot provides citations, links to websites, and suggested prompts.

> ⚠️ **IMPORTANT** Generative AI is creative by nature, so you will not always get the same response to the same prompt each time. That means you may also get different suggestions to continue the conversation each time, based on the response generated.

Copilot will also generate a list of suggested prompts to help you continue the conversation to get more information or refine the results. Select a suggested prompt to use it.

> 🔍 **SEE ALSO** You will find more information about how to iterate your prompts and continue the conversation with Copilot in Chapter 2, "Writing effective prompts."

How can I deal with distractions during a pomodoro?   What if my task takes longer than 25 minutes?

Are there any apps or tools to help me implement the Pomodoro Technique?

Ask me anything...

Select a suggested prompt to continue the conversation.

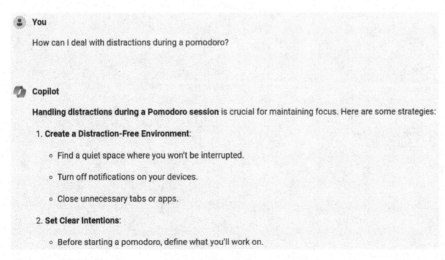

You

How can I deal with distractions during a pomodoro?

Copilot

Handling distractions during a Pomodoro session is crucial for maintaining focus. Here are some strategies:

1. **Create a Distraction-Free Environment**:
   - Find a quiet space where you won't be interrupted.
   - Turn off notifications on your devices.
   - Close unnecessary tabs or apps.

2. **Set Clear Intentions**:
   - Before starting a pomodoro, define what you'll work on.

Copilot generates a response from the selected prompt.

Edit or search based on your prompt

If you want to iterate using the same prompt with small changes, you can scroll back up to your prompt and hover just under the prompt to see more options that allow you to edit or search based on your prompt.

Select the **pencil** icon to edit your prompt.

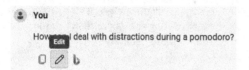

Hover under your prompt to reveal the option to edit.

Selecting this icon re-enters the original prompt into the prompt area, where you can make changes and send it to Copilot again.

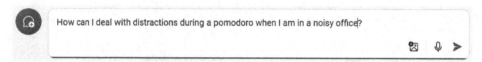

Make the changes to your prompt and select the arrow icon or press Enter to resend.

There is also an option to use the prompt to search the web using Bing.

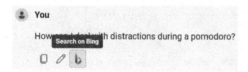

Hover under your prompt to reveal the option to search on Bing.

Selecting this icon will open Bing search in a new browser tab with your prompt automatically entered in the search box. You can easily switch back and forth between Bing and Copilot on the web using the tabs under the search box.

3

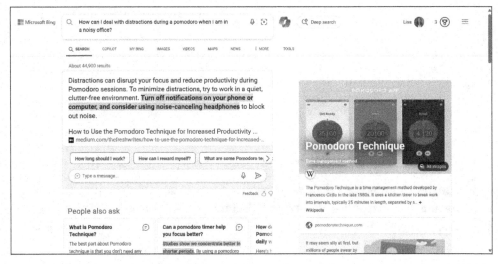

Search on Bing enters your prompt into Bing search in a new browser tab.

 TIP You can scroll back through the conversation to use the edit or search options with any of the prompts you've written in that conversation.

 TIP You can start a new Copilot session with the text in the search box by selecting the Copilot tab next to the search tab.

Select the Copilot tab next to the search tab in Bing search to start a new Copilot session based on the text in the Bing search box.

Work with the Copilot response

At the end of every response from Copilot you will also have the following options that you can use to work with the response.

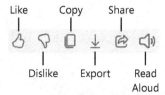

Copilot gives you options to work with the generated response.

- Use the **Thumbs up** icon to tell Copilot that you liked the response.

- Use the **Thumbs down** icon to provide feedback about that wasn't right or helpful in the response. When you select this option, you will see an expandable menu where you can provide additional feedback or report a legal or policy issue. This is optional.

Expand the Give Feedback menu to provide detailed feedback.

Report the response and add detailed feedback.

- Select the **Copy** icon to copy the content of the response to your clipboard.

■ Select the **Export** icon to download the content of the response in Word, PDF, or Text format.

You can download the response content in Word, PDF, or Text format.

■ Select the **Share** icon to get a link to the response that you can copy to your clipboard. You can send this to anyone, and they can paste the link into a browser and view the response, even without signing in to Copilot.

When you select the Share icon, you will see a pop-up window with a link you can copy to your clipboard.

■ Select the **Read aloud** icon to hear the response read aloud. This icon changes into a pause icon while the response is being read so that you can pause or stop listening at any time. You will also see a playback indicator in the prompt area.

When Copilot reads aloud, the speaker icon changes to a pause icon, and the playback indicator appears in the prompt area.

Generate code

You can ask Copilot to generate code in various programming languages. Copilot can help you write code for many scenarios, including for algorithms and data structures, creating code snippets, custom functions, SQL queries, web development code, and automation scripts.

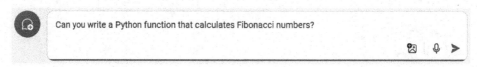

Can you write a Python function that calculates Fibonacci numbers?

You can ask Copilot to generate code.

When you use Copilot to generate code, the response is presented in a format that makes it easy for you to copy the code to use it where you need it. Select the copy icon in the top right of the response.

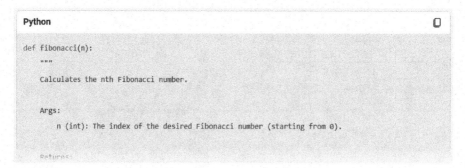

```
Python                                                              □

def fibonacci(n):
    """

    Calculates the nth Fibonacci number.

    Args:
        n (int): The index of the desired Fibonacci number (starting from 0).

    Returns:
```

Select the copy icon at the top right of the response to copy the code.

Add an image to your prompt

You can upload an image to use in your prompt. This is useful if you want Copilot to help you describe the image, answer questions about the image, use the image as inspiration for creative content or as source content for your prompt, or analyze or provide insights about your image.

In this example, you have an image of a collaborative office space that is available for lease, and you need to write marketing copy for the website. Rather than describing the aesthetic of the space in detail, you can add this image to your prompt.

3

You can upload an image to use as part of your prompt.

To add an image to your prompt

1. Select the **Add image** icon at the bottom right of the prompt area.

2. Add an image by pasting the image, pasting a link to an online image, uploading an image from your device, or using the camera on your device to take a photo.

 SEE ALSO You will learn how to use photos in prompts in Chapter 4, "Copilot mobile app."

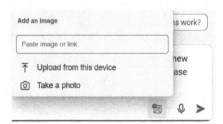

You can add an image by pasting the image or link, uploading an image, or taking a photo.

3. Write your prompt, including describing how you want Copilot to use the image as a source.

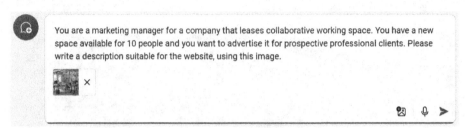

Write your prompt describing how you want Copilot to use the image as a source.

4. Copilot responds, using the image as source content.

Copilot uses the image to help generate the response.

> 🔍 **SEE ALSO** You can also upload images as part of a prompt when you are generating an image. You will learn more about that in the section on generating images later in this chapter.

Manage your chat history

Each time you chat with Copilot, the topic is saved in a list of recent chats, which you can view on the right side of the screen.

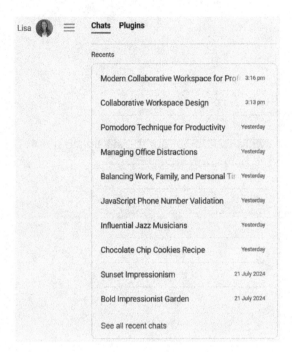

You can view your Copilot chat history on the right side of the screen.

Select any item in the chat history to return to the chat results you previously generated with Copilot.

Select an item in the chat history to return to that chat.

Hover over any item in the chat history for additional options:

- Select the **Pencil** icon to edit the name of the topic in the chat history.

- Select the **Trash can** icon to remove the topic from your chat history.

Hover over the chat history item for more options.

- In the **more options** (...) menu, you will also find options to get a link to share the topic or to export it in Word, PDF, or Text format.

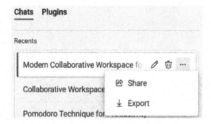

Select the more options menu to view options to share or export the chat history topic.

Choose a conversation style

When you chat with Copilot on the web, you can choose from three different conversation styles using the buttons above the prompt pane.

Copilot will start in **Balanced** style by default. This option is suitable for most scenarios, providing a balance between accuracy and creativity.

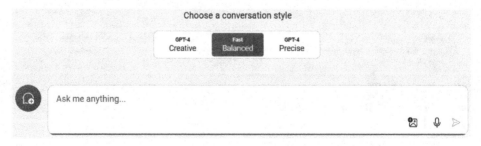

Copilot uses the Balanced option by default.

The **Creative** style will generate more imaginative responses. Use this option when you are working with Copilot on creative projects or when you want to generate humor or rhyme, or when you want it to be creative with language and ideas. It can also help with more creative thinking for your business scenarios.

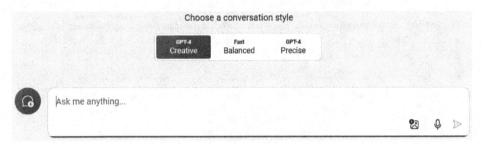

Use the Creative style to generate more imaginative responses.

The **Precise** style will prioritize accuracy over creativity and give you a more factual answer. Use this option when you are working with Copilot in scenarios where accuracy is the most important, such as asking it to write code, summarize content, or when you are asking about facts that don't change.

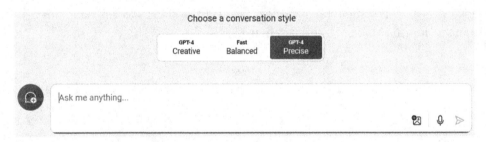

Use the Precise style when you want factual and accurate responses.

Compare the difference in the following responses to the same prompt in each style.

The prompt used is: "Describe a futuristic mode of transportation."

Balanced style provides a summarized list of futuristic modes of transportation that are in development or being prototyped, including citations and web references.

 Copilot

Certainly! Let's explore some exciting futuristic modes of transportation:

1. **Maglev Trains**: These high-speed trains use magnetic levitation from powerful electromagnets to travel at incredible speeds with less noise and vibration compared to traditional trains [1]. Imagine gliding silently along tracks, reaching destinations faster than ever before!

2. **Flying Taxis**: Already being prototyped by at least 20 companies, flying taxis aim to revolutionize urban transportation. These aerial vehicles combine the convenience of taxis with the freedom of flight, bypassing traffic and congestion [1]. Picture hopping into a compact aircraft for a quick commute above the cityscape!

3. **Driverless Cars**: Autonomous vehicles are becoming more common. These cars operate without human interference, relying on sensors, cameras, and AI algorithms to navigate roads safely. Imagine sitting back and relaxing while your car drives you to your destination.

4. **Delivery Drones**: Unmanned aerial vehicles (UAVs) designed for last-mile delivery. Controlled remotely or autonomously, these rechargeable drones use GPS and computer vision systems to drop off lightweight packages directly to your doorstep [1]. Say goodbye to waiting for delivery trucks!

In Balanced style, Copilot responds with a list of futuristic modes of transportation with references.

Creative style invents something that doesn't yet exist, asking us to "imagine" this innovative futuristic mode of transportation.

 Copilot

Imagine a mode of transportation called the **AeroLoop**. It's a sleek, autonomous vehicle that combines the best of high-speed rail and personal car comfort. The AeroLoop is a network of electrically powered, magnetically levitated pods that travel through low-pressure tubes at speeds exceeding **1,000 km/h**. Here's a glimpse into this futuristic transit system:

- **Design**: Each AeroLoop pod is designed with aerodynamics in mind, featuring a bullet-shaped body that reduces air resistance. The interior is spacious, with adjustable seating, ambient lighting, and virtual windows displaying scenic views or entertainment of choice.

- **Technology**: Utilizing magnetic levitation (maglev) technology, the pods float above the track, eliminating friction and allowing for incredibly high speeds. The entire system is powered by renewable energy sources, making it a green transportation option.

- **Network**: The AeroLoop network connects cities and even countries with stations located both within urban centers and at outskirts to minimize congestion. Passengers can board at any station and select their destination via an intuitive interface.

In Creative style, Copilot responds by describing an imagined futuristic mode of transportation.

Precise style describes in detail an actual futuristic transportation mode that is being prototyped by different companies.

Copilot

Sure, let's imagine a futuristic mode of transportation called the **Hyperloop Transit System**.

The Hyperloop Transit System is a ground-breaking transportation technology that propels passenger or cargo pods through a near-vacuum tube at speeds that could exceed **700 miles per hour**. This is faster than most commercial airplanes, making it possible to travel from Los Angeles to San Francisco in just 30 minutes!

The system operates on magnetic levitation technology, with the pods floating above the track, eliminating friction and allowing for smooth, efficient travel. The tubes are maintained at a low-pressure environment to minimize air resistance.

The Hyperloop is not only fast but also environmentally friendly. It's powered by renewable energy sources, including solar panels installed on the top of the tubes, making it a zero-emission transit system.

This futuristic mode of transportation could revolutionize how we travel, offering high-speed connections between cities and potentially transforming economic landscapes. Imagine living in one city and commuting to another hundreds of miles away on a daily basis!

In Precise style, Copilot responds with information about a real futuristic mode of transportation.

Depending on the kind of prompt you write, the responses using these three styles can be fairly similar or very different from each other. When you choose a style, you will remain in that style during your Copilot session, even when you start a new topic, until you choose a different style.

Balanced style is usually the best place to start, unless you know you are looking for a more creative or precise response. If you don't get the kind of response you wanted using Balanced mode, you can use the **New topic** button to start a new conversation with the same prompt in a different style.

3

Generate images

You can use Copilot on the web to generate images in any style using the DALL-E 3 image mode. With your Copilot Pro license, you get access to 100 "boosts" per day for faster image generation.

To generate an image, type the description of the image you want to create. It helps to think about the image in your mind and then describe it as if you were writing a caption. You can describe a general or specific artistic, photographic, or other creative medium as the style of the image. You can also start with a general prompt and use the options in Copilot to help you iterate and refine it.

> **SEE ALSO** You can learn more about writing prompts to generate images in Chapter 2.

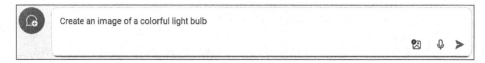

Describe the image you want to generate.

Copilot will generate four alternative images based on your prompt.

Copilot generates four images in response to your prompt.

At the bottom right of the generated images, you will see the number of boosts remaining for the day, indicated by a coin icon. Your Copilot Pro license gives you 100 boosts per day, so this will display as 99 the first time you generate an image, which uses the first boost for the day. Each time you iterate your prompt to generate a new image or write a new prompt to generate an image, you will use a boost, and you will see this count decrease.

3

You can see the remaining number of boosts available each time you generate an image.

Select the image you like best to see it in more detail and to access the options to copy, share, download, and edit your image.

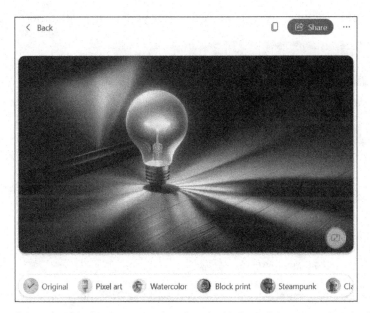

Select one of the images to open it and work with the options to copy, download, share, or edit your image.

Copy, share, and download your image

You can use the following options to save, share, download, or open your image in Microsoft Designer for further editing:

- Select the **Copy** icon to copy the image to your clipboard.

Copy the generated image to your clipboard.

- Select the **Share** button to get a link you can use to share your image with others.

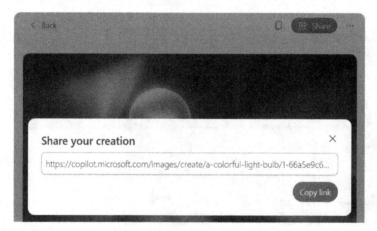

Select the Share button to get a sharable link for your image.

- Select the **more options** (...) menu to view options to edit in Designer, download your image, or view more information.

Select the more options menu to edit, download, or get more information about your image.

- Select **Edit in Designer** to open your image in a new tab in Microsoft Designer. You can use Microsoft Designer to create all sorts of designs, including greeting cards, stickers, collages, and invitations. You can also use Designer to edit and restyle your image.

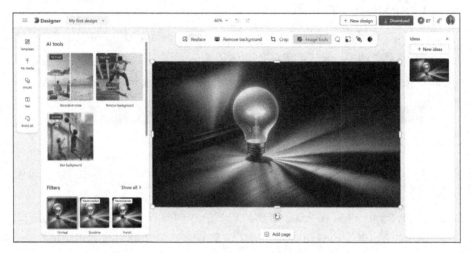

You can edit your image in Microsoft Designer to make further changes.

- Select the **Download** option to download the image to your device.

Select the Download option to download the image.

- The **More information** option will display the image size in pixels and the date and time of creation.

Select More information to view information about the image size and the time and date it was generated.

Edit your image in Copilot

You can use Copilot to change the artistic style and format of the image and apply some special effects.

To edit your image in Copilot

1. You will find a list of image styles below your selected image. Use the **left** and **right arrows** to scroll through the options.

2. Select the **Origami** style option to regenerate your image in that style.

Select a style option to re-create your image in that style.

3. After Copilot has re-created the image, you will have the option to keep it, by selecting the **Looks good** button, or to revert to the original image by selecting the **Undo** button.

Select the Looks good button to keep your new image.

4. Select the **resize** icon in the bottom right corner of your generated image to resize it.

Select the resize button to change your image into square or landscape format.

5. Choose **Square** to change your image to a square format.

Select the Square option to change the size of your image.

6. Keep the resized image by selecting the **Looks good** button. You also have the option to revert to the original format by selecting the **Undo** button.

Select the Looks good button to keep your resized image.

7. Hover over the image to select a section of the image, and then select it to add a color pop or blurred background effect.

Hover over and select a section of the image to apply a special effect.

8. Select **Color pop.**

Select the Undo button to return to the image without the color pop.

9. Select the **Undo** button to go back to the version of the image without the color pop.

You can continue the conversation with Copilot by using the suggested prompts and by writing your own prompt at any time to continue refining the image.

Use the suggested prompts or write a new prompt to refine your image.

If you create an image you want to keep, remember to download it, or open it in Microsoft Designer to save and continue editing.

Add an image to your prompt to generate an image

You can also use images as part of your prompt when asking Copilot to generate an image. Use this option when you have an image that is the starting point or inspiration for what you want to create or to give Copilot a visual description of what you have in mind without having to describe it in words.

In this example, you want to create an art deco style poster of an office space, using the same image of the office space you used earlier.

Use the **add image** icon to upload your image into the prompt, as shown earlier in this chapter, and then write a prompt to ask Copilot to generate an image in the style you want, using this image as the source.

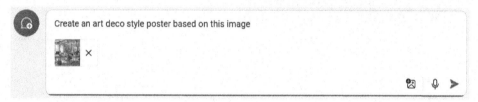

Select the add image icon to add an image to your prompt.

Copilot generates the image as requested, without you needing to describe the scene or any detail.

"Create an art deco style poster featuring a modern office interior ..."

Copilot uses the image in the prompt to generate the requested image.

Use plug-ins

Copilot on the web includes prebuilt plug-ins that allow you to connect your chat to services that can help with recipes, travel, restaurant bookings, shopping, and more. You can enable or disable these plug-ins using a toggle switch and choose up to three plug-ins at a time to use in your conversation.

3

> **TIP** The Search plug-in is enabled by default for all conversations. This plug-in means that Copilot finds information on the web when it responds to your prompts. You can choose to switch this off if you prefer for any conversation.

> ⚠ **IMPORTANT** Some of these plug-ins are available only in the US or work only with services in the US.

To use a plug-in with your chat

1. Select the **New topic** button to start a new conversation.

2. Select the **Plug-ins** option at the top right of the browser, next to the **Chats** option.

Select the Plug-ins option to view available plug-ins.

3. Scroll through the list of available plug-ins and select a plug-in by toggling the switch on the plug-in card to the **on** position.

Enable a plug-in using the toggle on the card.

4. Start your chat with a prompt that will make use of the selected plug-in(s).

Write a prompt to use the plug-in.

5. Copilot will indicate that it used a plug-in to generate the response by showing the plug-in icon at the top of the response.

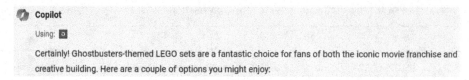

Copilot shows the Shop icon at the top of the prompt to indicate it has used that plug-in in the response.

6. You will also find links to the plug-in site at the end of the response, which you can follow to continue with your task, such as making a purchase or booking.

Select the links from the plug-in at the end of the response to continue your task.

Each time you want to change, add, or remove plug-ins, you will need to select the **New topic** button to start a new conversation.

Generating a song using the Suno plug-in

You can use the Suno plug-in with Copilot to generate up to five songs per day.

To ask Copilot to generate a song

1. Select the **New topic** button to start a new conversation.

2. Select the **Plug-ins** option at the top right of the browser, next to the **Chats** option.

3. Scroll down to find the **Suno** plug-in and switch the toggle to the **on** position. Switch off any other plug-ins except Search.

Enable the Suno plug-in to generate songs with Copilot.

4. Write a prompt to ask Copilot to generate a song.

> **TIP** Your prompt to generate a song can be a simple request that includes a theme and musical style, or you can provide more specific detail including phrases or lines to use in the lyrics, or the mood of the song. You should describe the style of music rather than naming a particular artist. You can also ask Copilot to help you write a good prompt to generate a song.

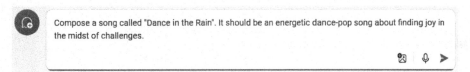

Write a prompt to ask Copilot to generate a song.

5. Copilot will indicate that it is using the Suno plug-in by showing the icon at the top of the response. It will generate the lyrics and then the music and will show a progress message while it is still working.

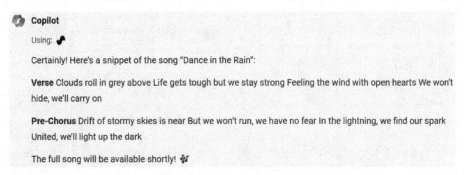

Copilot shows the Suno plug-in icon at the top of the response.

6. When Copilot has finished generating the song, you will see a confirmation message, and a card that shows the lyrics, with a Play button to listen to the song.

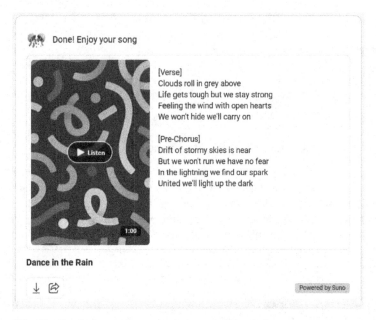

Select the Play button on the generated song to listen to it.

7. You can continue the conversation with Copilot to make changes to the song if you want.

8. When you are happy with the song, you can download it or get a link to share it using the icons at the bottom of the card.

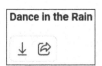

Select the icons to download or share your song.

Use the Notebook

The Notebook feature in Copilot on the web gives you a space to write and refine much longer prompts, with a single persistent box for the response instead of a chat experience. Use this when you want to include much longer source content in your prompt (up to 18,000 characters), such as very long blocks of text.

To use the Notebook

1. Select the **Notebook** option at the top left of the screen.

Select the Notebook option at the top left of the screen.

2. Type your prompt in the prompt area at the top, including pasting in any long blocks of text you want to use as the source in the prompt.

Write your prompt and paste in a long block of text.

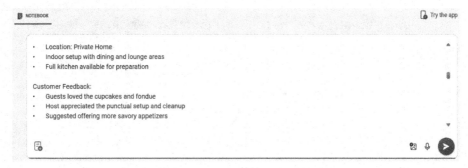

You can include up to 18000 characters in your prompt using Notebook.

3. Select the **arrow** icon to submit your prompt.

4. Copilot responds in the area at the bottom of the screen.

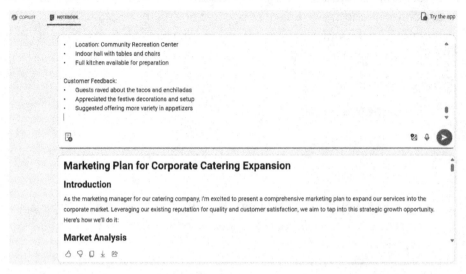

Copilot responds in the bottom section of the Notebook.

5. You can refine your prompt and resubmit to view the new response

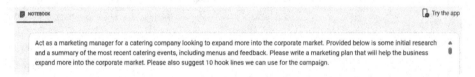

Change or refine your prompt to get a better response.

6. Copilot generates a new response in the bottom section.

Copilot generates a new response in the bottom section of the Notebook.

7. Use the icons under the response to provide feedback, copy, or download the response.

Provide feedback, copy, or download the response.

3

Use the Copilot in Edge sidebar

When you use Copilot in the Microsoft Edge browser, you have access to additional features using Copilot from the sidebar. With the Copilot in Edge sidebar, you can chat with the content open in your browser, which allows you to ask questions about or summarize websites, PDF documents, and YouTube videos. There is also a Compose feature that makes it quick and easy to generate emails, ideas, and social media posts in different tones and lengths without needing to write long prompts.

Chat with website content

To use the Copilot in Edge sidebar to summarize website content

1. With a website open in your browser, select the **Copilot** button at the top of the Edge sidebar.

Select the Copilot icon at the top of the Edge sidebar.

2. The Copilot pane will pop out on the right side of the browser.

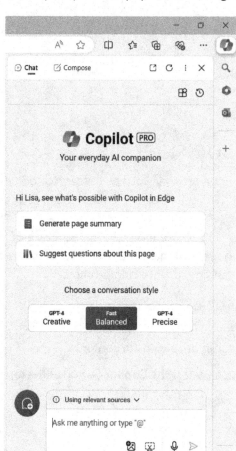

Copilot will open in a panel at the right side of the Edge browser.

3. Select the **Generate page summary** button.

4. Copilot shows a summary of the webpage open in your browser. At the top of the response, it indicates that it is using that website for the response.

Copilot summarizes the content of the website open in the browser.

The first time you use this feature, you will get a notification telling you that Copilot is using "context clues," meaning it has access to the webpage and browser history when generating a response. There is a link in this notification to help you manage your settings if you prefer to turn off this option.

Copilot is using context clues

Copilot gives better answers based on the current webpage, browser history, or your preferences in Microsoft Edge. This data only applies to context clues and won't be used otherwise.

Manage settings

Follow this notification link to manage your settings if you prefer to turn off this feature.

You can use Copilot chat in the Edge sidebar to chat with reference to the website content, or for general questions and prompts, or mix up the conversation between these things. Copilot will default to using "Relevant sources," which means it decides from the context of your prompt whether to use the website content or to respond with general knowledge and web search.

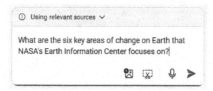

Copilot defaults to using relevant sources to decide what to use based on the context of your prompt.

If you want to be sure that Copilot will use the content of the website open in your browser, you can change this setting using the expandable menu at the top of the prompt area to select whether it should use the current page or the current website.

Tell Copilot to use this website when generating the response.

 TIP You can also type @ in the prompt to bring up this menu to select the source you want Copilot to use.

Add a screenshot to your prompt

You can take a screenshot of any part of the open website and add that to your prompt. This is useful if you want to ask a question about or identify something in an image on the website.

To add a screenshot into your prompt

1. In the prompt area, select the **snip** icon.

Select the snip icon to add a screenshot.

2. Drag your mouse to select the image or area of the website you want to take as a screenshot.

3. Select the **green check mark** to finalize your selection.

Drag your mouse to select the screenshot area and select the green check mark when done.

4. This puts the image into the prompt area. Type your question to complete your prompt and send it to Copilot by pressing **Enter** or selecting the **arrow** icon.

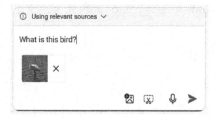

Type your prompt to go with the selected screenshot.

5. Copilot responds using the screenshot as the source information in the prompt.

Copilot uses the screenshot to provide a response.

 TIP You can use the other prompting features you learned about earlier in the chapter here too, including adding an image to your prompt and selecting the conversation style.

Chat with a PDF document

You can open a PDF document in your Edge browser and use Copilot in Edge sidebar to generate a summary of the document, ask questions about the document, generate key insights from the document, or write prompts to extract specific information in the format you need.

To use the Copilot in Edge sidebar with a PDF document

1. Open a PDF document in Edge.

2. Select the **Copilot** button at the top of the Edge sidebar.

Open a PDF in Edge and then open the Copilot in Edge sidebar to chat with the document.

3. Select any of the suggested prompts or type your own prompt in the prompt area to ask for specific information from the document.

 TIP You can use the phrase "in this document" in your prompt instead of switching the source menu.

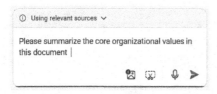

Type your prompt to ask questions about the document.

3

4. Copilot responds showing that it has used the PDF as the source for the response.

Copilot shows at the top of the response that it has used the PDF as the source.

Chat with a YouTube video

You can also use Copilot to understand or ask questions about a YouTube video, based on the video transcript, without needing to watch the whole video.

To use the Copilot in Edge sidebar with a YouTube video

1. Open a YouTube video in Edge.

2. Select the **Copilot** button at the top of the Edge sidebar.

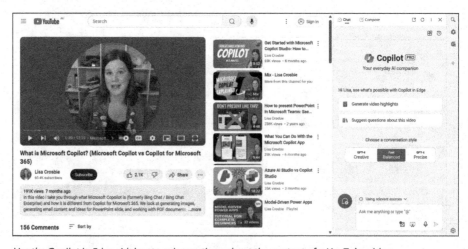

Use the Copilot in Edge sidebar to ask questions about the content of a YouTube video.

3. Select the **Generate video highlights** prompt button.

4. Copilot responds with a video summary and time-stamped highlights of the video.

Copilot uses the transcript of the video to generate highlights.

Use the Compose feature to draft content

The Copilot in Edge sidebar has a separate Compose feature that gives you a quick way to create content in any length and tone using quick button selections rather than needing to type out a full prompt.

To use the Copilot in Edge sidebar Compose feature

1. Select the **Copilot** button at the top of the Edge sidebar.

2. Select the **Compose** option at the top of the Copilot pane.

Select the Compose option at the top of the Copilot pane.

3. Type what you want to write about in the prompt box at the top.

4. Select your tone, format, and length from the options.

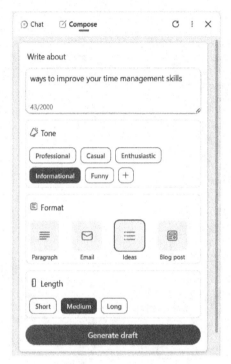

Describe what you want to write about, and then select tone, format, and length options.

5. Select the **Generate draft** button.

6. Copilot drafts a response in the **Preview** window below the prompt area, in the selected tone, format, and length.

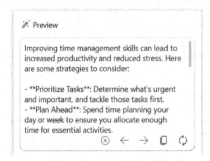

Copilot generates a response based on your prompt and the options selected.

7. Below the response, Copilot provides suggested prompts to rewrite your content. Select one of these to use it.

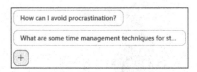

Copilot suggests prompts to help you change or refine your content.

8. Select the **plus** icon to open the option to write your own prompt to ask Copilot to change the content.

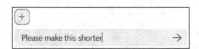

Select the plus icon to write your own prompt to refine the content.

9. Use the icons under the prompt to stop generating, scroll back and forth between the different drafts, copy the content, or regenerate the content.

Use the icons to stop generating, browse between drafts, copy, or regenerate the content.

10. If you want to use the content on something open in your browser, such as for a social media post, place your cursor where you want to use the content and select the **Add to site** button.

11. Copilot copies the content into that area in your browser.

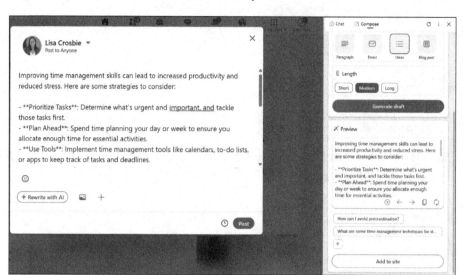

Use the Add to site button to copy the content to the location of your cursor in the browser.

Skills review

In this chapter, you learned how to:

- Chat with Copilot on the web and understand all the options available to you for working with prompts and responses.

- Work with the different conversation styles to make the Copilot responses more creative, balanced, or precise.

- Generate images, change artistic styles, apply formatting, and add special effects.

- Use plug-ins to connect to other web services and generate songs.

- Create and refine longer prompts using the Notebook.

- Chat with content in your web browser, including PDF documents, and compose content using the Copilot in Edge sidebar.

Practice tasks

Before you can complete these tasks, you must copy the book's practice files to your computer. The practice files for these tasks are in the CopilotProSBS\Ch03 folder.

The introduction includes a complete list of practice files and download instructions.

Get started with Copilot Pro on the web

Open the Edge browser, and then complete the following tasks:

1. Navigate to the Copilot home page: *https://copilot.microsoft.com*.

2. Select **Sign in**, and sign in with the Microsoft account you used to sign up for Copilot Pro.

3. Use the **arrows** to browse through the carousel of suggested prompts.

4. Select any prompt.

5. View the response and note any citations and links.

6. Select one of the suggested prompts to continue the conversation.

Chat with Copilot

Continue working from where you finished the previous task, and then complete the following tasks:

1. Select the **New topic** button to start a new conversation.

2. Type the following prompt into the prompt area: Please help me understand calendar blocking.

3. Scroll back up to your prompt and select the **Edit** button, which appears when you hover under the prompt.

4. Edit your prompt to the following: Please help me understand how calendar blocking can make me more productive.

5. Scroll back up and down through the conversation to notice the difference in the responses.

6. Select the **Export** icon, and then select **Word**. The content will open in a Word document in a new tab. Save it if you want to keep it or close the tab without saving.

7. Find this conversation at the top of your Chat history on the right side of the screen and select the **Edit** icon that appears when you hover over the name.

8. Change the name of the conversation history item to: Productivity and Calendar Blocking.

Choose a conversation style

Continue working from where you finished the previous task, and then complete the following tasks:

1. Select the **New topic** button to start a new conversation.

2. Choose the **Creative** conversation style.

3. Type the following prompt into the prompt area: Please write a funny poem about working from home.

4. Open a new tab in your Edge browser and navigate to the Copilot home page: *https://copilot.microsoft.com*.

5. Select the **New topic** button to start a new conversation.

6. Choose the **Precise** conversation style.

7. Type the same prompt into the prompt area: Please write a funny poem about working from home.

8. Wait for Copilot to finish generating the poem, and then switch back and forth between the browser tabs to compare the results between the two different conversation styles.

9. Close the second browser tab.

Generate Images

Continue working from where you finished the previous task, and then complete the following tasks:

1. Select the **New topic** button to start a new conversation.

2. Select the **Balanced** conversation style.

3. Enter the following prompt: Generate an image of a sunrise, using bright colors and an inspirational aesthetic.

4. Wait for Copilot to finish generating the images. Note the number of boosts you have available next to the coin icon at the bottom right of the generated images.

5. Select the image you like best to open it.

6. In the options for the different artistic styles below the image, select **Pixel Art**.

7. When the image has finished regenerating, select the **Looks good** button to keep it.

8. At the top of the image, select the **more options** (...) menu, and then select **Download**.

9. Open the image from your Downloads folder to view it.

Use plug-ins

Continue working from where you finished the previous task, and then complete the following tasks:

1. Select the **New topic** button to start a new conversation.

2. Select the **Plug-ins** option at the top right of the screen.

3. Scroll down to find the **Suno** plug-in and switch the toggle to the **on** position.

4. Enter the following prompt: Write an upbeat and catchy tune that I can use for the introduction to a podcast about productivity.

5. Wait for Copilot and Suno to finish generating the song. Select the **Play** button to listen to the generated song.

Use the Notebook

Continue working from where you finished the previous task, and then complete the following tasks:

1. Select the **Notebook** option at the top left of the screen.

2. In the top section, type the following prompt: Act as a marketing copywriter. Your tone is enthusiastic, professional, and fun. Below is some information about a catering business. Please write some marketing copy for a brochure to help promote the business, including the types of catering offered.

3. Open the Word document called "Corporate Catering Practice Task" from the files provided with this chapter. Select all the text from that document and paste it below your prompt.

4. Select the **arrow** icon in Copilot to submit the prompt.

5. Review the response generated in the bottom section of the Notebook.

6. Select the main **Copilot** option in the top left of the screen.

Use the Copilot in Edge sidebar

Continue working from where you finished the previous task, and then complete the following tasks:

1. From the files provided with this chapter, open the PDF called "Contoso Ltd Digital Transformation" in the Edge browser.

2. Select the **Copilot** icon at the top of the Edge sidebar to open the Copilot pane on the right of the screen.

3. In the prompt area, type the following prompt: What are the main goals of this project? Change the **Using relevant sources** option to **This page**.

4. Select the **arrow** icon to enter your prompt.

5. Copilot will respond showing that it has used the information from the PDF document to generate the response.

Copilot mobile app

You can work with Copilot Pro using your mobile device to search and chat with Copilot on the go, taking advantage of the capabilities of your device. You can chat using voice with the microphone and add images to your prompts using your camera or photo library, helping you search for information and get answers using your surrounding context when you are traveling or just out and about. You can create images and save them to your device and create written content on the go for social media posts and messages.

In this chapter, you'll learn how to download and use the Copilot mobile app for iOS and Android devices; learn how to use this app to ask questions, generate images, and write content; and discover scenarios for which you can benefit from using Copilot Pro on your mobile device.

In this chapter

- Get started with the Copilot mobile app
- Chat and search on the go
- Generate images
- Write content

Practice files

No practice files are necessary to complete the practice tasks in this chapter.

Get started with the Copilot mobile app

The best way to use Copilot Pro on your mobile device is through the Copilot mobile app, which is available for free for iOS and Android devices.

Use the QR code or links below to open and install the Copilot mobile app on your device.

Scan this QR code to download the Copilot mobile app on your device.

- iOS: *https://apps.apple.com/us/app/microsoft-copilot/id6472538445*

- Android: *https://play.google.com/store/apps/details?id=com.microsoft.copilot*

> ✓ **TIP** The Copilot app is the recommended way to work with Copilot Pro on your mobile device, but you can also access Copilot on the Microsoft 365 mobile app, the Bing mobile app, the Microsoft Start mobile app, the Edge mobile app, or when using a mobile web browser.

Sign in to the Copilot mobile application

Once you have downloaded the app to your mobile device, you must sign in to get access to the full features of your Copilot Pro license. Your desktop and mobile experiences are directly connected through your account, so any chat history you have from your desktop web browser will show in the chat history on the mobile app, and vice versa.

To sign in to the Copilot mobile application

1. Open the app you just downloaded on your mobile device.

> ⚠️ **IMPORTANT** You may get a sign-in prompt on your device when you first open the app. Follow the prompts to sign in and skip to the next section. This section shows you how to sign in if you do not get that prompt or if you want to switch or add a new account.

2. The heading will show "Copilot," with a message recommending that you sign in to ask more questions and have more conversations. Select the **Sign in** icon at the top left of the app.

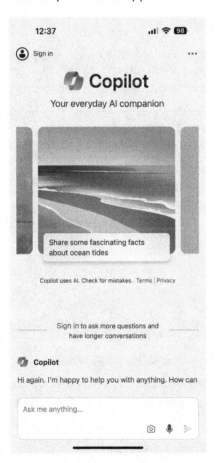

Open the Copilot mobile app on your device and sign in to get the full features of Copilot Pro.

3. The Settings menu will open from the left side of the screen. Under the **Accounts** section, select the **Sign in** option. Sign in with the personal Microsoft account you used to sign up for Copilot Pro.

Sign in using the personal Microsoft account you used to sign up for Copilot Pro.

4. When you have signed in, you will see your Microsoft account email shown in the accounts section, with a check mark next to it, and the option to sign out.

 TIP If you also use Copilot or Microsoft 365 Copilot with a work account, you can sign in with your work account as well and use this menu to switch between them.

When you have signed in, you will see your Microsoft account email with a check mark next to it.

5. Select the **arrow** icon at the top left of the menu to return to the main Copilot screen. Now that you are logged in, you will see that the main header shows "Copilot Pro."

When you have signed in, you will see the heading "Copilot Pro."

Navigate the Copilot mobile app

You have access to all the same features on the Copilot mobile app that you have on the desktop web browser.

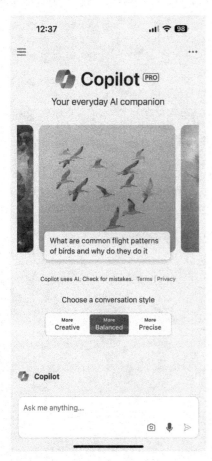

The Copilot mobile app gives you all the same features as you have available on the desktop web browser.

You can select any of the suggested prompts from the carousel to start a conversation or type your prompt into the prompt area. You can choose between creative, balanced, and precise conversation styles.

 SEE ALSO You will learn more about how to use images from your device, camera, or image library in your prompt in the next section.

 SEE ALSO You can learn more about using the carousel and working with different conversation styles in Chapter 3, "Copilot on the web."

Select the menu icon at the top left of the app to access the account and settings menu.

Select the menu icon to open the account and settings menu.

The account and settings menu will pop out on the left of the app, where you can see your logged-in account details, switch between accounts, and view your chat history.

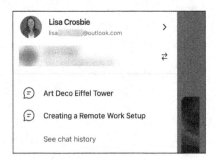

Select the right arrow next to the logged-in account to navigate to the settings menu.

Select the right arrow next to your account to open the settings menu. Here you will find options to set your preferences for notifications, themes, region and language, and more.

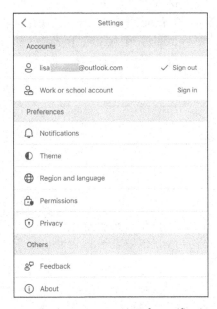

You can change your settings for notifications, theme,
region and language, and more in the settings menu.

Select the arrow at the top left to return to the main Copilot area in the app.

Select the more options menu (...) at the top right of the app to get to the Plugins, Notebook, and Feedback options.

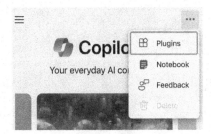

Select the more options menu to get to
Plugins, Notebook, and Feedback.

 SEE ALSO You will learn more about using plug-ins in the Copilot mobile app later in this chapter. To learn about the Notebook feature, see Chapter 3.

Chat and search on the go

You can work with the Copilot mobile app in the same way that you use the desktop web browser experience, to select a prompt suggestion from the carousel or type your prompt in the prompt area. However, when using the mobile app, you can take advantage of searching and chat with Copilot using the capabilities of your mobile device. In this section, you will learn how to use your device's microphone, camera, and image library with your prompts.

 IMPORTANT You will need to give the Copilot mobile app permission to use your device microphone, camera, and photos to use these features.

Chat with Copilot using voice

You can use the microphone on your device to chat with Copilot with your voice. When you use this feature, Copilot will automatically respond by reading out the response using voice, as well as responding in text.

 TIP Using Copilot voice responses can be very useful for translations.

To chat with Copilot using voice

1. Select the **microphone** icon in the prompt area or select the large microphone icon.

Select the microphone icon in the prompt area to chat with Copilot using voice.

2. The icon will change to a larger microphone icon, and the prompt will change to "I'm listening...."

A larger microphone icon appears, and the prompt changes to "I'm listening...."

3. Start speaking to your device immediately to ask your question. You don't need to press on or hold down the microphone icon. Copilot will transcribe your voice (including adding punctuation and capital letters) and add it to the prompt area. As soon as you stop speaking, the prompt will automatically be sent, without you needing to press send.

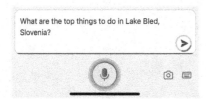

Copilot will transcribe your voice and automatically send the prompt when you stop speaking.

4. Copilot will display the text of the response and read it out using voice. You will see a playback indicator at the bottom of the screen.

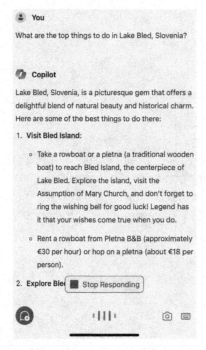

Copilot responds and reads out the response using voice.

5. You can continue the conversation with voice or select the keyboard icon to switch back to typing prompts.

Select the keyboard icon to switch back to typing prompts.

Work with the Copilot response

Copilot will respond to your prompt with citations and web links, the same way it does using Copilot in the desktop web browser. Follow any of these links to open them in your mobile browser.

Copilot responds with citations and links and gives you options to provide feedback, copy, share, or read the response using the speaker.

Use the icons to provide feedback or work with the results:

- Select the **thumbs up** icon if you like the response.
- Select the **thumbs down** icon if there is a problem with the response. This will open an additional pop-up option to provide specific feedback.
- Select the **copy** icon to copy the response to the clipboard on your device.
- Select the **share** icon to open the sharing options on your device, to share it in another app or in a message.
- Select the **speaker** icon to hear the response read out using voice.

Use your camera to add an image to the prompt

When you are travelling or just out and about, you can use Copilot with the camera on your device to ask questions or understand more about what you see around you.

To use your camera with a Copilot prompt

1. Select the **camera** icon in the prompt area.

*Select the camera icon at the bottom
right of the prompt area.*

> ✅ **TIP** In this example, asking Copilot for a translation or a fact, you are likely to
> get a more accurate response by switching to the More Precise mode.

2. This will open the camera on your device. Line up your camera and press the
    button to capture the photo.

Line up your camera and take the photo.

3. You have the option to mark up the image to highlight any key areas to focus on. Slide the scale to choose your color, and then draw on the screen.

Use the maker to highlight important parts of the image.

4. Select the **check mark** when you are ready to add the photo with any markup to your prompt.

5. You will be returned to the prompt area with the image attached to the prompt. Type in a question or additional details about the image or context and select the **arrow** in the prompt area or the **send** button on your mobile keyboard.

> **TIP** To get the best response, provide Copilot with additional details and context about where you are or what you already know.

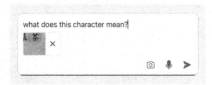

Type in your question or additional context to accompany the image to complete your prompt.

6. Copilot responds, using the photo as source content in the prompt.

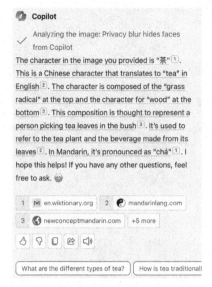

Copilot responds with citations and references.

Add an image from your photo library to your prompt

You can also upload an image from your device's photo library to use as part of your prompt.

To add an image to your prompt from the device's photo library

1. Select the **camera** icon in the prompt area

Select the camera icon in the prompt area to add an image from your photo library.

2. This will open the camera on your device. Select the image icon at the bottom left of the screen to switch from the camera to your photo library.

Select the image icon to switch from the camera to the photo library on your device.

4

3. Select the image you want to add from your photo library. You have the option to add any markup to highlight key areas of the image.

4. When you are done, select the **check mark** to add the image to your prompt.

Choose an image from your photo library and select the blue check mark to add it to your prompt.

5. Type your question or add any additional details or context to your prompt and select the **send** button on your device keyboard.

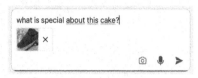

Type your question and any additional details and send your prompt.

6. Copilot responds, using the photo as source content in the prompt.

Copilot analyzes the image and responds.

Use Plug-ins

You have access to all the same plug-ins on the mobile app that you can use on the desktop web browser, to connect your chat to services that can help with shopping, travel, restaurant reservations, generating songs, and more.

To use plug-ins

1. Select the **more options** (...) icon at the top right of the app and then select **Plugins**.

Select the more options menu to navigate to Plugins.

2. Scroll up and down the list of plug-ins and set the **toggle switch** to the on position to enable each plug-in you want to use. You can choose up to three. When you have made your selections, select the **X** icon at the top left to close the Plugins menu.

Set the toggle switch to the on position to enable a plug-in.

IMPORTANT Some plug-ins are only available or useful in the United States.

 TIP Select "New topic" to add or remove plug-ins for each conversation.

3. Enter your prompt to make use of the plug-in(s) selected. In this example, the OpenTable plug-in provides restaurant recommendations with a direct link for booking reservations.

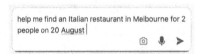

Enter your prompt with details that will be used by the plug-in.

4. Copilot indicates in the response that it is using the plug-in by showing an icon. The response is returned using OpenTable with suggested restaurants and a link for each to make a reservation.

Copilot shows that it is using a plug-in by displaying an icon at the top of the response. The response provides links to the service connected with the plug-in.

5. The links take you to the website or service connected by the plug-in. Select a link to open the OpenTable reservation page for that restaurant. Notice that the details you added to your prompt, such as the reservation date and number of people, have been automatically added to the form.

The link takes you to the website or service connected by the plug-in and automatically adds details from your prompt.

Generate images

You can use the Copilot mobile application to generate images, save them to your device, or copy them to use in other mobile apps such as chats and social media posts. You have the same features available to generate images on the mobile app that you have with the desktop web browser, including changing the artistic style and formatting and adding special effects.

To generate images with the Copilot mobile application

1. In the prompt area, describe the image you want to create by typing or using your voice.

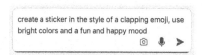

Describe the image you want to generate.

2. Copilot will generate four images based on your prompt, as well as some prompt suggestions to help you refine the image.

Copilot generates four images based on your prompt and suggests prompts to help you refine the image.

3. Select the image you like best to open and edit it.

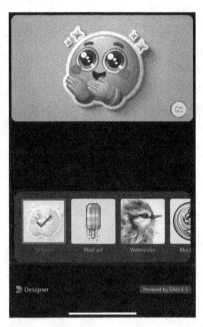

Select an image to open it and view the editing options.

4. Scroll through the carousel of options for different artistic styles and choose the one you want to use. This example uses the Pixel art option. Copilot will show a progress message while it re-creates the image.

Select Undo to go back to your original image or select Looks good to keep the new image.

5. Select the **Undo** button to return to your original image or select the **Looks good** button to keep this new version.

6. Select the resize icon at the bottom right of the image to change the format of your image.

Select the resize icon at the bottom right corner of your image to change the format of your image.

7. Choose between square and landscape format by selecting the option you prefer.

Copilot gives you the option to format your image as square or landscape.

8. When you are happy with your image, select the more options menu (...) at the top right to download your image.

Select the more options menu to get to the option to download the image to your device.

9. The image will be saved to the photo library on your device, and you will see a confirmation message.

You will see a message confirming that the image has been saved to your photo library.

10. To get a link to share the image, select the **Share** button at the top right of the screen next to the more options menu.

Select the Share button to get a shareable link for your image.

4

11. When the link appears on the screen, select the **Copy link** button to copy it to the clipboard on your device. You can paste this link into a message or email to share with someone else. They will be able to access the image via the link even without logging in to Copilot.

Select the Copy link button to copy the shareable link to your device's clipboard.

Write content

You can use the Copilot mobile application to draft content on the go, which you can copy and paste into other apps on your phone, such as Microsoft Teams, email, social media, or messaging apps.

> **SEE ALSO** You can use Copilot to help draft emails using the Outlook mobile app. You can learn how to do this in Chapter 6, "Copilot in Outlook."

To write content with the Copilot mobile application

1. In the prompt area, describe what you want to write by typing or using your voice.

My colleagues Steph and Bridget just closed a huge deal with Contoso for a million dollars. They have worked extremely well together and collaborated with the rest of the team to win against strong competition. Write a congratulatory message to show appreciation for their work that I can share with the wider team. The tone should be professional, proud, and casual.

Enter a description of what you want to write in the prompt area.

2. Copilot will generate a draft of the content for you.

Copilot drafts the content based on your prompt.

3. Copilot finishes with a message summarizing the task and offering suggested prompts if you want to refine the content further.

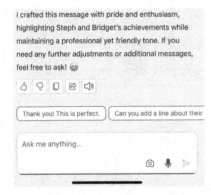

Copilot confirms the task completed and offers suggested prompts to continue the conversation.

4. To use this content in another app on your device, select the **copy** button to copy it to your clipboard.

Select the copy icon next to the thumbs up and thumbs down icons to copy the content to your device's clipboard.

5. You will get a confirmation message that the content has been copied. You can now switch to another application to paste and use the content there.

Copilot confirms that the content has been copied to the clipboard.

Skills review

In this chapter, you learned how to:

- Install and log in to the Copilot mobile application on your iOS or Android device.
- Chat and search using the Copilot mobile application, using the microphone to interact with voice, and using the camera and photo library on your device to add images to your prompt.
- Enable plug-ins to use with your chat.
- Generate and edit images and save them to your device.
- Write content and copy it to use with other applications on your device.

Practice tasks

No practice files are necessary to complete the practice tasks in this chapter.

Get started with the Copilot mobile app

Scan the QR code from the first section of this chapter, install the Copilot mobile app on your iOS or Android device, and then perform the following tasks:

1. Open the Copilot mobile app on your device.

2. Select the **Sign in** button at the top left of the app.

3. Sign in with the Microsoft account you used to sign up for Copilot Pro.

4. Select any of the suggested prompts from the carousel.

5. Select the **menu** icon at the top left of the app to view your conversation history.

6. Close the menu to return to the main Copilot area of the app.

7. Select the **New topic** button next to the prompt area.

Chat and search on the go

Open the Copilot mobile app on your mobile device, and then perform the following tasks:

1. Select the **camera** icon in the prompt area. If prompted by your device, allow Copilot to use the camera.

2. Take a photo of something nearby, such as an object, plant, animal, artwork, or landmark you want to identify.

3. Select the button to take the photo, and then return to the prompt. You will see the thumbnail of the photo in the prompt area.

4. Type a prompt into the prompt area to ask Copilot to identify or tell you about the image. Use a prompt such as "Can you tell me what this is" or "Can you tell me about this." Add any other details for context, such as your location or any clues about the object you already know.

5. Copilot will respond with the information based on your photo and prompt.

Generate images

Continue working from where you finished the previous task, and then perform the following tasks:

1. Select the **New topic** button to start a new conversation.

2. Select the **microphone** icon to enable voice. If prompted by your device, allow Copilot access to the microphone. (If you prefer, you can skip this step and just type your prompt in the prompt area.)

3. Say (or type) the following: Create an emoji of a glittery star that I can use to celebrate an achievement. If you are using voice, stop speaking, and Copilot will automatically send the prompt. If you are typing, select the **arrow** to enter your prompt.

4. Select the image you like best to open it.

5. Select the **more options** icon at the top right of the app.

6. Select **Download.**

7. Wait for the Downloaded confirmation message. If prompted, allow Copilot access to your photos.

8. Switch to the photo library in your app to view the generated image.

Write content

Open the Copilot mobile application on your device, and then perform the following tasks:

1. Select the **New topic** button to start a new conversation.

2. Select the **More Creative** style.

3. Enter the following prompt into the prompt area: Write an inspirational message about dreaming big and reaching for the stars.

4. Select the **copy** icon.

5. Wait for the confirmation message that the content has been copied to your clipboard.

6. If you want, you can copy this inspirational message into the notes on your phone, or you can paste it into an email or a chat message to send to someone.

Part 3

Use Copilot Pro in Microsoft 365 applications

Copilot in Excel

5

Copilot in Excel can help you format, understand, and gain insights into data in your Excel data tables. You can use prompts to ask Copilot to sort your data by a specific column, filter the data, or apply conditional formatting to cells to help you easily identify key data points.

You can ask Copilot to suggest and write formulas for you, without needing to understand how to make the calculations or write the formulas yourself. Copilot will create formulas and new columns in your table based on your description and explain the logic behind the formulas to help you understand the suggestion and learn more about formulas if you wish.

You can also ask Copilot to help you understand your data by identifying trends, patterns, and outliers. Copilot can analyze your data to provide a range of instant insights or perform calculations to answer specific questions you have about your data. It will automatically create charts, PivotTables, and descriptions to help you visualize the insights.

Copilot also provides built-in help for how to use Excel. You can ask questions in natural language, such as how to write a specific formula, and get answers in context as you work with your spreadsheet.

In this chapter

- Get started with Copilot in Excel
- Highlight, sort, and filter your data
- Generate formula columns
- Understand your data

Practice files

You will need to use the practice files provided with this chapter to complete the practice tasks.

You remain in control every step of the way. Copilot in Excel responds to your prompts with a suggestion for you to review before applying it to your data tables, and always provides an easy undo option to reverse the changes it makes.

Get started with Copilot in Excel

To get started with Copilot in Excel, you will need to open an existing spreadsheet that is saved in the cloud in your personal OneDrive.

> ⚠️ **IMPORTANT** Your spreadsheet must be saved in the personal OneDrive associated with the Microsoft account that you used to sign up for Copilot Pro. Copilot in Excel also works with files in OneDrive for Business and SharePoint, but you need a business account and a Microsoft 365 Copilot license to work with those options.

You can launch Copilot from the button at the right side of the **Home** ribbon.

You can launch Copilot from the button at the right end of the Home ribbon.

Copilot will appear in a pane pinned to the right side of the app, showing suggested prompts and a prompt area where you can type in the details of what you want to ask Copilot to do with your data.

> ✅ **TIP** You can move and resize the Copilot pane using the icons at the top right of the Copilot pane. See Chapter 1, "Introduction to Copilot Pro," for step-by-step instructions on how to do this.

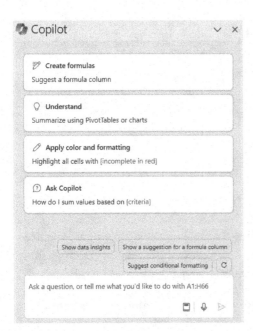

Copilot in Excel helps you create formulas, understand your data, apply color and formatting to your spreadsheet, and ask for help about how to use Excel.

If you open a spreadsheet that isn't saved in your personal OneDrive, when you launch Copilot, you will get a message that tells you Copilot can only work with files that have AutoSave turned on. You will need to save your spreadsheet to your OneDrive before you can continue.

Copilot will only work with files saved in the cloud, with AutoSave turned on.

Select the **Turn on AutoSave** button to get more instructions, telling you where you need to save your file to continue.

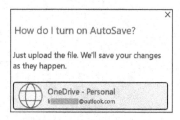

To work with Copilot, your spreadsheet must be saved in your personal OneDrive.

Copilot works best with structured data formatted as a table, but it can also work with a table-like range. A table-like range has a single header row with different column names, no empty rows or columns, consistent data formatting per column, and no subtotals.

If your data is in a supported table-like range, you will see the range in the prompt area, and you can work with it in Copilot.

If your data is in a supported range, you will see the data range in the prompt area.

If your data does not meet these criteria, then when you try to use Copilot, you will get the following message.

If your data is not in a supported range, you will get a message describing the requirements and suggesting that you can format your data as a table.

In this case, you will need to format your data as a table to work with Copilot.

To format your data as a table

1. Select the range of cells you want to work with.

2. Select the **Format as Table** button on the **Home** ribbon.

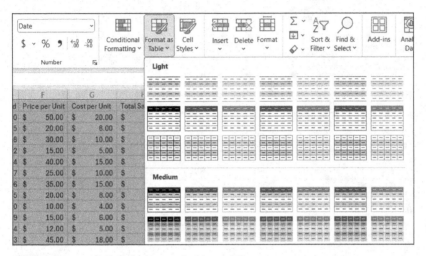

Select the Format as Table button on the Home ribbon.

3. Choose the table style you want.

4. Confirm the selected range and select the checkbox to indicate that your table has headers.

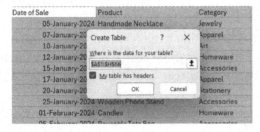

Confirm the data range and select the checkbox to indicate that your table has headers.

5. Select the **OK** button.

6. Your data is now formatted as a table.

Date of Sale	Product	Category	Sales Channel	Units Sold	Price per Unit	Cost per Unit	Total Sales
05-January-2024	Handmade Necklace	Jewelry	Online Store	10	$ 50.00	$ 20.00	$ 500.00
07-January-2024	Custom T-shirt	Apparel	Social Media	5	$ 20.00	$ 8.00	$ 100.00
10-January-2024	Digital Art Print	Art	Online Store	8	$ 30.00	$ 10.00	$ 240.00
12-January-2024	Ceramic Mug	Homeware	In-Person Sales	12	$ 15.00	$ 5.00	$ 180.00
15-January-2024	Leather Wallet	Accessories	Online Store	4	$ 40.00	$ 15.00	$ 160.00
17-January-2024	Knitted Scarf	Apparel	Social Media	7	$ 25.00	$ 10.00	$ 175.00
20-January-2024	Handcrafted Journal	Stationery	Online Store	6	$ 35.00	$ 15.00	$ 210.00
25-January-2024	Wooden Phone Stand	Accessories	In-Person Sales	15	$ 20.00	$ 8.00	$ 300.00
01-February-2024	Candles	Homeware	Online Store	20	$ 10.00	$ 4.00	$ 200.00
05-February-2024	Reusable Tote Bag	Accessories	Social Media	9	$ 15.00	$ 6.00	$ 135.00
07-February-2024	Phone Case	Electronics	In-Person Sales	14	$ 12.00	$ 5.00	$ 168.00
10-February-2024	Wall Art Print	Art	Online Store	3	$ 45.00	$ 18.00	$ 135.00
12-February-2024	Handmade Earrings	Jewelry	Social Media	11	$ 25.00	$ 10.00	$ 275.00
15-February-2024	Personalized Keychain	Accessories	In-Person Sales	25	$ 10.00	$ 4.00	$ 250.00
18-February-2024	Throw Pillow	Homeware	Online Store	18	$ 20.00	$ 8.00	$ 360.00
19-February-2024	Digital Art Print	Homeware	Social Media	30	$ 50.00	$ 10.00	$ 1,500.00
20-February-2024	Digital Art Print	Accessories	Social Media	19	$ 50.00	$ 8.00	$ 950.00
21-February-2024	Handcrafted Journal	Apparel	In-Person Sales	5	$ 40.00	$ 4.00	$ 200.00
22-February-2024	Throw Pillow	Accessories	Social Media	1	$ 30.00	$ 18.00	$ 30.00
23-February-2024	Handmade Earrings	Accessories	In-Person Sales	16	$ 10.00	$ 25.00	$ 160.00
24-February-2024	Wall Art Print	Accessories	In-Person Sales	1	$ 10.00	$ 25.00	$ 10.00
25-February-2024	Handcrafted Journal	Accessories	In-Person Sales	6	$ 10.00	$ 8.00	$ 60.00
26-February-2024	Handmade Earrings	Apparel	Online Store	2	$ 15.00	$ 18.00	$ 30.00
27-February-2024	Digital Art Print	Art	Social Media	23	$ 10.00	$ 15.00	$ 230.00
28-February-2024	Handmade Earrings	Art	Online Store	20	$ 15.00	$ 25.00	$ 300.00
29-February-2024	Wooden Phone Stand	Jewelry	Social Media	100	$ 12.00	$ 10.00	$ 1,200.00

Your data is now formatted as a table.

Highlight, sort, and filter your data

Copilot makes it quick and easy to highlight, sort, and filter the data in your spreadsheet using natural language prompts.

Highlight with conditional formatting

Copilot can help you apply conditional formatting to highlight key points, trends, or outliers in your data. This is particularly useful when you have a large data table, and you want to quickly identify the outliers. You can use a wide range of formatting options, from basic formatting like bold or italic, highlighting cells in different fill and font colors, or using more sophisticated conditional formatting options like data bars and icon sets.

To highlight cells in your data

1. Describe the rule and the type of highlighting you want to apply to your data, and then select the **arrow** to send your prompt.

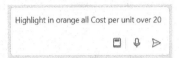

Write a prompt that describes the rule and the formatting you want to apply to your data.

2. Copilot will respond by confirming your request and describing the details of the cells that will be changed and the formatting that will be applied, for you to review before the changes are made.

Copilot responds by confirming and describing the formatting changes in detail.

3. If you are happy with the details, select the **Apply** button to apply the changes to your spreadsheet. If the details are not as you expected, rewrite your prompt.

4. Copilot applies the requested formatting to your spreadsheet.

> ⚠ **IMPORTANT** Copilot will only highlight cells in a column, not entire rows.

> ✓ **TIP** You will get the best results from Copilot if you use the exact name of your column headers in your prompt.

Date of Sale	Product	Category	Sales Channel	Units Sold	Price per Unit	Cost per Unit	Total Sales
05-January-2024	J34 Handmade Necklace	Jewelry	Online Store	10	$ 50.00	20	$ 500.00
07-January-2024	A23 Custom T-shirt	Apparel	Social Media	5	$ 20.00	8	$ 100.00
10-January-2024	A12 Digital Art Print	Art	Online Store	8	$ 30.00	10	$ 240.00
12-January-2024	H90 Ceramic Mug	Homeware	In-Person Sales	12	$ 15.00	5	$ 180.00
15-January-2024	C88 Leather Wallet	Accessories	Online Store	4	$ 40.00	15	$ 160.00
17-January-2024	A21 Knitted Scarf	Apparel	Social Media	7	$ 25.00	10	$ 175.00
20-January-2024	S77 Handcrafted Journal	Stationery	Online Store	6	$ 35.00	15	$ 210.00
25-January-2024	C23 Wooden Phone Stand	Accessories	In-Person Sales	15	$ 20.00	8	$ 300.00
01-February-2024	H11 Candles	Homeware	Online Store	20	$ 10.00	4	$ 200.00
05-February-2024	C66 Reusable Tote Bag	Accessories	Social Media	9	$ 15.00	6	$ 135.00
07-February-2024	C32 Phone Case	Accessories	In-Person Sales	14	$ 12.00	5	$ 168.00
10-February-2024	A16 Wall Art Print	Art	Online Store	3	$ 45.00	18	$ 135.00
12-February-2024	J90 Handmade Earrings	Jewelry	Social Media	11	$ 25.00	10	$ 275.00
15-February-2024	C45 Personalized Keychain	Accessories	In-Person Sales	25	$ 10.00	4	$ 250.00
18-February-2024	H22 Throw Pillow	Homeware	Online Store	18	$ 20.00	8	$ 360.00
19-February-2024	A23 Digital Art Print	Art	Social Media	30	$ 50.00	10	$ 1,500.00
20-February-2024	A24 Digital Art Print	Art	Social Media	19	$ 50.00	8	$ 950.00
21-February-2024	S77 Handcrafted Journal	Stationery	In-Person Sales	5	$ 40.00	4	$ 200.00
22-February-2024	H08 Throw Pillow	Homeware	Social Media	1	$ 30.00	18	$ 30.00
23-February-2024	J09 Handmade Earrings	Jewelry	In-Person Sales	16	$ 10.00	25	$ 160.00
24-February-2024	A17 Wall Art Print	Art	In-Person Sales	1	$ 10.00	25	$ 10.00
25-February-2024	S24 Handcrafted Journal	Stationery	In-Person Sales	6	$ 10.00	8	$ 60.00
26-February-2024	J15 Handmade Earrings	Jewelry	Online Store	2	$ 15.00	18	$ 30.00
27-February-2024	A65 Digital Art Print	Art	Social Media	23	$ 10.00	15	$ 230.00
28-February-2024	J06 Handmade Earrings	Jewelry	Online Store	20	$ 15.00	25	$ 300.00
29-February-2024	C33 Wooden Phone Stand	Accessories	Social Media	100	$ 12.00	10	$ 1,200.00

Copilot applies the requested highlights to your data.

You can ask Copilot to apply conditional formatting to an entire column to help you visualize your data, without describing a rule. This is useful if you want to use conditional formatting such as data bars or icon sets. Copilot will automatically determine the patterns to use with these types of formatting, based on the values in the column.

Describe the type of conditional formatting pattern you want in the prompt area.

Add data bars to the Total Sales column

*Ask Copilot to apply conditional formatting
to an entire column without adding a rule.*

Copilot responds with confirmation and a description of the changes, including a visual representation of the formatting you've requested.

Copilot describes the changes for your review, showing a visual representation of the data bar with gradient green.

Select **Apply** to apply the formatting changes to your spreadsheet.

Date of Sale	Product	Category	Sales Channel	Units Sold	Price per Unit	Cost per Unit	Total Sales
05-January-2024	J34 Handmade Necklace	Jewelry	Online Store	10	$ 50.00	20	$ 500.00
07-January-2024	A23 Custom T-shirt	Apparel	Social Media	5	$ 20.00	8	$ 100.00
10-January-2024	A12 Digital Art Print	Art	Online Store	8	$ 30.00	10	$ 240.00
12-January-2024	H90 Ceramic Mug	Homeware	In-Person Sales	12	$ 15.00	5	$ 180.00
15-January-2024	C88 Leather Wallet	Accessories	Online Store	4	$ 40.00	15	$ 160.00
17-January-2024	A21 Knitted Scarf	Apparel	Social Media	7	$ 25.00	10	$ 175.00
20-January-2024	S77 Handcrafted Journal	Stationery	Online Store	6	$ 35.00	15	$ 210.00
25-January-2024	C23 Wooden Phone Stand	Accessories	In-Person Sales	15	$ 20.00	8	$ 300.00
01-February-2024	H11 Candles	Homeware	Online Store	20	$ 10.00	4	$ 200.00
05-February-2024	C66 Reusable Tote Bag	Accessories	Social Media	9	$ 15.00	6	$ 135.00
07-February-2024	C32 Phone Case	Accessories	In-Person Sales	14	$ 12.00	5	$ 168.00
10-February-2024	A16 Wall Art Print	Art	Online Store	3	$ 45.00	18	$ 135.00
12-February-2024	J90 Handmade Earrings	Jewelry	Social Media	11	$ 25.00	10	$ 275.00
15-February-2024	C45 Personalized Keychain	Accessories	In-Person Sales	25	$ 10.00	4	$ 250.00
18-February-2024	H22 Throw Pillow	Homeware	Online Store	18	$ 20.00	8	$ 360.00
19-February-2024	A23 Digital Art Print	Art	Social Media	30	$ 50.00	10	$ 1,500.00
20-February-2024	A24 Digital Art Print	Art	Social Media	19	$ 50.00	8	$ 950.00
21-February-2024	S77 Handcrafted Journal	Stationery	In-Person Sales	5	$ 40.00	4	$ 200.00
22-February-2024	H08 Throw Pillow	Homeware	Social Media	1	$ 30.00	18	$ 30.00
23-February-2024	J09 Handmade Earrings	Jewelry	In-Person Sales	16	$ 10.00	25	$ 160.00
24-February-2024	A17 Wall Art Print	Art	In-Person Sales	1	$ 10.00	25	$ 10.00
25-February-2024	S24 Handcrafted Journal	Stationery	In-Person Sales	6	$ 10.00	8	$ 60.00
26-February-2024	J15 Handmade Earrings	Jewelry	Online Store	2	$ 15.00	18	$ 30.00
27-February-2024	A65 Digital Art Print	Art	Social Media	23	$ 10.00	15	$ 230.00
28-February-2024	J06 Handmade Earrings	Jewelry	Online Store	20	$ 15.00	25	$ 300.00
29-February-2024	C33 Wooden Phone Stand	Accessories	Social Media	100	$ 12.00	10	$ 1,200.00

Copilot applies the data bar formatting to the Total Sales column as requested.

5

Sometimes when you apply the formatting changes you've requested, the results may not be as you expected when they are applied to your actual data, and you will want to undo the formatting changes made by Copilot.

In this example, the prompt asks Copilot to add an icon set to the Units Sold column to help identify patterns in the sales data.

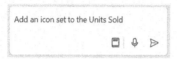

Write a prompt to ask Copilot to add conditional formatting to a column.

Copilot responds with a suggestion to add an icon set of three arrows to the column and shows a visual representation of the icons it will use. Select **Apply** to make the changes.

Copilot describes the changes for your review, showing a visual representation of the three arrows in the suggested icon set.

When the formatting is applied to the spreadsheet, the results are not useful in identifying patterns with this dataset. When the conditional formatting is added, there is one outlier that skews the pattern so that almost everything is highlighted with a down arrow icon.

	A	B	C	D	E	F	G	H
1	Date of Sale	Product	Category	Sales Channel	Units Sold	Price per Unit	Cost per Unit	Total Sales
2	05-January-2024	J34 Handmade Necklace	Jewelry	Online Store	10	$ 50.00	20	$ 500.00
3	07-January-2024	A23 Custom T-shirt	Apparel	Social Media	5	$ 20.00	8	$ 100.00
4	10-January-2024	A12 Digital Art Print	Art	Online Store	8	$ 30.00	10	$ 240.00
5	12-January-2024	H90 Ceramic Mug	Homeware	In-Person Sales	12	$ 15.00	5	$ 180.00
6	15-January-2024	C88 Leather Wallet	Accessories	Online Store	4	$ 40.00	15	$ 160.00
7	17-January-2024	A21 Knitted Scarf	Apparel	Social Media	7	$ 25.00	10	$ 175.00
8	20-January-2024	S77 Handcrafted Journal	Stationery	Online Store	6	$ 35.00	15	$ 210.00
9	25-January-2024	C23 Wooden Phone Stand	Accessories	In-Person Sales	15	$ 20.00	8	$ 300.00
10	01-February-2024	H11 Candles	Homeware	Online Store	20	$ 10.00	4	$ 200.00
11	05-February-2024	C66 Reusable Tote Bag	Accessories	Social Media	9	$ 15.00	6	$ 135.00
12	07-February-2024	C32 Phone Case	Accessories	In-Person Sales	14	$ 12.00	5	$ 168.00
13	10-February-2024	A16 Wall Art Print	Art	Online Store	3	$ 45.00	18	$ 135.00
14	12-February-2024	J90 Handmade Earrings	Jewelry	Social Media	11	$ 25.00	10	$ 275.00
15	15-February-2024	C45 Personalized Keychain	Accessories	In-Person Sales	25	$ 10.00	4	$ 250.00
16	18-February-2024	H22 Throw Pillow	Homeware	Online Store	18	$ 20.00	8	$ 360.00
17	19-February-2024	A23 Digital Art Print	Art	Social Media	30	$ 50.00	10	$ 1,500.00
18	20-February-2024	A24 Digital Art Print	Art	Social Media	19	$ 50.00	8	$ 950.00
19	21-February-2024	S77 Handcrafted Journal	Stationery	In-Person Sales	5	$ 40.00	4	$ 200.00
20	22-February-2024	H08 Throw Pillow	Homeware	Social Media	1	$ 30.00	18	$ 30.00
21	23-February-2024	J09 Handmade Earrings	Jewelry	In-Person Sales	16	$ 10.00	25	$ 160.00
22	24-February-2024	A17 Wall Art Print	Art	In-Person Sales	1	$ 10.00	25	$ 10.00
23	25-February-2024	S24 Handcrafted Journal	Stationery	In-Person Sales	6	$ 10.00	8	$ 60.00
24	26-February-2024	J15 Handmade Earrings	Jewelry	Online Store	2	$ 15.00	18	$ 30.00
25	27-February-2024	A65 Digital Art Print	Art	Social Media	23	$ 10.00	15	$ 230.00
26	28-February-2024	J06 Handmade Earrings	Jewelry	Online Store	20	$ 15.00	25	$ 300.00
27	29-February-2024	C33 Wooden Phone Stand	Accessories	Social Media	100	$ 12.00	10	$ 1,200.00

Copilot applies the icon set formatting to the Units Sold column as requested.

Copilot will always suggest an undo option when it confirms that it has made the requested changes so that you can immediately undo the formatting if it isn't helpful. Select the **Undo** button to remove the formatting changes.

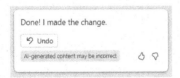

Select the Undo button in the Copilot confirmation message to undo the changes.

Copilot confirms that it has completed the undo action.

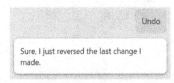

Copilot confirms that it has reversed the last change.

In this example, describing a specific rule and using basic formatting provides a better result than applying the conditional formatting pattern. You can ask Copilot to iden-tify the top values in a column automatically.

Describe the formatting and a rule to apply it.

Copilot responds with confirmation and details of the request.

Copilot describes the changes for your review, showing a visual representation of the formatting requested.

Select **Apply** to accept and apply the new formatting. The top 20 values in the Units Sold column are now shown in bold.

	Date of Sale	Product	Category	Sales Channel	Units Sold	Price per Unit	Cost per Unit	Total Sales
2	05-January-2024	J34 Handmade Necklace	Jewelry	Online Store	10	$ 50.00	20	$ 500.00
3	07-January-2024	A23 Custom T-shirt	Apparel	Social Media	5	$ 20.00	8	$ 100.00
4	10-January-2024	A12 Digital Art Print	Art	Online Store	8	$ 30.00	10	$ 240.00
5	12-January-2024	H90 Ceramic Mug	Homeware	In-Person Sales	12	$ 15.00	5	$ 180.00
6	15-January-2024	C88 Leather Wallet	Accessories	Online Store	4	$ 40.00	15	$ 160.00
7	17-January-2024	A21 Knitted Scarf	Apparel	Social Media	7	$ 25.00	10	$ 175.00
8	20-January-2024	S77 Handcrafted Journal	Stationery	Online Store	6	$ 35.00	15	$ 210.00
9	25-January-2024	C23 Wooden Phone Stand	Accessories	In-Person Sales	15	$ 20.00	8	$ 300.00
10	01-February-2024	H11 Candles	Homeware	Online Store	20	$ 10.00	4	$ 200.00
11	05-February-2024	C66 Reusable Tote Bag	Accessories	Social Media	9	$ 15.00	6	$ 135.00
12	07-February-2024	C32 Phone Case	Accessories	In-Person Sales	14	$ 12.00	5	$ 168.00
13	10-February-2024	A16 Wall Art Print	Art	Online Store	3	$ 45.00	18	$ 135.00
14	12-February-2024	J90 Handmade Earrings	Jewelry	Social Media	11	$ 25.00	10	$ 275.00
15	15-February-2024	C45 Personalized Keychain	Accessories	In-Person Sales	25	$ 10.00	4	$ 250.00
16	18-February-2024	H22 Throw Pillow	Homeware	Online Store	18	$ 20.00	8	$ 360.00
17	19-February-2024	A23 Digital Art Print	Art	Social Media	30	$ 50.00	10	$ 1,500.00
18	20-February-2024	A24 Digital Art Print	Art	Social Media	19	$ 50.00	8	$ 950.00
19	21-February-2024	S77 Handcrafted Journal	Stationery	In-Person Sales	5	$ 40.00	4	$ 200.00
20	22-February-2024	H08 Throw Pillow	Homeware	Social Media	1	$ 30.00	18	$ 30.00
21	23-February-2024	J09 Handmade Earrings	Jewelry	In-Person Sales	16	$ 10.00	25	$ 160.00
22	24-February-2024	A17 Wall Art Print	Art	In-Person Sales	1	$ 10.00	25	$ 10.00
23	25-February-2024	S24 Handcrafted Journal	Stationery	In-Person Sales	6	$ 10.00	8	$ 60.00
24	26-February-2024	J15 Handmade Earrings	Jewelry	Online Store	2	$ 15.00	18	$ 30.00
25	27-February-2024	A65 Digital Art Print	Art	Social Media	23	$ 10.00	15	$ 230.00
26	28-February-2024	J06 Handmade Earrings	Jewelry	Online Store	20	$ 15.00	25	$ 300.00
27	29-February-2024	C33 Wooden Phone Stand	Accessories	Social Media	100	$ 12.00	10	$ 1,200.00

Copilot applies the bold formatting to the Units Sold column as requested.

 TIP You can ask for multiple formatting changes in a single prompt—for example, "Highlight the top 20 Units Sold in bold and highlight all Cost per Unit above 20 in orange."

You can also ask Copilot to apply other formatting changes to your data, such as changing a column to currency format.

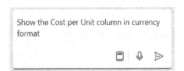

Show the Cost per Unit column in currency format

Write a prompt to ask Copilot to change a column to currency format.

Copilot confirms the requested change before giving you the option to apply it.

OK! Looking at **A1:H66**, here are 2 changes to review and apply:

- Apply a currency format on the column 'Cost per Unit'
- Autofit column(s) in G2:G66

✓ Apply

AI-generated content may be incorrect

Copilot describes the changes for your review.

The Cost per Unit column is now shown in currency format, and the column widths have been adjusted to fit.

Units Sold	Price per Unit	Cost per Unit	Total Sales
10	$ 50.00	$ 20.00	$ 500.00
5	$ 20.00	$ 8.00	$ 100.00
8	$ 30.00	$ 10.00	$ 240.00
12	$ 15.00	$ 5.00	$ 180.00
4	$ 40.00	$ 15.00	$ 160.00
7	$ 25.00	$ 10.00	$ 175.00
6	$ 35.00	$ 15.00	$ 210.00
15	$ 20.00	$ 8.00	$ 300.00
20	$ 10.00	$ 4.00	$ 200.00
9	$ 15.00	$ 6.00	$ 135.00
14	$ 12.00	$ 5.00	$ 168.00

Copilot formats the column in currency format.

Sort your data

You can ask Copilot to sort your data by a specific column and describe the sort order. You can use simple language to describe the sort, such as "largest to smallest," or you can describe what you want using Excel terminology, such as "descending order."

To sort your data with Copilot

1. Write a prompt to describe the column you want to sort and the way you want to sort it, and then select the arrow to send your prompt.

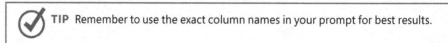

TIP Remember to use the exact column names in your prompt for best results.

Sort Total Sales from largest to smallest

*Write a prompt asking Copilot to sort
a column from largest to smallest.*

2. Copilot confirms the changes for your review. Select **Apply** to accept the changes.

Sure! Looking at **A1:H66**, here's 1 change
to review and apply:

- Apply a custom sort on column
  'Total Sales' in table Table1

✓ Apply

AI-generated content may be incorrect

*Copilot describes the changes for
your review.*

3. Copilot has now sorted the data by the Total Sales column, in descending order.

	Date of Sale	Product	Category	Sales Channel	Units Sold	Price per Unit	Cost per Unit	Total Sales
1								
2	19-February-2024	A23 Digital Art Print	Art	Social Media	30	$ 50.00	$ 10.00	$ 1,500.00
3	08-March-2024	A99 Digital Art Print	Art	Online Store	29	$ 50.00	$ 4.00	$ 1,450.00
4	08-April-2024	J01 Handmade Necklace	Jewelry	Online Store	26	$ 50.00	$ 10.00	$ 1,300.00
5	24-March-2024	A78 Wall Art Print	Art	In-Person Sales	25	$ 50.00	$ 15.00	$ 1,250.00
6	29-February-2024	C33 Wooden Phone Stand	Accessories	Social Media	100	$ 12.00	$ 10.00	$ 1,200.00
7	19-March-2024	C14 Phone Case	Accessories	In-Person Sales	28	$ 40.00	$ 20.00	$ 1,120.00
8	13-March-2024	S02 Handcrafted Journal	Stationery	In-Person Sales	27	$ 40.00	$ 4.00	$ 1,080.00
9	15-March-2024	J66 Handmade Necklace	Jewelry	In-Person Sales	21	$ 50.00	$ 25.00	$ 1,050.00
10	07-April-2024	A89 Custom T-shirt	Apparel	In-Person Sales	25	$ 40.00	$ 10.00	$ 1,000.00
11	20-February-2024	A24 Digital Art Print	Art	Social Media	19	$ 50.00	$ 8.00	$ 950.00
12	04-April-2024	H89 Throw Pillow	Homeware	Online Store	23	$ 40.00	$ 15.00	$ 920.00
13	02-March-2024	A19 Digital Art Print	Art	In-Person Sales	28	$ 30.00	$ 5.00	$ 840.00
14	06-March-2024	S01 Handcrafted Journal	Stationery	Online Store	24	$ 30.00	$ 8.00	$ 720.00
15	03-March-2024	C90 Reusable Tote Bag	Accessories	In-Person Sales	17	$ 30.00	$ 15.00	$ 510.00
16	05-January-2024	J34 Handmade Necklace	Jewelry	Online Store	10	$ 50.00	$ 20.00	$ 500.00
17	25-March-2024	H03 Candles	Homeware	Online Store	25	$ 20.00	$ 20.00	$ 500.00
18	28-March-2024	H92 Candles	Homeware	In-Person Sales	25	$ 20.00	$ 4.00	$ 500.00
19	04-March-2024	J03 Handmade Necklace	Jewelry	Online Store	30	$ 15.00	$ 4.00	$ 450.00
20	05-April-2024	C34 Phone Case	Accessories	Social Media	21	$ 20.00	$ 8.00	$ 420.00
21	06-April-2024	J89 Handmade Necklace	Jewelry	In-Person Sales	9	$ 45.00	$ 20.00	$ 405.00
22	10-March-2024	H02 Throw Pillow	Homeware	In-Person Sales	2	$ 200.00	$ 50.00	$ 400.00
23	18-February-2024	H22 Throw Pillow	Homeware	Online Store	18	$ 20.00	$ 8.00	$ 360.00
24	18-March-2024	S89 Handcrafted Journal	Stationery	Social Media	11	$ 30.00	$ 5.00	$ 330.00
25	25-January-2024	C23 Wooden Phone Stand	Accessories	In-Person Sales	15	$ 20.00	$ 8.00	$ 300.00
26	28-February-2024	J06 Handmade Earrings	Jewelry	Online Store	20	$ 15.00	$ 25.00	$ 300.00

Copilot sorts the data by the Total Sales column, from largest to smallest.

You can also sort by other types of columns, including those with text and dates.
In this example, the prompt asks Copilot to sort by the Category column, without

describing the sort order. When you ask Copilot to sort by a text column, it will automatically sort in alphabetical order.

Ask Copilot to sort by a text column without describing the sort order.

Copilot confirms the changes for your review. Select **Apply** to accept the changes.

Copilot describes the changes for your review.

The data is now sorted in alphabetical order by the Category column.

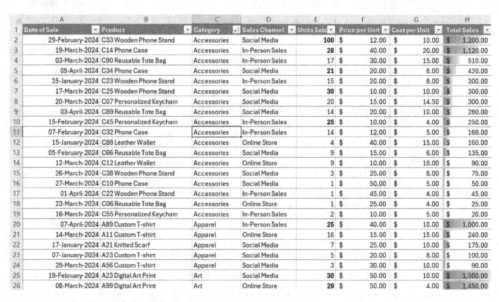

	A	B	C	D	E	F	G	H
1	Date of Sale	Product	Category	Sales Channel	Units Sold	Price per Unit	Cost per Unit	Total Sales
2	29-February-2024	C33 Wooden Phone Stand	Accessories	Social Media	100	$ 12.00	$ 10.00	$ 1,200.00
3	19-March-2024	C14 Phone Case	Accessories	In-Person Sales	28	$ 40.00	$ 20.00	$ 1,120.00
4	03-March-2024	C90 Reusable Tote Bag	Accessories	In-Person Sales	17	$ 30.00	$ 15.00	$ 510.00
5	05-April-2024	C34 Phone Case	Accessories	Social Media	21	$ 20.00	$ 8.00	$ 420.00
6	25-January-2024	C23 Wooden Phone Stand	Accessories	In-Person Sales	15	$ 20.00	$ 8.00	$ 300.00
7	17-March-2024	C25 Wooden Phone Stand	Accessories	Social Media	30	$ 10.00	$ 10.00	$ 300.00
8	20-January-2024	C07 Personalized Keychain	Accessories	Social Media	20	$ 15.00	$ 14.50	$ 300.00
9	03-April-2024	C89 Reusable Tote Bag	Accessories	Social Media	14	$ 20.00	$ 10.00	$ 280.00
10	15-February-2024	C45 Personalized Keychain	Accessories	In-Person Sales	25	$ 10.00	$ 4.00	$ 250.00
11	07-February-2024	C32 Phone Case	Accessories	In-Person Sales	14	$ 12.00	$ 5.00	$ 168.00
12	15-January-2024	C88 Leather Wallet	Accessories	Online Store	4	$ 40.00	$ 15.00	$ 160.00
13	05-February-2024	C66 Reusable Tote Bag	Accessories	Social Media	9	$ 15.00	$ 6.00	$ 135.00
14	12-March-2024	C12 Leather Wallet	Accessories	Online Store	9	$ 10.00	$ 18.00	$ 90.00
15	26-March-2024	C38 Wooden Phone Stand	Accessories	Social Media	3	$ 25.00	$ 8.00	$ 75.00
16	27-March-2024	C10 Phone Case	Accessories	Social Media	1	$ 50.00	$ 5.00	$ 50.00
17	01-April-2024	C22 Wooden Phone Stand	Accessories	In-Person Sales	1	$ 45.00	$ 4.00	$ 45.00
18	23-March-2024	C06 Reusable Tote Bag	Accessories	Online Store	1	$ 25.00	$ 4.00	$ 25.00
19	16-February-2024	C55 Personalized Keychain	Accessories	In-Person Sales	2	$ 10.00	$ 5.00	$ 20.00
20	07-April-2024	A89 Custom T-shirt	Apparel	In-Person Sales	25	$ 40.00	$ 10.00	$ 1,000.00
21	14-March-2024	A11 Custom T-shirt	Apparel	Online Store	16	$ 15.00	$ 15.00	$ 240.00
22	17-January-2024	A21 Knitted Scarf	Apparel	Social Media	7	$ 25.00	$ 10.00	$ 175.00
23	07-January-2024	A23 Custom T-shirt	Apparel	Social Media	5	$ 20.00	$ 8.00	$ 100.00
24	29-March-2024	A56 Custom T-shirt	Apparel	Social Media	3	$ 30.00	$ 10.00	$ 90.00
25	19-February-2024	A23 Digital Art Print	Art	Social Media	30	$ 50.00	$ 10.00	$ 1,500.00
26	08-March-2024	A99 Digital Art Print	Art	Online Store	29	$ 50.00	$ 4.00	$ 1,450.00

Copilot sorts the data alphabetically by the Category column.

> ✓ **TIP** Copilot can't apply multilevel sorting. For example, if you ask Copilot in a single prompt to sort by Category then by Units Sold, the result will be sorted only by the Units Sold column.

Filter your data

Copilot can help you apply or remove filters on the columns in your data so that you can focus on the data that matters most.

To filter your data with Copilot

1. Describe the filter you want to apply and select the **arrow** to send your prompt.

Write a prompt to ask Copilot to filter the data by the sales date.

2. Select **Apply** to accept the changes.

> ✓ **TIP** Although it is best to use exact column names, in this example the prompt asks Copilot to filter by the date of sale, and Copilot is able to correctly interpret the request.

Copilot describes the changes for your review.

3. Copilot filters the data by the Date of Sale column so that you now only see rows where the sale occurred in March 2024.

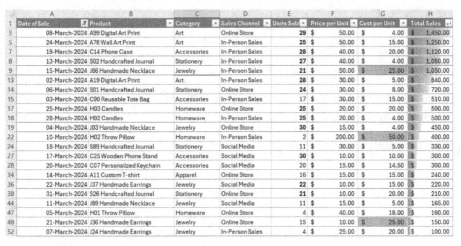

	A	B	C	D	E	F	G	H
1	Date of Sale	Product	Category	Sales Channel	Units Sold	Price per Unit	Cost per Unit	Total Sales
3	08-March-2024	A99 Digital Art Print	Art	Online Store	29	$ 50.00	$ 4.00	$ 1,450.00
5	24-March-2024	A78 Wall Art Print	Art	In-Person Sales	25	$ 50.00	$ 15.00	$ 1,250.00
7	19-March-2024	C14 Phone Case	Accessories	In-Person Sales	28	$ 40.00	$ 20.00	$ 1,120.00
8	13-March-2024	S02 Handcrafted Journal	Stationery	In-Person Sales	27	$ 40.00	$ 4.00	$ 1,080.00
9	15-March-2024	J66 Handmade Necklace	Jewelry	In-Person Sales	21	$ 50.00	$ 25.00	$ 1,050.00
13	02-March-2024	A19 Digital Art Print	Art	In-Person Sales	28	$ 30.00	$ 5.00	$ 840.00
14	06-March-2024	S01 Handcrafted Journal	Stationery	Online Store	24	$ 30.00	$ 8.00	$ 720.00
15	03-March-2024	C90 Reusable Tote Bag	Accessories	In-Person Sales	17	$ 30.00	$ 15.00	$ 510.00
17	25-March-2024	H03 Candles	Homeware	Online Store	25	$ 20.00	$ 20.00	$ 500.00
18	28-March-2024	H92 Candles	Homeware	In-Person Sales	25	$ 20.00	$ 4.00	$ 500.00
19	04-March-2024	J03 Handmade Necklace	Jewelry	Online Store	30	$ 15.00	$ 4.00	$ 450.00
22	10-March-2024	H02 Throw Pillow	Homeware	In-Person Sales	2	$ 200.00	$ 50.00	$ 400.00
24	18-March-2024	S89 Handcrafted Journal	Stationery	Social Media	11	$ 30.00	$ 5.00	$ 330.00
27	17-March-2024	C25 Wooden Phone Stand	Accessories	Social Media	30	$ 10.00	$ 10.00	$ 300.00
28	20-March-2024	C07 Personalized Keychain	Accessories	Social Media	20	$ 15.00	$ 14.50	$ 300.00
34	14-March-2024	A11 Custom T-shirt	Apparel	Online Store	16	$ 15.00	$ 15.00	$ 240.00
36	22-March-2024	J37 Handmade Earrings	Jewelry	Social Media	22	$ 10.00	$ 15.00	$ 220.00
38	31-March-2024	S26 Handcrafted Journal	Stationery	Online Store	21	$ 10.00	$ 20.00	$ 210.00
44	11-March-2024	J89 Handmade Necklace	Jewelry	Social Media	11	$ 15.00	$ 5.00	$ 165.00
47	05-March-2024	H01 Throw Pillow	Homeware	Online Store	4	$ 40.00	$ 18.00	$ 160.00
48	21-March-2024	J36 Handmade Earrings	Jewelry	Online Store	15	$ 10.00	$ 25.00	$ 150.00
52	07-March-2024	J24 Handmade Earrings	Jewelry	In-Person Sales	4	$ 25.00	$ 20.00	$ 100.00

Copilot filters the data by the Date of Sale column.

If you ask Copilot to apply another filter, it will apply that as a second filter, with the first one still in place.

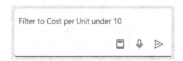

Filter to Cost per Unit under 10

Ask Copilot to apply a second filter to your data.

Copilot confirms the details. Select **Apply** to accept the changes.

Sure! Looking at **A1:H66**, here's 1 change to review and apply:

- Apply a filter on 'Cost per Unit' to show only rows where the value is less than 10

✓ Apply

AI-generated content may be incorrect

Copilot describes the changes for your review.

The data is now filtered both by the date of sale and the cost per unit, showing only those rows where the cost per unit is under 10 and the sale was in March 2024.

	A	B	C	D	E	F	G	H
1	Date of Sale	Product	Category	Sales Channel	Units Sold	Price per Unit	Cost per Unit	Total Sales
3	08-March-2024	A99 Digital Art Print	Art	Online Store	29	$ 50.00	$ 4.00	$ 1,450.00
8	13-March-2024	S02 Handcrafted Journal	Stationery	In-Person Sales	27	$ 40.00	$ 4.00	$ 1,080.00
13	02-March-2024	A19 Digital Art Print	Art	In-Person Sales	28	$ 30.00	$ 5.00	$ 840.00
14	06-March-2024	S01 Handcrafted Journal	Stationery	Online Store	24	$ 30.00	$ 8.00	$ 720.00
18	28-March-2024	H92 Candles	Homeware	In-Person Sales	25	$ 20.00	$ 4.00	$ 500.00
19	04-March-2024	J03 Handmade Necklace	Jewelry	Online Store	30	$ 15.00	$ 4.00	$ 450.00
24	18-March-2024	S89 Handcrafted Journal	Stationery	Social Media	11	$ 30.00	$ 5.00	$ 330.00
44	11-March-2024	J89 Handmade Necklace	Jewelry	Social Media	11	$ 15.00	$ 5.00	$ 165.00
55	26-March-2024	C38 Wooden Phone Stand	Accessories	Social Media	3	$ 25.00	$ 8.00	$ 75.00
59	27-March-2024	C10 Phone Case	Accessories	Social Media	1	$ 50.00	$ 5.00	$ 50.00
63	23-March-2024	C06 Reusable Tote Bag	Accessories	Online Store	1	$ 25.00	$ 4.00	$ 25.00
64	16-March-2024	C55 Personalized Keychain	Accessories	In-Person Sales	2	$ 10.00	$ 5.00	$ 20.00
66	01-March-2024	H76 Candles	Homeware	Social Media	1	$ 10.00	$ 5.00	$ 10.00
67								

Copilot filters the data by the Cost per Unit column.

You can also ask Copilot to remove the filters.

 TIP You can ask Copilot to remove specific filters by specifying the columns, with a prompt like "Remove the filters from the Cost per Unit and Date of Sale columns."

Remove all filters

Write a prompt to ask Copilot to remove all filters.

Copilot describes the requested changes. Select **Apply** to accept the changes.

Sure! Looking at **A1:H66**, here's 1 change to review and apply:

- Remove all filters on table Table1

✓ Apply

AI-generated content may be incorrect

Copilot describes the changes for your review.

The filters have now been removed from your table.

	A	B	C	D	E	F	G	H
1	Date of Sale	Product	Category	Sales Channel	Units Sold	Price per Unit	Cost per Unit	Total Sales
2	19-February-2024	A23 Digital Art Print	Art	Social Media	30	$ 50.00	$ 10.00	$ 1,500.00
3	08-March-2024	A99 Digital Art Print	Art	Online Store	29	$ 50.00	$ 4.00	$ 1,450.00
4	08-April-2024	J01 Handmade Necklace	Jewelry	Online Store	26	$ 50.00	$ 10.00	$ 1,300.00
5	24-March-2024	A78 Wall Art Print	Art	In-Person Sales	25	$ 50.00	$ 15.00	$ 1,250.00
6	29-February-2024	C33 Wooden Phone Stand	Accessories	Social Media	100	$ 12.00	$ 10.00	$ 1,200.00
7	19-March-2024	C14 Phone Case	Accessories	In-Person Sales	28	$ 40.00	$ 20.00	$ 1,120.00
8	13-March-2024	S02 Handcrafted Journal	Stationery	In-Person Sales	27	$ 40.00	$ 4.00	$ 1,080.00
9	15-March-2024	J66 Handmade Necklace	Jewelry	In-Person Sales	21	$ 50.00	$ 25.00	$ 1,050.00
10	07-April-2024	A89 Custom T-shirt	Apparel	In-Person Sales	25	$ 40.00	$ 10.00	$ 1,000.00
11	20-February-2024	A24 Digital Art Print	Art	Social Media	19	$ 50.00	$ 8.00	$ 950.00
12	04-April-2024	H89 Throw Pillow	Homeware	Online Store	23	$ 40.00	$ 15.00	$ 920.00
13	02-March-2024	A19 Digital Art Print	Art	In-Person Sales	28	$ 30.00	$ 5.00	$ 840.00
14	06-March-2024	S01 Handcrafted Journal	Stationery	Online Store	24	$ 30.00	$ 8.00	$ 720.00

Copilot removes the filters from the columns.

Generate formula columns

Copilot can help you write formulas to perform calculations on your data. You can describe what you want in natural language without knowing any details of the formula, and Copilot will suggest and explain the formula to you, giving you a button to instantly add it to your table as a new column.

You can start by asking Copilot to suggest a formula column that would be a good fit for your data by using the suggested prompt. This prompt appears at the top of the Copilot pane when you first launch Copilot. You can find it again by scrolling to the top of the chat history in the pane, or you can type "Suggest a formula column" in the prompt area.

Scroll to the top of the conversation history to find the prompt button to suggest a formula column.

Copilot will respond by suggesting a formula column, providing a description and a sample of the output. In this example, where the data contains sales and unit costs, Copilot suggests a formula to calculate the profit for each product.

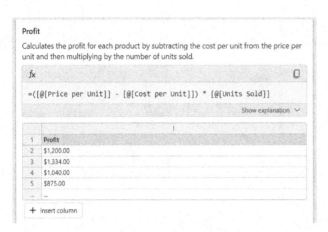

Copilot suggests a formula and provides a description of the formula and sample output.

Expand the **Show explanation** option under the formula to get a full explanation of what the formula is and what it will do.

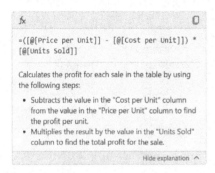

Expand the Show explanation menu to see a full explanation of the formula.

You can select the **Copy** icon at the top right of the formula to copy the formula if you want to work with it yourself in the formula bar or use it elsewhere.

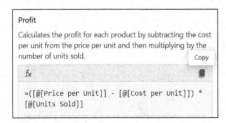

Select the Copy icon to copy the formula to your clipboard.

Hover over the **Insert column** button at the bottom of the Copilot response to get a preview of the new column before adding it to your table.

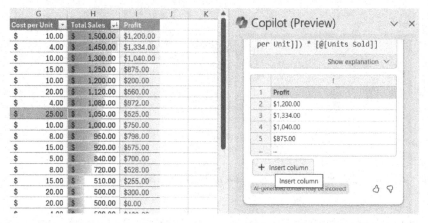

Hover over the Insert column button to get a preview of the column in your table.

Select the **Insert column** button to add the column to your table. Copilot adds the column and responds with a confirmation message.

 TIP You can select the Undo button in the Copilot response to remove the new column.

Copilot adds the column to your table and confirms with a message that includes an Undo button.

You can ask Copilot to help you with any formula you want to create by describing what you want in the prompt area. In this example, the prompt asks Copilot to split an existing column into two separate columns of data.

Split the product column into two separate columns for product code and product name

Describe the formula you want to create in the prompt area.

Copilot responds with a description of the formula needed to make the change. In this example, two formulas are needed, and Copilot breaks down the explanation for each.

Copilot describes that it will create a formula for the Product Code column by extracting the product code from the product name by taking the text before the first space. It also describes that it will create a formula for the Product Name column by extracting the name of each product by removing the initial code from the Product column, providing a clearer view of the product names in the table.

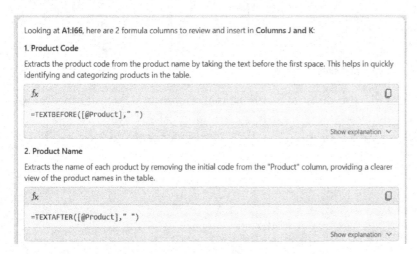

Looking at **A1:I66**, here are 2 formula columns to review and insert in **Columns J and K**:

1. Product Code

Extracts the product code from the product name by taking the text before the first space. This helps in quickly identifying and categorizing products in the table.

fx

```
=TEXTBEFORE([@Product]," ")
```

Show explanation ⌄

2. Product Name

Extracts the name of each product by removing the initial code from the "Product" column, providing a clearer view of the product names in the table.

fx

```
=TEXTAFTER([@Product]," ")
```

Show explanation ⌄

Copilot suggests the formula and provides an explanation for each part.

Copilot also shows a preview of the two new columns for Product Code and Product Name, with sample data from the table.

Copilot shows a preview of the data in the two new columns.

Select the **Insert columns** button to add the new columns to your table.

Copilot adds the new columns to the table.

You can ask Copilot to help you write a formula that references data in another table in your workbook. In this example, there is another table called "Inventory" in a separate sheet, which contains data about the stock on hand for each product.

Copilot can help you write formulas that reference other tables in your workbook.

Write a prompt to ask Copilot to write the formula, describing the data you want to get from the other table. To get the best result, include details such as the table name and column where Copilot will find the data you want to add.

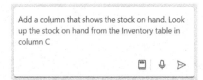

Write a prompt that describes the formula you want to create.

Copilot responds with a suggested formula for you to review before accepting it. Select the **Insert column** button to accept the suggested formula and create the new column.

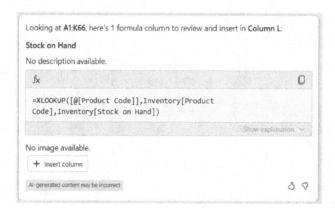

Copilot suggests a formula for your review before accepting it.

Copilot adds the formula and the new column to your table.

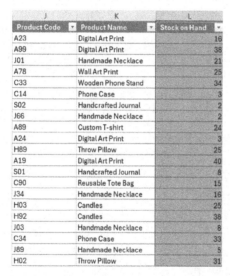

Copilot adds the new column to your table.

> ✅ **TIP** You can also ask Copilot for help with constructing or understanding formulas, or how to do things in Excel, with prompts such as "Can you give me an example of how to use =XLOOKUP" or "How do I add subtotals?"

Understand your data

Copilot can help you gain insights and identify patterns, trends, or outliers in your data. You can ask Copilot to give you general insights, or you can ask a specific question about your data.

You can start by asking Copilot to automatically analyze your data and discover insights by using the prompt "show data insights." You can enter this into the prompt area or select it when Copilot suggests it as a prompt.

Select the suggested prompt or enter
"show data insights" into the prompt area.

> ✓ **TIP** You can also scroll back to the top of the Copilot chat and select the **Understand** suggested prompt to ask Copilot to summarize your data using PivotTables or charts. This more specific prompt asks Copilot to provide a summary, while the broader prompt "show data insights" will help you discover insights in your data. Depending on your dataset, you may get similar or very different results from each of these options.

Copilot will respond with insights from your data, which may include a preview of a chart and a description. In this example, Copilot returns a chart showing sales by date.

Copilot responds with insights from your data,
which may include a chart.

Copilot also provides a description of the insight provided. Depending on the insights, this message can be a simple confirmation or may include a description of specific insights. There is a Copy button that you can use to copy the description to your clipboard if you find it useful and want to use it somewhere else.

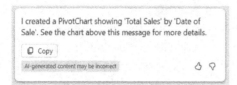

Copilot provides a description of the insight as part of the response.

Select the **Add to a new sheet** button under the preview of the chart to create a new sheet in your workbook and add this PivotChart with the related data to that new sheet.

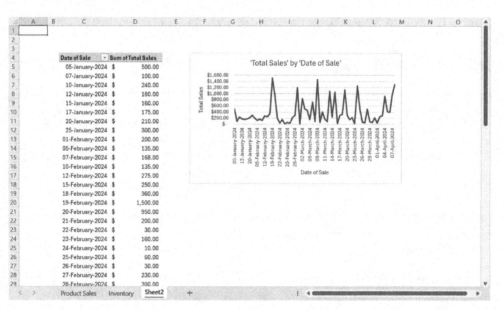

Copilot adds the data and the PivotChart to a new sheet.

Copilot confirms the action and includes buttons you can use to undo the change or navigate back to your data. Select the **Go back to data** button to return to your original sheet.

*Copilot confirms the action and gives you options
to Go back to data or Undo.*

You can ask Copilot for another insight, or you can ask for all the insights it can find
in a single action. You may see this as a suggested prompt that you can select, or you
can type the prompt "Add all insights to grid" in the prompt area.

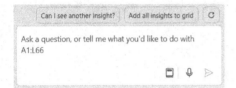

Copilot suggests the "Add all insights to grid" prompt.

Copilot creates a new sheet in your workbook and adds charts for all the insights it
can find in your data.

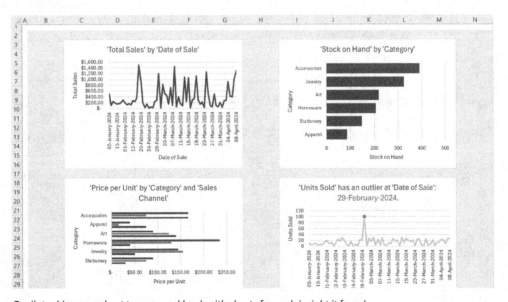

Copilot adds a new sheet to your workbook with charts for each insight it found.

5

Select the **Go back to data** button in the Copilot chat or select the tab for the sheet that contains your original table.

You can ask Copilot about specific data points or insights in your data, including asking questions that require Copilot to perform calculations or generate charts.

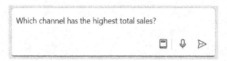

You can ask Copilot a specific question about your data.

Copilot analyzes your data and presents the results with an explanation. You can choose to add the results to a new sheet or copy the details, or you can just read the insights in the chat and move on to the next question.

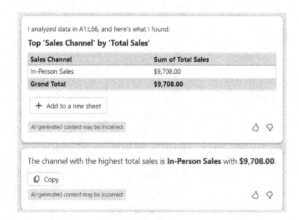

Copilot analyzes your data and answers the question.

You can ask questions that involve multiple dimensions in your data.

Ask Copilot a question that involves multiple dimensions in your data.

Copilot presents the results in a table, together with a summary description of the results in natural language.

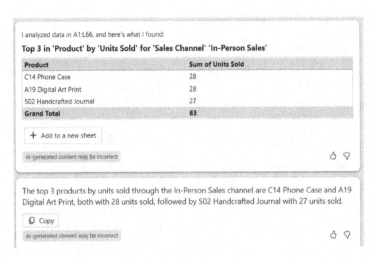

Copilot returns the results as a table and description.

You can also ask Copilot a more general question to help you understand your data across different dimensions.

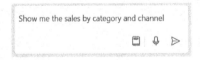

Ask Copilot a more general question to help understand your data.

In response to this type of prompt, Copilot will generate a PivotChart to help you visualize and analyze your data, and a description of the insights.

I analyzed data in A1:L66, and here's what I found:

'Total Sales' by 'Category' and 'Sales Channel'
Sum of Total Sales

+ Add to a new sheet

AI-generated content may be incorrect

The total sales by category and channel are as follows: Accessories - In-Person Sales: $2,413.00, Online Store: $275.00, Social Media: $2,760.00. See the PivotChart above for more details.

Copy

AI-generated content may be incorrect

Copilot creates a PivotChart and description of the insights to help you visualize and understand your data.

Select **Add to a new sheet** to create a new sheet in your workbook and add this PivotTable and chart to that sheet.

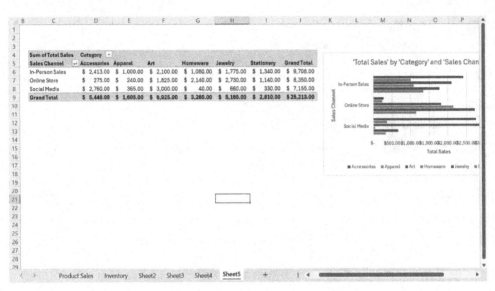

Select Add to new sheet to add the PivotTable and chart to a new sheet in your workbook.

Skills review

In this chapter, you learned how to:

- Get started with Copilot in Excel, understand the requirements for working with Copilot in Excel, and format your data as a table.

- Apply conditional formatting to your data, and sort and filter data using Copilot.

- Generate formula columns by describing the formula in natural language.

- Understand your data by asking Copilot to automatically analyze your data for insights and by asking specific questions about your data.

Practice tasks

Before you can complete these tasks, you must copy the book's practice files to your computer. The practice files for these tasks are in the CopilotProSBS\Ch05 folder.

The introduction includes a complete list of practice files and download instructions.

Get started with Copilot in Excel

Using the file "Packaging Inventory.xlsx" provided in the practice files, perform the following tasks:

1. Save the file to your personal OneDrive that you used to sign up for Copilot Pro.

2. Open the file in Excel.

3. Select the data in the sheet.

4. On the **Home** ribbon, select **Format as Table**.

5. Select a style of your choice. Choose a style that leaves the main rows of the table in white so that you can see the highlights that you will add later.

6. Launch Copilot by selecting the icon at the right end of the **Home** ribbon.

Highlight, sort, and filter your data

Continue working from where you finished the previous task, and then perform the following tasks:

1. Enter the following prompt into the Copilot prompt area: Highlight the highest values in Reorder Quantity in yellow.

2. Wait for Copilot to respond, and then select **Apply** to add the highlights to your sheet.

3. Enter the following prompt: Add data bars to the Quantity in Stock column.

4. Wait for Copilot to respond, and then select **Apply** to add the highlights to your sheet.

5. Enter the following prompt: Sort by Quantity in Stock in descending order.

6. Wait for Copilot to respond, and then select **Apply** to apply the sort to your table.

7. Enter the following prompt: Filter by Supplier ID SUP1004.

8. Wait for Copilot to respond, and then select **Apply** to apply the filter to your table.

9. Select the **Undo** button in the Copilot confirmation message to remove the filter.

10. Enter the following prompt: Show items with Description that includes Bubble Wrap.

11. Wait for Copilot to respond, and then select **Apply** to apply the filter to your table.

12. Select the **Undo** button in the Copilot confirmation message to remove the filter.

13. Enter the following prompt: Format unit price as currency.

14. Wait for Copilot to respond, and then select **Apply** to accept the formatting changes.

Generate formula columns

Continue working from where you finished the previous task, and then perform the following tasks:

1. Scroll to the top of the Copilot chat and select the button **Suggest a formula column** (or type Suggest a formula column into the prompt area).

2. Wait for Copilot to respond, and then select **Insert column** to add the column to your table.

3. Enter the following prompt: Split the Location column into separate columns for Section and Shelf.

4. Wait for Copilot to respond, and then select **Insert columns** to add the columns to your table.

Understand your data

Continue working from where you finished the previous task, and then perform the following tasks:

1. Scroll to the top of the Copilot chat and select the button **Show data insights** (or type Show data insights into the prompt area).

2. Wait for Copilot to respond, and then select **Add to new sheet** to add the chart and related data to a new sheet in your workbook.

3. Select **Go back to data** in the Copilot confirmation message.

4. Select the suggested prompt **Add all insights to grid** (or type Add all insights to grid in the prompt area).

5. Wait for Copilot to create a new sheet showing a range of charts and insights. Review the created charts.

6. Select **Go back to data** in the Copilot confirmation message.

7. Enter the following prompt: Show me reorder quantity by Supplier ID.

8. Wait for Copilot to respond, and then select **Add to new sheet** to add the chart and related data to a new sheet in your workbook.

9. Select **Go back to data** in the Copilot confirmation message.

10. Enter the following prompt: Which cardboard box has the highest unit price.

11. Wait for Copilot to respond, and then view the results.

Copilot in Outlook

Copilot in Outlook can help you save time when working with email by helping you create a first draft of a new email or reply. You can use a natural language prompt to describe what kind of email you want and choose from a list of quick options for tone and length or describe your own style in detail. You can work with Copilot to redraft your email by adding additional information or by changing the tone and length until you are happy with it. You are always in control, choosing when to keep or discard the email drafts and making final edits before sending.

You can also use Copilot in Outlook to help you catch up on long email threads, using the Summary by Copilot feature. Copilot will identify and summarize the main points of the email thread for you, providing citations to help you refer back to the original email source for each point in the summary. You can copy the summary to use somewhere else, such as in your notes or in another email.

Copilot can also help you write better emails by offering coaching suggestions to improve the tone, reader sentiment, and clarity of your emails. You will get suggestions about different words and phrases to use that help you write clearer, more positive emails that encourage responses and ongoing collaboration.

In this chapter

- Get started with Copilot in Outlook
- Draft an email
- Summarize an email thread
- Improve your emails with Coaching by Copilot
- Use Copilot in the Outlook mobile app

Practice files

No practice files are necessary to complete the practice tasks in this chapter.

In this chapter, you will learn how to use Copilot in Outlook on both desktop and mobile experiences to draft emails, summarize email threads, and improve your emails with coaching.

Get started with Copilot in Outlook

You can use Copilot in Outlook in web, Windows, Mac, and mobile experiences when drafting a new email, replying to an email, or reading an email thread. In this section, you will learn how to access Copilot in Outlook on the web and desktop experiences.

 SEE ALSO You will learn how to use Copilot in the Outlook mobile app in the last section of this chapter.

IMPORTANT To use Copilot in Outlook with your Copilot Pro license, your Microsoft account that you used to sign up for Copilot Pro must be an email address from outlook.com, hotmail.com, live.com, or msn.com. Microsoft accounts using Outlook with an account from a third-party provider such as Gmail or Yahoo won't have access to Copilot in Outlook. You cannot use your work account for Copilot in Outlook with your Copilot Pro license.

You will find Copilot in Outlook when you are drafting a new email or reading an email thread.

When you are drafting an email, you will find Copilot on the Message ribbon.

- The Draft with Copilot option will help you draft a new email or a reply to an existing email.

- Coaching by Copilot will help you rewrite the content in your draft.

Start a new email and select the Copilot icon on the Message ribbon.

You will also find the Summary by Copilot feature at the top of any email thread. This can help you quickly understand the context of a long email thread with multiple replies without needing to read through all of them.

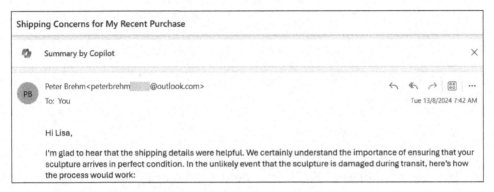

Shipping Concerns for My Recent Purchase

Select an email thread to view the Summary by Copilot feature.

Draft an email

You can save time when writing emails by describing the email you want to write and asking Copilot to write the first draft. Copilot can help you write a new email from scratch or reply to an existing email using the context of that email.

Use Copilot to draft a new email

In this section, you will learn how to use a prompt to ask Copilot to draft an email for you. You will also learn how to select the tone and length, and how to regenerate and refine the draft until you are ready to send it.

To draft an email message with Copilot in Outlook

1. Start a new email message.

2. Select the **Copilot** icon on the Message ribbon and select **Draft with Copilot**.

> **TIP** You will only see the Copilot icon when you have a new or draft email open. It does not appear on the main Home ribbon in Outlook.

Select the Copilot icon and select Draft with Copilot.

3. This opens a Draft with Copilot pane. Describe the email you want to draft. In this example, you are writing an email to your contact at Wide World Importers, an import company that buys and sells unique pieces of art from around the world, to ask about new pieces coming in.

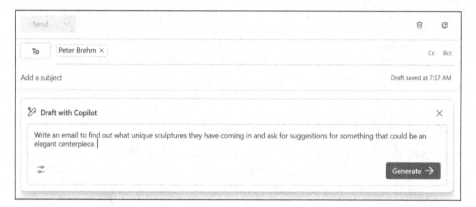

Describe the email you want Copilot to help you draft.

> **TIP** The Draft with Copilot feature works best with a short general prompt. If you write a longer prompt with a lot of detail, Copilot will tend to just repeat what you've written. If you have a longer and more descriptive prompt in mind, write that as a draft and use the Coaching by Copilot feature described later in this chapter to help you improve it.

4. Select the **slider** icon to select the tone and length of your email.

> ✅ **TIP** If you want a more specific tone or style than what is offered in this list, describe it in your prompt. You can also refine and change the tone and length selections after the first draft.

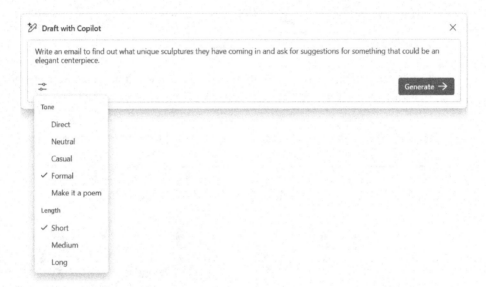

Select the tone and length you want for your draft.

5. When you have made your selections, select the **Generate** button to send the prompt to Copilot.

6. Copilot responds with a draft email based on the prompt and the options you selected for tone and length.

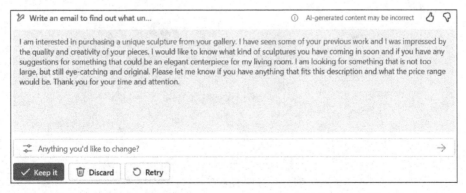

Copilot generates a draft email based on your prompt and selections for tone and length.

7. You can choose to iterate on the draft by describing any changes you want to make, keep it, discard it, or generate a new version. Select the **Retry** button to regenerate a new draft using the same prompt and selections for tone and length.

Select the Retry button to regenerate a new draft of the email.

8. Copilot generates a new draft of the email. Depending on your prompt, this may or may not be very different from the first version.

 TIP The broader or more general your prompt, the more differences you will see in automatically generating a new draft this way.

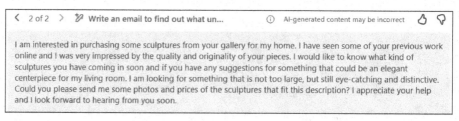

Copilot generates a new draft of the email.

9. Select the **slider** icon to expand the list of options to change the length and tone. You can choose one of these options if you want to generate a quick new draft of your email. Select the option **Make it sound more casual.**

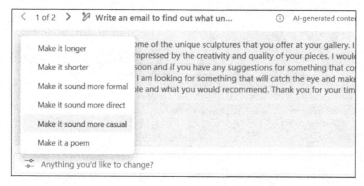

Select the slider icon to select from quick options to change the tone and length.

10. Copilot generates a draft of the email using the selected tone.

Copilot regenerates the draft in a more casual tone.

11. Use the **left and right arrows** to navigate between and view the different versions of the draft.

Select the left arrow to navigate back to the previous version of the draft.

12. Choose the draft you like best to continue working. In this example, go back to the first version of the draft. Rather than choosing from the preset options, you can refine your draft by describing exactly how you want to change the tone, style, or length of the email. You can also describe additional detail or content you want to add to the draft.

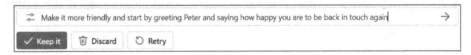

Describe how you want Copilot to redraft your email by describing what you want.

13. Copilot drafts a new version of the email based on your prompt.

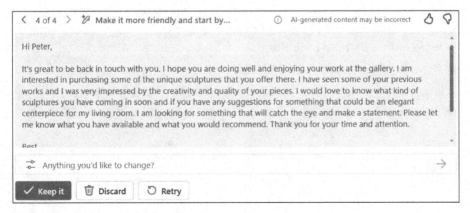

Copilot drafts a new version of the email.

14. When you are happy with the draft, select the **Keep it** button to add it to your email.

The draft content is added to your email.

15. Add a subject line and make any edits to the draft before sending.

> ⚠️ **IMPORTANT** Copilot in Outlook does not send emails for you; it only creates a draft. You are in control of adding the draft content to the email and sending the email when you are happy with it.

Use Copilot to draft a reply to an email

You can use Copilot to draft a reply to an email using one of the quick prompts or by describing what you want to write. Copilot uses the context of the open email and your prompt to draft the response.

To use Copilot in Outlook to draft a reply to an email

1. Open an existing email message that you want to reply to and select the **Reply** button.

2. Copilot will suggest some prompts to generate a draft reply based on the email content.

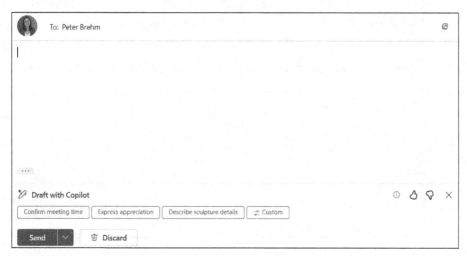

Copilot suggests prompts to help you draft a reply.

3. Select any of these suggested prompts to generate a reply.

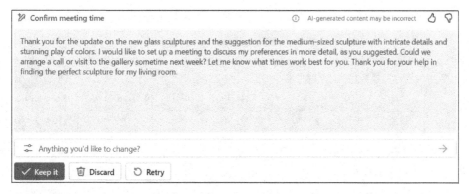

Copilot generates a response to confirm a meeting time.

4. You can choose to keep it, discard it, or regenerate a different version. You can also select a different tone or length or describe what you want to change, as shown in the previous section. **Discard** this draft to return to the email.

5. Select the **Custom** option.

Select the Custom option to open the Draft with Copilot pane.

6. This opens the Draft with Copilot pane, where you can describe the email reply that you want to draft. You can also select the length and tone as shown in the previous section.

7. Write the prompt to generate the reply and select the **Generate** button.

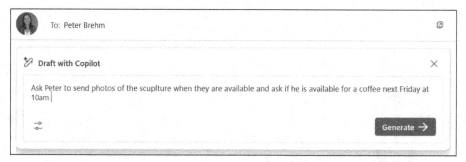

Describe the reply you want Copilot to draft.

8. Copilot generates a reply based on the context of the original email and your prompt.

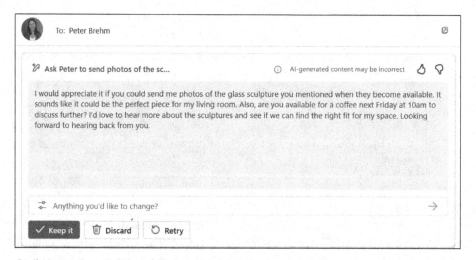

Copilot generates a reply based on the original email and your prompt.

9. You can discard, regenerate, or adjust for length and tone in the same way you did when drafting a new email. When you are happy with the final draft, select the **Keep it** button to add it to the email, edit, and send.

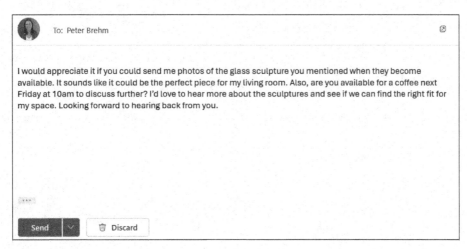

The draft content is added to your email.

Summarize an email thread

Copilot can help you catch up on long email threads or find information in an email thread quickly using the Summary by Copilot feature.

> ⚠️ **IMPORTANT** The content of your email is not shared outside your tenant or with Microsoft when you use this feature. The summary and the emails used in the summary remain private and secure.

To use Summary by Copilot to summarize an email thread

1. Open an existing email that is part of an email thread.

2. You will find Summary by Copilot at the top of the email thread.

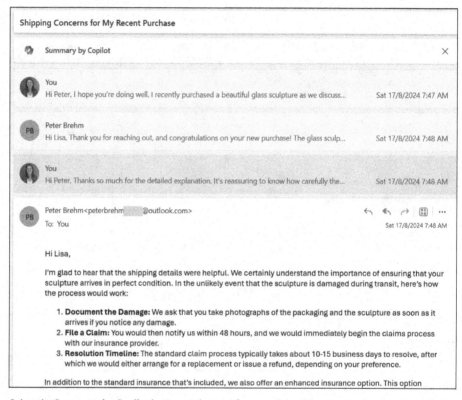

*Select the **Summary by Copilot** button at the top of an email thread to summarize that thread.*

3. Select the **Summary by Copilot** button to generate a summary of the email thread.

4. Copilot summarizes the email thread and provides citations to where each point in the summary came from.

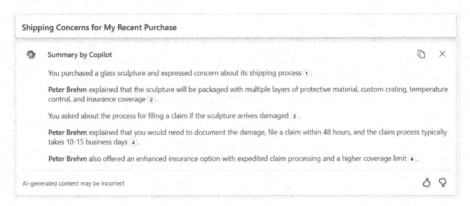

Copilot summarizes the email thread and provides citations.

> ✓ **TIP** You can select the copy icon at the top right of the summary to copy the content of the email summary to use somewhere else, such as copying it to a notebook or using it in another email.

5. Select any of the citation numbers to be taken directly to the email that was the source of that part of the summary.

> **Peter Brehm** explained that you would need to document the damage, file a claim within 48 hours, and the claim process typically takes 10-15 business days 4 .

Select the citation number at the end of any point in the summary to go to the relevant email.

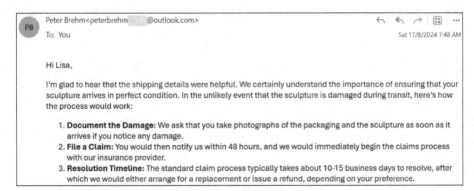

The original email is opened so that you can check the source of the summary.

Improve your emails with Coaching by Copilot

Copilot can help you write better emails by offering suggestions to improve the tone, reader sentiment, and clarity of your draft before you send it. This is useful when you want to write your own first draft and then have Copilot check it for you and coach you with ideas to make it better. Coaching by Copilot will offer suggestions in these three categories:

- *Tone* suggestions help you rephrase parts of your email to use language that is more polite, friendly, or professional. You will find suggestions here about adding a greeting, setting a positive or collaborative tone, or using softer or stronger language.

- *Reader Sentiment* suggestions help improve empathy, ask open-ended questions, encourage open dialog, help the reader feel involved in next steps, and facilitate ongoing communication or collaboration.

- *Clarity* suggestions help you reword parts of your email to provide context or to provide more specific details to make the email clearer.

To use Coaching by Copilot to improve your emails

1. Draft an email with at least 100 characters.

> **TIP** Coaching by Copilot only works with drafts that are at least 100 characters long. If you write a draft shorter than that, you will get a message that tells you to write at least 100 characters. You will get more value from Coaching by Copilot with longer drafts.

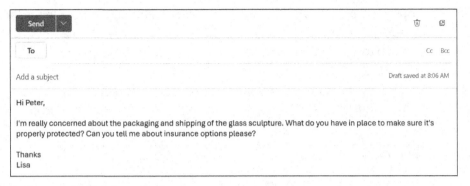

Draft an email with at least 100 characters.

2. Select the **Copilot** icon on the Message ribbon, and then select the **Coaching by Copilot** option.

Select the Coaching by Copilot option from the Message ribbon.

3. Copilot shows a series of progress messages while it analyzes your draft and generates coaching suggestions.

 TIP Select the **Stop generating** button if you want to stop the process and redraft your email.

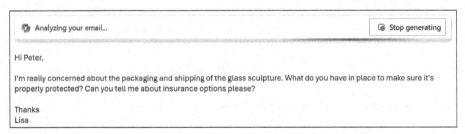

Copilot shows a series of progress messages while it generates coaching suggestions.

4. Copilot will present a pop-up window with coaching suggestions in the three categories: Tone, Reader Sentiment, and Clarity. Select each category and scroll through to review the suggestions. The Tone suggestions are open first.

 TIP You can generate new coaching suggestions by selecting the **Regenerate** button.

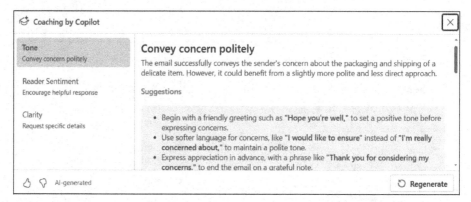

Copilot generates coaching suggestions for Tone, Reader Sentiment, and Clarity. The Tone suggestion is to convey concern politely.

5. Select **Reader Sentiment** on the left side to view the suggestions to improve in that category.

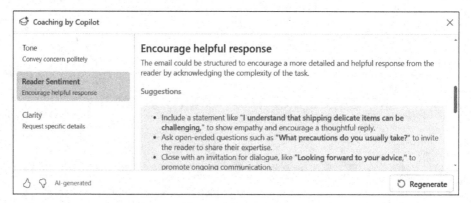

The Reader Sentiment suggestion is to encourage helpful response.

6. Select **Clarity** on the left side to view the suggestions to improve in that category.

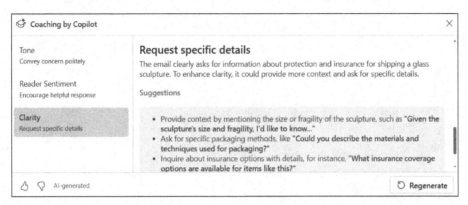

The Clarity suggestion is to request specific details.

> ⚠️ **IMPORTANT** Copilot does not automatically make these changes to your email. You decide which suggestions to follow and manually rewrite your draft based on those suggestions.

Use Copilot in the Outlook mobile app

You can use all the same features of Copilot in Outlook on the Outlook mobile app to get help with drafting emails, summarizing email threads, and getting coaching suggestions while you are working with email on the go.

Draft a new email with Copilot in the Outlook mobile app

Copilot can help you draft emails in the Outlook mobile app, with options to adjust the tone, length, and content of the draft until you are happy with it.

To draft an email message with Copilot in the Outlook mobile app

1. Open the Outlook mobile app on your device and start a new email message.

2. Select the **Draft with Copilot** option that appears in the body of the email.

*Select the **Draft with Copilot** option in the body of the email.*

 TIP You can also select the Copilot icon in the menu bar to get to the Draft with Copilot option.

3. This will open the Draft with Copilot pane. Write a prompt describing the email you want to draft.

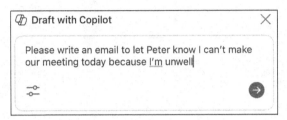

Write your prompt in the Draft with Copilot pane.

4. Select the **slider** icon to open the menu of options to set the tone and length of the email.

5. Select the options you want, and then select the **Apply** link at the top right of the panel.

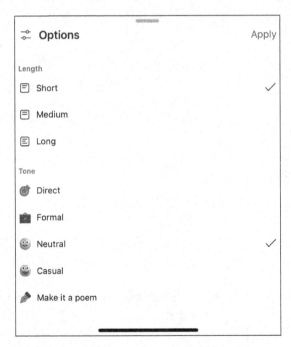

Select the length and tone of your email draft, and then select Apply.

6. You will see a series of progress messages as Copilot drafts your email.

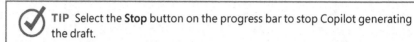

> ✓ **TIP** Select the **Stop** button on the progress bar to stop Copilot generating the draft.

Copilot shows a series of progress messages and an option to stop generating.

7. When Copilot has finished generating, you will see the draft content in the body of your email. The text is highlighted to indicate that you haven't yet accepted the content.

Copilot generates the draft and adds it to the body of the email. The text is highlighted to indicate that you haven't yet accepted it.

8. At the bottom of the email, you will see the prompt you used to generate the draft, a prompt area where you can describe what you want to change, and options to keep, discard, or regenerate the draft.

9. Select the **Options** button to open the menu of options to change the length and tone.

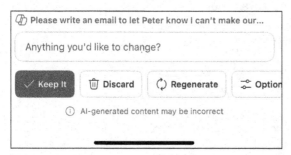

You can write a prompt to change the draft; keep, discard, or regenerate it; or open the menu of options to change the length and tone.

10. Select a different length or tone for your email. In this example, choose the **Casual** tone.

Choose a different length or tone to regenerate the email.

6

11. Copilot will regenerate your email draft using the selected option. This new draft will replace the previous draft in the body of the email. The text is highlighted to indicate that you haven't yet accepted it.

Hey, I'm sorry to say that I can't make it to our meeting today. I'm feeling sick and I need to lie down. I hope this doesn't mess up your plans too much. Thanks for being understanding and flexible. I'll get in touch with you when I'm better and we can reschedule our meeting.

Copilot replaces the first draft with the new draft. The text is highlighted to indicate that you haven't yet accepted the draft.

12. At the bottom of the email, you will find the option to scroll between the different versions of the draft, an option to write a prompt to change any version of the draft, and the options to keep it, discard, or regenerate.

*Select the **Keep It** button to add the draft content to the body of your email.*

13. When you are happy with the draft, select the **Keep It** button to add the draft content to your email, and then continue to edit, add a subject line, and send.

The content of the draft is now in your email ready for you to edit and send.

Use Summary by Copilot in the Outlook mobile app

Copilot can help you summarize email threads in the Outlook mobile app, providing you with the key points in the thread and citations to view the original email for each point.

To summarize an email thread using the Outlook mobile app

1. Open an existing email that is part of an email thread.

2. Select the **Copilot** icon in the menu at the top right of the app.

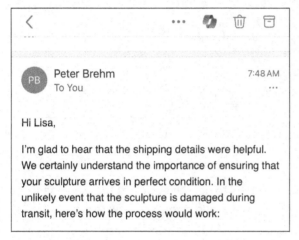

Open an email that is part of an email thread, and then select the Copilot icon in the top menu of the app to generate a summary of the thread.

3. Copilot shows a series of progress messages and then displays the generated summary.

Copilot shows a series of progress messages while it generates the summary.

6

TIP Select the **Stop** button to stop Copilot from generating the summary.

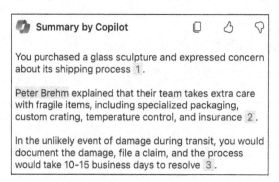

Copilot generates a summary of the email thread with citations for each part of the summary.

 TIP You can select the **copy** icon to copy the summary content to your device clipboard.

4. Select any of the citation numbers to get the details of the message that is the source for that part of the summary, and a link to follow to view it.

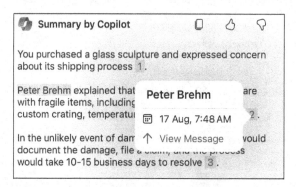

Select the citation number to view the message that was used for that part of the summary.

Use Coaching by Copilot in the Outlook mobile app

Copilot can coach you to write better email messages by analyzing your draft for tone, reader sentiment, and clarity.

To improve your email draft with Coaching by Copilot in the Outlook mobile app

1. Draft an email message with at least 100 characters.

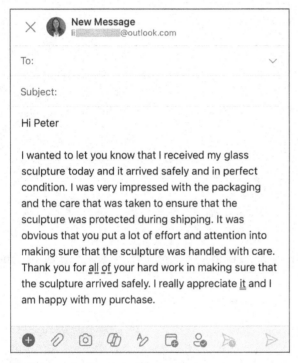

Draft an email with at least 100 characters.

2. Select the **Copilot** icon on the menu at the bottom of the email to expand the options.

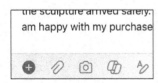

Select the Copilot icon at the bottom of the email.

239

3. Select the **Coaching by Copilot** option.

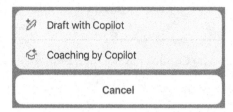

Select the Coaching by Copilot option.

4. Copilot shows a series of progress messages while it generates the coaching suggestions.

TIP Select the **Stop** button to stop Copilot generating the coaching suggestions at any point.

Copilot shows a series of progress messages while it generates the coaching suggestions.

5. Copilot generates suggestions to help you improve the tone, reader sentiment, and clarity.

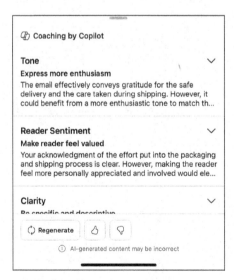

Copilot generates coaching suggestions to help you improve tone, reader sentiment, and clarity.

6. Select the **expand** icon next to each section to read the full list of suggestions.

> ⑦ **Coaching by Copilot**
>
> could benefit from a more enthusiastic tone to match the positive sentiment behind the message.
>
> Suggestions
>
> - Start with **"I'm thrilled to inform you"** instead of **"I wanted to let you know"** to immediately express excitement.
> - Use **"I'm absolutely delighted with my purchase"** instead of **"I am happy with my purchase"** to enhance the positive feedback.
> - Include a sentence like **"Your dedication shines through in every detail!"** to add a personal touch and reinforce the appreciation.

Expand the section to view the full list of suggestions for that category.

7. You can choose to use any of these suggestions in your email draft before sending it.

> ⚠ **IMPORTANT** Copilot does not automatically make these changes to your email. You decide which suggestions to follow and manually rewrite your draft based on those suggestions.

Skills review

In this chapter, you learned how to:

- Draft an email in Outlook by describing the email you want and then selecting and adjusting the tone and length.

- Regenerate email drafts by writing a prompt to change the content, tone, or length, or by choosing from the preset options.

- Summarize an email thread and view the original emails used for each part of the summary.

- Improve the tone, reader sentiment, and clarity of your emails by using Coaching by Copilot.

- Use Copilot in the Outlook mobile app to draft emails, summarize email threads, and improve your emails with coaching.

Practice tasks

No practice files are necessary to complete the practice tasks in this chapter.

Get started with Copilot in Outlook

Open your preferred Outlook application on the web, Windows, or Mac, and then perform the following tasks:

1. Start a new email.

2. Select the **Copilot** icon on the Message ribbon to view the options to **Draft with Copilot** or use **Coaching by Copilot**.

3. Select any email in your inbox that is part of an email thread.

4. Notice the **Summary by Copilot** option at the top of the email thread.

Draft an email

In your preferred Outlook application on the web, Windows, or Mac, perform the following tasks:

1. Start a new email.

2. Select the **Copilot** icon on the Message ribbon and select **Draft with Copilot**.

3. In the **Draft with Copilot** prompt area, enter the following prompt: Write an email inviting a group of friends to my place for a casual pizza dinner on Saturday night.

4. Select the **slider** icon to open the options to set the Tone and Length. Choose **Casual** tone and **Medium** length.

5. Select the **Generate** button and wait for Copilot to finish generating the email draft.

6. In the **Anything you'd like to change** area, write the following prompt and then select the arrow to submit the prompt to Copilot: Ask people to share their favorite pizza related songs by email to add to a playlist.

7. Wait for Copilot to finish generating the draft. Use the **left and right arrows** to switch between the first draft and the new draft.

8. Choose the one you like best, and then select the **Keep it** button to add it to an email.

9. **Discard** the email draft.

Summarize an email thread

In your preferred Outlook application on the web, Windows, or Mac, perform the following tasks:

1. Select any email in your Inbox that is part of an email thread.

2. Select the **Summary by Copilot** button at the top of the email thread.

3. Wait for Copilot to generate the summary and then view the results.

4. Select one of the citation numbers and view the email that was used for that part of the summary.

Improve your emails with Coaching by Copilot

In your preferred Outlook application on the web, Windows, or Mac, perform the following tasks:

1. Start a new email.

2. Enter the following text in the body of the email: Thank you so much for helping me put together the annual report. That was a huge job, and I couldn't have done it on my own.

3. In the Message ribbon, select the **Copilot** icon, and then select **Coaching by Copilot.**

4. Review the coaching tips by selecting each of the categories (Tone, Reader Sentiment, Clarity) on the left side of the coaching panel and scrolling through each to read the details.

5. Choose one of the suggestions and edit your original email to improve the tone, reader sentiment, or clarity.

Use Copilot in the Outlook mobile app

Open the Outlook mobile app on your device, and then perform the following tasks:

1. Start a new email.

2. Select the link to **Draft with Copilot** in the body of the email.

3. Enter the following into the Draft with Copilot prompt area: Thank my friends for coming to my place for pizza and music.

4. Select the arrow to send the prompt to Copilot.

5. Wait for Copilot to finish generating the draft.

6. Select the **Options** button at the bottom of the email, and then select **Make it a poem.**

7. Wait for Copilot to finish generating the draft.

8. Select **Discard all** to discard the draft.

9. Close the email draft.

Copilot in Word

7

Copilot in Word can help you quickly and easily draft content for your documents, rather than starting with a blank page. You can use a natural language prompt to describe what you want to write, and Copilot will write a first draft for you. You can use Copilot to help you write any type of content—for example, a simple paragraph or list of bullet points, an outline for a story, a business proposal, a piece of creative writing, or even a whitepaper. You can also use Copilot to rewrite existing content, immediately giving you multiple alternative versions of text that you can use in your document. Copilot can help you transform text into a table and then add, remove, or merge columns in your table, adding additional content using context. You can also chat with Copilot to summarize an existing document, ask questions about the content of a document, or generate answers to general questions to help you as you write.

This chapter guides you through using Copilot to generate documents across a range of different scenarios, showing the variety of results you can get with different prompts. You will learn how to use Copilot to edit and transform your document, and the ways you can chat with Copilot to get answers to your questions while working with an existing document or generating new content.

In this chapter

- Start Copilot in Word
- Create a draft of your document
- Draft additional content in an existing document
- Rewrite content
- Transform content into a table
- Chat with Copilot

Practice files

No practice files are necessary to complete the practice tasks in this chapter.

🔍 **SEE ALSO** You can learn more about how to write effective prompts to generate content in Word in Chapter 2, "Writing effective prompts for Copilot."

Start Copilot in Word

There are two ways to work with Copilot in Word.

When you open a new document, you will see a prompt on the blank document with a Copilot icon, where you can click or tap to start drafting content with Copilot. You will use this way of starting Copilot whenever you are drafting, editing, or adding new content in your document. This is the main way to work with Copilot in Word, and you will work with Copilot here for most of this chapter to draft, rewrite, and transform content.

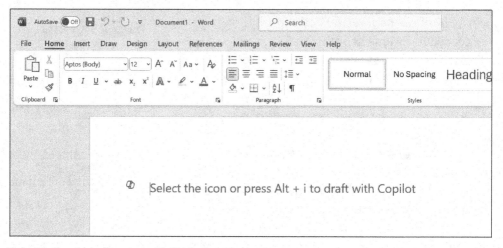

Select the icon to draft content with Copilot in your document.

There is also a Copilot chat experience, which you can open by selecting the Copilot icon at the right end of the Home tab of the ribbon.

Select the Copilot button on the ribbon.

This will launch the Copilot pane, which is docked to the right side of your screen, allowing you to chat with Copilot while working on your document. You will use this to ask questions about your document or other information you might need while working. You will use this part of Copilot in Word in the final section of this chapter, where you learn to chat with Copilot.

 TIP You can close the Copilot pane using the close icon or move or resize it using the dropdown arrow.

 TIP You can also use Copilot in Word on the web, Word for Microsoft 365 for Mac, and Word for iPad.

7

Create a draft of your document

In this section, you will learn how to draft documents in Word using Copilot, as well as how to use Copilot to help you refine the draft and add more content.

Draft content using a prompt

To draft new content for your document

1. Select the **Copilot** icon on your document to open the Copilot prompt pane.

2. Describe what you'd like to write with a simple phrase.

3. Select the **Generate** button in the prompt area.

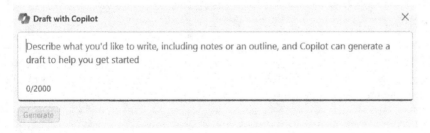

Type your prompt into the Copilot prompt area.

Write a simple prompt

Start by writing a simple prompt to get Copilot to help you write a draft—for example, "Help me write about the benefits of graphic novels for children."

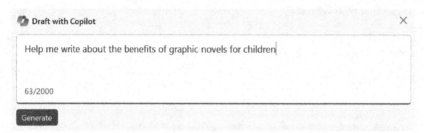

Type in your prompt and select the Generate button.

You will see a series of progress messages, such as "Creating a draft," "Pulling things together," and "Working on it," while your document remains blank.

Copilot shows a series of progress messages while it drafts the content.

> **TIP** If you make a mistake or change your mind about your prompt, you can select the Stop generating button or hit the Esc keyboard button at any time to stop Copilot and enter a new prompt.

After a moment, you will start to see Copilot generating the content in chunks while the progress messages keep running. The length and style of the generated content will depend on your prompt, but for a simple general prompt like the one shown here, you will usually get a document of about 1–2 pages. Wait for Copilot to finish generating the draft.

> 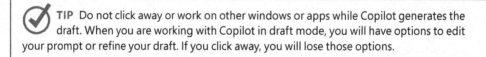 **TIP** Do not click away or work on other windows or apps while Copilot generates the draft. When you are working with Copilot in draft mode, you will have options to edit your prompt or refine your draft. If you click away, you will lose those options.

> **IMPORTANT** The nature of generative AI is that it is creative, so you will not always get the same results from the same prompt every time.

Why Graphic Novels Are Good for

🔵 Working on it...   [🔵 Stop generating] ESC

A brief overview of the advantages of reading graphic novels for young readers

◢ Introduction

Graphic novels are a form of literature that combines text and images to tell a story. They are often associated with genres such as fantasy, science fiction, horror, and superheroes, but they can also cover a wide range of topics and themes. Graphic novels are not just for adults; they can also be a great way to engage children in reading and

Copilot generates the content in chunks while showing a progress message.

When Copilot has finished generating the content, you will be taken to the end of the draft, and you will see a prompt ready for you to choose your next step. Note that the generated text is highlighted in pale blue. This is because it is still only a suggested draft from Copilot, which you haven't yet decided to keep or add to your document.

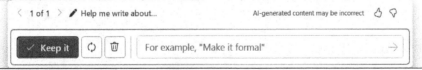

Graphic novels can also satisfy children by providing them with a sense of accomplishment and reward, and by fostering their confidence and self-esteem. By reading graphic novels, children can have fun and enjoy reading, and feel proud and happy about their reading achievements.

Conclusion

Graphic novels are a form of literature that can benefit children in many ways. Graphic novels can improve children's reading comprehension and vocabulary, develop their visual literacy and critical thinking skills, encourage their creativity and imagination, and increase their motivation and engagement. Graphic novels can also provide children with a diverse and enriching reading experience, and with a lifelong love of reading and learning. Graphic novels are not just for adults; they are for children too.

‹ 1 of 1 › ✏ Help me write about...   AI-generated content may be incorrect 👍 👎

[✓ Keep it] ↻ 🗑   For example, "Make it formal"   →

Copilot has finished drafting the content.

You now have the following options available:

- Select the **Edit** icon to change your prompt and redraft the content.

- Select the **Keep it** button to accept the draft as it is and add it to your document.

- Select the **Regenerate** icon to prompt Copilot to generate a different draft based on the same prompt.

- Select the **Delete** icon to delete the draft.

- Type an additional prompt in the **prompt area** to refine or change the draft—for example, for length, tone, or audience.

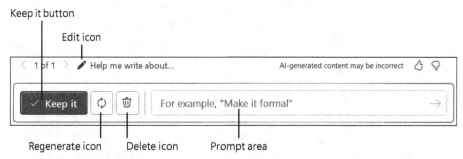

You can choose to edit, keep, regenerate, delete, or refine your draft.

To generate a different draft with the same prompt

1. Select the **Regenerate** icon.

2. Wait for Copilot to finish generating the new draft. You will know this is done when the progress messages stop and you see the same edit pane.

The regenerated content will be different from the first version—it can be quite similar or very different depending on your prompt.

When the new draft is completed, you have the same options to edit, keep, regenerate, delete, or refine your draft. Note that this time next to the edit icon there are two versions of the draft, and you can switch back and forth between the first version and the regenerated version using the left and right arrows. At this stage, neither draft is part of your document because you haven't kept either one.

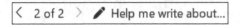

You can switch back and forth between the first draft and the regenerated draft.

To generate a different draft with a change to your prompt

1. Select the **edit** icon.

2. The Draft with Copilot pane will appear with your original prompt.

3. Edit the prompt to change the word "children" to "young adults."

4. Select the **Generate** button.

You are still in drafting mode because you haven't yet selected the Keep it button to add the content to your document. Use this option when you want to make a small change to your original prompt and keep the previous version(s) of the drafts to compare and make your final selection.

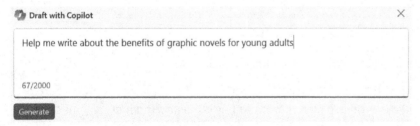

Edit your Copilot prompt to create a new draft.

Copilot will generate a new draft based on your edited prompt. Note the change in heading and content. You now have three different drafts, and you can switch back and forth to compare the original draft, the regenerated draft, and this new draft with the edited prompt.

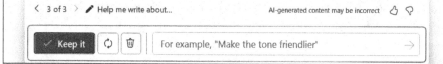

The Benefits of Graphic Novels for Young Adults

How reading comics can boost literacy, creativity, and engagement

Introduction

Graphic novels, or comics, are often dismissed as a lowbrow or childish form of reading. However, research has shown that graphic novels can have many benefits for young adults' learning and development. Graphic novels combine text and images to create a rich and immersive storytelling experience that can appeal to a wide range of readers. In this document, we will explore some of the benefits of graphic novels for young adults, such as:

⟨ 3 of 3 ⟩ ✏ Help me write about...   AI-generated content may be incorrect 🖒 🖓

✓ Keep it   ↻ 🗑   For example, "Make the tone friendlier"   →

Copilot generates a new draft based on your edited prompt.

To fine-tune the draft by providing additional prompts

1. Click or tap in the prompt box on the edit pane. This will open a prompt area where you can type in a new prompt to fine-tune and regenerate your draft.

2. Select the arrow to regenerate your draft.

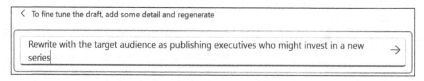

⟨ To fine tune the draft, add some detail and regenerate

Rewrite with the target audience as publishing executives who might invest in a new series   →

Type in a new prompt to refine and regenerate your draft.

You can fine-tune your draft with common prompts such as "make it shorter," "make it longer," or "change to a more professional tone." You can also fine-tune with more specific prompting, such as asking for it to be a particular length or style, to use simpler or more complex language, to include or exclude specific content, or to target the content to a particular audience. Your options and the results you get will vary depending on your content. Try different things to see what works.

Use this option when you want to provide additional or different information to refine the draft. This prompt iterates your draft, working with the context of what you have already prompted and drafted. You don't need to restate the content from your original prompt.

> ✅ **TIP** Starting with a general prompt and then using this feature is an effective way to work with Copilot to get the final content you want. You can go through multiple iterations to continue to refine and then select whichever version of the draft you prefer.

Copilot generates a new draft based on your refined prompt. You now have four versions of the draft to select from, and you can scroll back and forth to select the one you want using the left and right arrows.

Copilot generates a new draft based on your edited prompt.

To add the draft content to your document

1. Scroll back and forth through the different versions of the draft, using the left and right arrows, until you find the one that is the best fit.

2. Select the **Keep it** button to keep that version of the draft.

3. That draft content will now be added to your document, and the other versions of the draft will be discarded.

Notice that the pale blue highlighting is gone, and the Copilot editing pane is no longer there.

 IMPORTANT Once you select the **Keep it** button, you will not be able to go back to your prompt or to the other versions of the draft.

How Graphic Novels Can Boost Your Publishing Business

A brief overview of the market potential and educational value of graphic novels for young adults

Introduction

Graphic novels are a form of literature that combines text and images to tell a story. They are often associated with genres such as fantasy, science fiction, horror, and superheroes, but they can also cover a wide range of topics and themes. Graphic novels are not just for adults; they are also a popular and profitable choice for young adults, who are looking for engaging and diverse reading experiences. In this document, we will

The draft has been added to your Word document.

Draft content using a detailed prompt with context

In this example, you will see how a general prompt and a more detailed prompt can make a huge difference to the results when drafting content with Copilot. Let's start with a simple prompt in a different scenario, this time writing a business case to go to a conference.

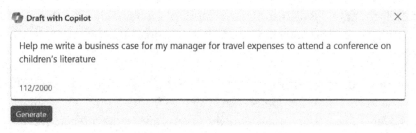

*Type in your prompt and select the **Generate** button.*

Copilot will generate the draft for you. The danger of a general prompt like this is that Copilot will generate fictional details to build out the draft. For instance, in this example, it has added the name, dates, and location of a conference that doesn't exist. While this can be useful as a template that you can use to replace and fill in the correct information, there is a danger of leaving AI-generated content in your document that isn't real and shouldn't be there, or worse, not realizing that the content is fictional.

> **IMPORTANT** Generative AI can generate content that isn't real. Always read and check the content generated by Copilot before using it.

Background and Rationale

- The ICCL is the most influential and respected conference in the field of children's literature, attracting over 2,000 participants from more than 50 countries every year.
- The theme of the 2024 ICCL is "Children's Literature in a Changing World: Challenges and Opportunities", which reflects the current and future issues and trends affecting the creation, production, and consumption of children's books.
- The conference program covers a wide range of topics and perspectives, such as:
- The impact of digital technologies, social media, and online platforms on children's reading habits and preferences.
- The role of children's literature in fostering diversity, inclusion, and social justice.
- dia
- ting

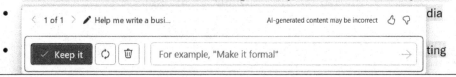

Copilot has generated a draft that includes details of a conference that doesn't exist.

You can give Copilot a more detailed and specific prompt for a situation like this, using up to 2000 characters. Examine the detail, context, and instructions provided to Copilot in this prompt.

> Help me write a business case for my manager for travel expenses to attend The Ultimate Children's Literature Conference in Sydney from 1-2 April. The conference runs over 2 days and includes all meals. I am asking for $2000, to cover air fares ($500), accommodation for 2 nights ($500), and conference ticket ($1000). Focus on the business benefits of me attending the conference. The biggest benefit will be that it can help us with our goal to introduce a new series of graphic novels for young adults - I will be able to meet and network with potential authors and major booksellers to learn about this. Make it concise, no more than 2 pages.

This prompt includes the name of the conference, the location, the dates, and the details of the expenses being requested. It asks Copilot to focus the draft on the business benefits. It provides a particular benefit to focus on and specifies the length of the desired output.

 TIP Use a more specific and detailed prompt when you want more control over the content of the draft. Copilot will be more creative with a more general or simple prompt.

 TIP You can also include instructions in your prompt about what not to include—for example, do not include any details about the conference location or venue.

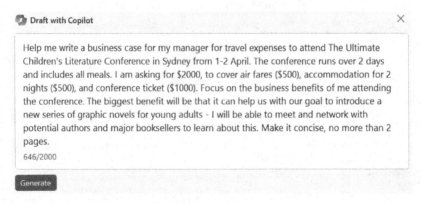

*Type in your prompt and select the **Generate** button.*

This prompt generates a business case using the details provided.

Executive Summary

- This document presents a business case for requesting $2000 to cover the travel expenses to attend The Ultimate Children's Literature Conference in Sydney from 1-2 April.
- The conference is a premier event for children's literature professionals, featuring keynote speakers, workshops, panels, and networking opportunities with authors, publishers, booksellers, and educators.
- The main business benefit of attending the conference is that it can help us with our strategic goal to introduce a new series of graphic novels for young adults, a growing and lucrative market segment.
- By attending the conference, I will be able to meet and network with potential authors and major booksellers, learn about the latest trends and best practices in graphic novel creation and distribution, and gain insights and feedback from the target audience.

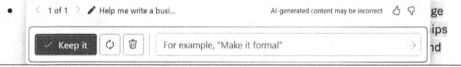

< 1 of 1 > ✏ Help me write a busi...   AI-generated content may be incorrect 👍 👎   ge
✓ Keep it   ↻   🗑   For example, "Make it formal"   →   ips
  nd

Copilot has generated a draft based on the detail and context provided in the prompt.

Draft creative content

Copilot can also help you draft or come up with ideas for creative writing and content. In this example, we will use Copilot to help with ideas for a novel for teenage readers.

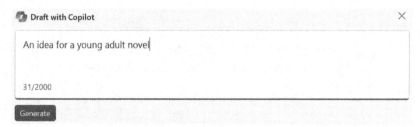

Draft with Copilot   ✕

An idea for a young adult novel

31/2000

Generate

Type in your prompt and select the Generate button.

Copilot generates a document with a plot summary, a list of characters, and an outline of suggested chapters. You can edit and refine your prompt as shown earlier to iterate on this draft and come up with different ideas.

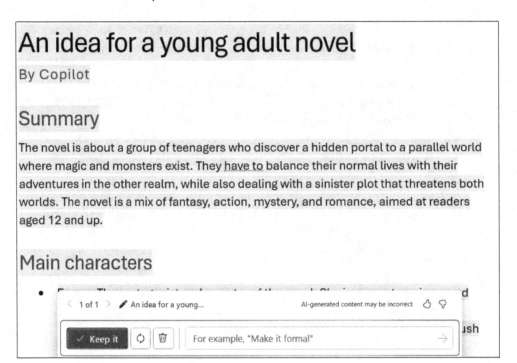

An idea for a young adult novel

By Copilot

Summary

The novel is about a group of teenagers who discover a hidden portal to a parallel world where magic and monsters exist. They have to balance their normal lives with their adventures in the other realm, while also dealing with a sinister plot that threatens both worlds. The novel is a mix of fantasy, action, mystery, and romance, aimed at readers aged 12 and up.

Main characters

Copilot generates a draft outlining an idea for a novel.

Draft additional content in an existing document

In the previous section, you learned how to draft content in a blank document. You can also use Copilot to draft new content in a document, using the content already in the document as a source.

> ⚠ **IMPORTANT** To generate content from other Word documents or PowerPoint presentations, you need a Microsoft 365 Copilot license. With your Copilot Pro license, you can use the techniques shown here to generate content based on whatever you have in the document you are working on.

Draft additional content in an existing document

To draft new content in an existing document

1. Place your cursor in the document at the start of a new blank line, or press Enter to create a new paragraph in the position where you want to add the new content.

2. Select the **Copilot** icon on your document to open the Copilot prompt pane.

3. Describe what you'd like to write using a simple or more detailed prompt.

4. Select the **Generate** button in the prompt area.

Change Management: A Guide for Organizations

How to plan, implement, and sustain change initiatives

Introduction

Change is inevitable in today's dynamic and competitive business environment.

The Copilot icon appears when your cursor is at the start of a new blank paragraph.

> ✅ **TIP** If you don't have an existing document to work with, you can create a document similar to the one used in this section by starting with a blank document and using the prompt: Write a whitepaper on change management.

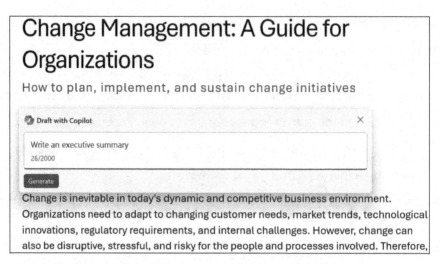

Select the Copilot icon to open the Copilot pane and enter your prompt.

Copilot will generate the draft based on your prompt. You have the same options to edit, keep, regenerate, discard, or refine your prompt as you did when you created a draft in a blank document.

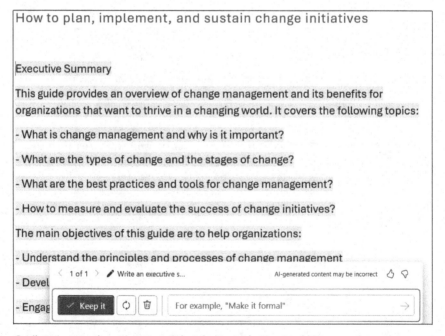

Copilot generates the new content. Select the Keep it button to add it to your document.

5. Select the **Keep it** button to add the new content to your document.

Draft ideas based on the existing document

You can use the same technique to draft content or ideas related to the document that you might use elsewhere, such as ideas for titles, tags, or social media posts.

Start a new paragraph at the end of your document and enter your prompt. In this example, we ask Copilot to write 10 suggested titles for the whitepaper. This prompt is working with the content and context of this document.

Conclusion

Change management is a vital skill for organizations that want to survive and thrive in the fast-changing and uncertain world. Change management can help organizations plan, implement, and sustain change initiatives, and achieve their desired goals and benefits. Change management can also help organizations engage and empower their stakeholders, and foster a culture of continuous improvement and innovation. By following the best practices of change management, organizations can increase their chances of success and enhance their performance and competitiveness.

> **Draft with Copilot** ✕
>
> Write 10 suggested titles for this whitepaper
> 45/2000
>
> Generate

Open the Copilot pane inside an existing document and enter a prompt to generate content or ideas related to the document content.

⚠️ **IMPORTANT** Copilot can work with documents up to about 80,000 words. If your document is longer than this, Copilot will work from the beginning of the document up to that limit and may not use the content in the rest of the document beyond that.

7

Copilot generates the draft content based on the prompt.

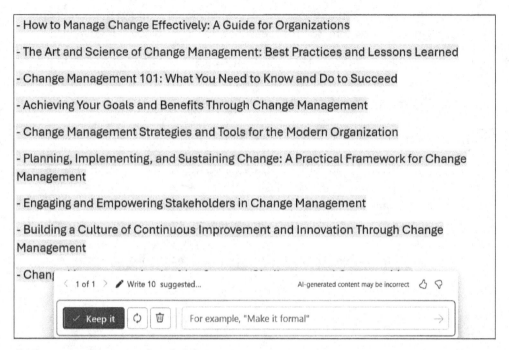

- How to Manage Change Effectively: A Guide for Organizations

- The Art and Science of Change Management: Best Practices and Lessons Learned

- Change Management 101: What You Need to Know and Do to Succeed

- Achieving Your Goals and Benefits Through Change Management

- Change Management Strategies and Tools for the Modern Organization

- Planning, Implementing, and Sustaining Change: A Practical Framework for Change Management

- Engaging and Empowering Stakeholders in Change Management

- Building a Culture of Continuous Improvement and Innovation Through Change Management

- Chan

‹ 1 of 1 › ✎ Write 10 suggested...   AI-generated content may be incorrect

✓ Keep it ↻ 🗑   For example, "Make it formal" →

Copilot generates the content based on the prompt.

Here is another example of how you can use Copilot to generate new content based on your document. You can ask Copilot to write a social media post based on the whitepaper. Note that you don't have to specify the source, because you are using this prompt inside the existing document, so it will automatically use that content.

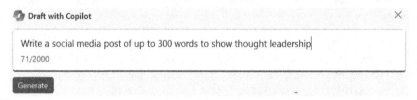

Draft with Copilot   ✕

Write a social media post of up to 300 words to show thought leadership
71/2000

Generate

Ask Copilot to generate a social media post based on the content in the document.

Copilot responds with the content as requested.

Change is inevitable, but not always easy. How can leaders and managers navigate the complex and dynamic environments of the 21st century and foster a culture of continuous improvement and innovation in their organizations?

These are some of the questions that we explore in our latest publications on change management, which offer insights, tools, and best practices for leading and managing change effectively. Whether you are facing a major transformation, a small adjustment, or an ongoing challenge, you will find valuable guidance and inspiration in these resources.

Here are some of the topics that we cover:

- Building a Culture of Continuous Improvement and Innovation Through Change Management: This report explains how to create a culture that embraces change as an opportunity for learning and growth, rather than a threat or a burden. It also provides a framework and a checklist for assessing and developing your organization's change readiness and capability.

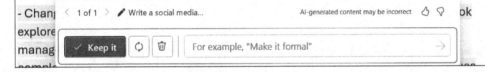

Copilot drafts a social media post based on the document content.

You can regenerate and refine your draft and select the **Keep it** button when you want to add it to your document. You can then cut, copy, paste, edit, and use that content in the document or elsewhere.

Draft additional content without using a prompt

You may want to add more to your draft without really knowing what to ask for. Copilot can suggest additional content for you with the "Inspire me" option. The "Inspire me" option will only appear under the prompt when you already have some content in your Word document; you will not be able to use this option with a blank document.

 TIP You can have a blank document with just a title and use the "Inspire me" option as a way to get started.

To draft additional content without a prompt

1. Place your cursor in the document at the start of a new blank line, or press Enter to create a new paragraph in the position where you want to add the new content.

2. Select the Copilot icon on your document to open the Copilot prompt pane.

3. Select the **Inspire me** button.

Use this option when you need inspiration or ideas to build on your existing content.

Select the Inspire me button to generate content in an existing document, without using a prompt.

Copilot will draft new content to continue the writing. You can keep, discard, refine, or edit as you want.

- Assess the readiness and capacity for change: analyze the current state of the organization and its stakeholders, and their willingness and ability to adopt the change. Identify the potential barriers and enablers of change, and how to address them.

- Engage and communicate with stakeholders: identify the key stakeholder groups and their roles, expectations, and concerns regarding the change. Establish a clear and consistent communication plan that informs, educates, and involves them throughout the change process. Use various channels and methods to deliver tailored and relevant messages that appeal to the stakeholder's needs and interests.

- Provide training and support: design and deliver appropriate training programs that equip the stakeholders with the knowledge and skills they need to perform their new roles and tasks. Provide ongoing coaching, feedback, and assistance to help them overcome challenges and difficulties during the transition. Recognize and reward their efforts and achievements.

- Monit
outcon   port
on the   s.

‹ 1 of 1 ›   ✏ Inspire me   AI-generated content may be incorrect 👍 👎

✓ Keep it   ↻   🗑   │   For example, "Make it formal"   →

Copilot generates additional content in the context of the document.

> ✅ **TIP** Try the "Inspire me" option in different places in your document, and with different types of content to see the different results. It works more effectively with shorter content than with very long and detailed content.

Rewrite Content

Copilot can help you rewrite the content in your document in different lengths, tones, and styles, or simply give you an automatic rewording. In this section, you will learn how to use Copilot to rewrite content using a prompt to describe how you want it rewritten and how to use Copilot to automatically generate rewrites without using a prompt.

Ask Copilot to rewrite content using a prompt

To rewrite content already in your document using a prompt

1. Highlight the content you want to rewrite.

2. Select the **Copilot** icon on your document to open the Copilot options to transform your content.

3. Select **Write a Prompt....**

4. Describe the changes you want to make to the highlighted content.

5. Select the **Generate** button.

Nutrition Education Program

A guide to help people learn about healthy eating habits

Introduction

Nutrition is the science of how food affects our health and well-being. It involves ...ling the nutrients that our bodies need, the sources of these nutrients, and the effects of different dietary patterns on our health. Nutrition education is the process of providing information and skills to help people make informed and healthy food choices. It can help prevent and manage chronic diseases, improve physical and mental performance, and enhance quality of life.

Highlight the content you want to rewrite and select the Copilot icon in the document.

TIP To create a document similar to the one used in this section, start with a blank document and use the prompt "Create a program to help educate people on good nutrition."

Copilot gives you options to write a prompt, auto rewrite, or visualize as a table. Start by selecting **Write a Prompt**. Use this option when you can describe the changes you want to make to the content, such as the length, tone, audience, content, or language used.

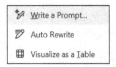

*Select **Write a Prompt**.*

Provide a simple or detailed prompt to describe how you want to change or rewrite the highlighted content. The prompt is working in the context of what is already written, so you can use prompts such as "Make it longer" or "Rewrite so that a child of 10 could understand." You don't need to include details about the existing content.

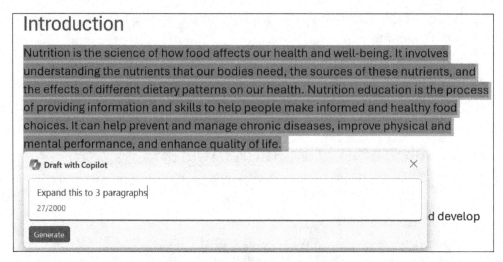

Type your prompt into the Copilot pane and select the Generate button.

Copilot drafts the rewrite based on your prompt. Use the options provided to edit your prompt, keep the draft, regenerate, discard, or provide another prompt, as described earlier in this chapter.

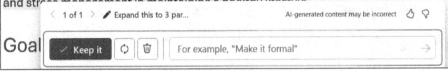

the effects of different dietary patterns on our health. Nutrition is important for everyone, regardless of age, gender, or health status. It can influence our growth, development, immunity, and metabolism.

Nutrition education is the process of providing information and skills to help people make informed and healthy food choices. It can help prevent and manage chronic diseases, such as diabetes, heart disease, and obesity. It can also improve physical and mental performance, such as energy, concentration, and mood. Nutrition education can be delivered through various settings, such as schools, workplaces, health care facilities, and community organizations.

The main goal of this program is to help people learn about good nutrition and develop healthy eating habits. By participating in this program, you will gain knowledge and skills on how to plan, prepare, and enjoy nutritious meals and snacks. You will also learn how to read and interpret food labels, compare different food products, and make smart choices when eating out. You will also discover the role of physical activity, hydration, and str~~~~

⟨ 1 of 1 ⟩ ✏ Expand this to 3 par...   AI-generated content may be incorrect 👍 👎

Goal | ✓ Keep it | ○ | 🗑 | | For example, "Make it formal" →

Copilot generates a rewrite based on your prompt.

Automatically generate alternative drafts without a prompt

To generate rewrites of your content without using a prompt

1. Highlight the content you want to rewrite.

2. Select the **Copilot** icon on your document to open the Copilot options to transform your content.

3. Select **Auto Rewrite.**

Select Auto Rewrite.

Copilot will automatically draft three different versions of the highlighted content. You can scroll through them using the left and right arrows at the top of the pane. Use this option when you want ideas about how to rewrite your existing content, without making specific changes to the tone, length, or substance of the content.

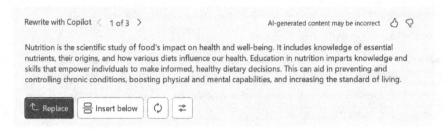

Select the left and right arrows to review the three rewrites generated by Copilot.

When you have browsed through the rewrite options, you can:

- Select the **Replace** button to replace your original content with the rewrite.

- Select the **Insert below** button to add the rewrite to your document while keeping your original content.

- Select the **Regenerate** icon to generate three new rewrite options.

- Select the **Tone** icon to rewrite based on a list of tone options.

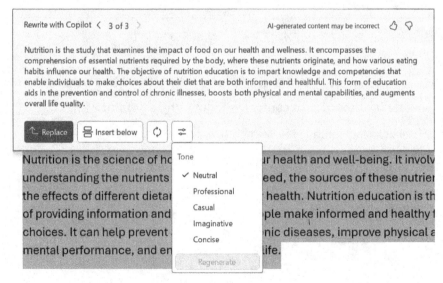

Select the Tone icon to select from a list of tones to rewrite the content.

Select the **Professional** tone and then select **Regenerate**.

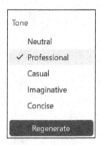

Select the Professional tone and then select Regenerate.

You will now have another three rewrites of your content in the tone chosen. There is a header above the text indicating the tone used in the rewrite. You can scroll through the options and continue to regenerate or add the content to your document with the **Replace** or **Insert below** buttons.

7

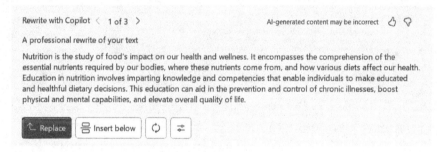

Copilot provides three more rewrites in a professional tone.

Fine-tuning the automatically generated rewrites

> ⚠️ **IMPORTANT** This option is only available when using Word for the web. It is not available in the Word desktop app.

If you use the web version of Word, you will find an additional option to fine-tune the rewrites with an additional prompt.

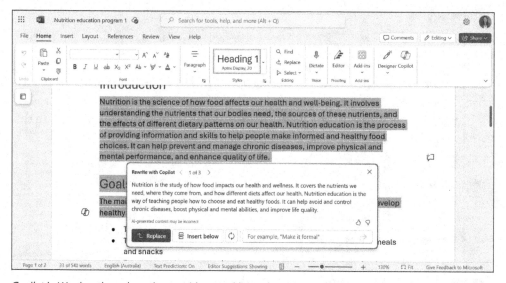

Copilot in Word on the web version provides an additional option to refine the rewrite with a prompt.

This can be used in the same way as described earlier in this chapter for fine-tuning your draft of new content using prompts.

Transform content into a table

Copilot can help you transform large blocks of text or bullet points in your document into a table format. This is useful when you have a list of items with a similar structure that would be clearer as a table. You can also use Copilot to fill the table with additional related content.

Visualize your content in table format

To transform your content into a table

1. Highlight the content you want to transform into a table.

2. Select the **Copilot** icon on your document to open the Copilot options to transform your content.

3. Select **Visualize as a Table**.

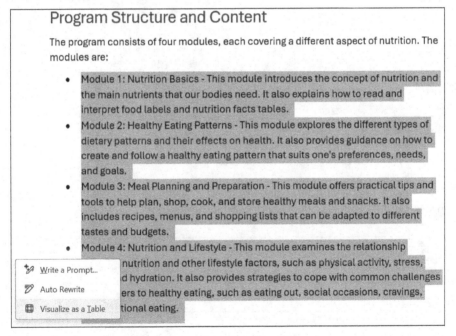

*Select the content, open Copilot, and select **Visualize as a Table**.*

Use this option for content that can naturally be presented in a table, such as lists of items or repeated descriptions that could be grouped together.

Copilot will arrange your content into a table with headings. You can select the **Keep it** button to add the table to your document, regenerate, discard, or refine the table with additional prompts.

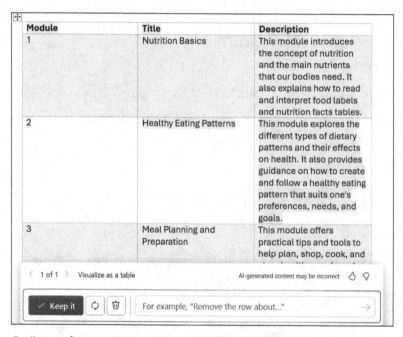

Copilot transforms your content into a table with headings.

You can use the prompt here to ask Copilot to make changes to the table, including removing or merging columns or adding new columns.

> ✅ **TIP** You can ask for multiple changes to the table in a single prompt.

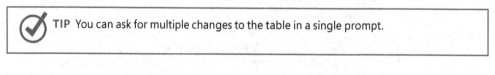

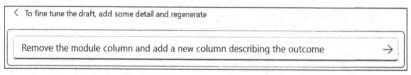

Describe the changes you want to make to the table in the prompt area.

Copilot can generate new content in the table that wasn't already in your document, based on what you describe in the prompt. In this case, it has written new content using the context to describe the outcome of each module.

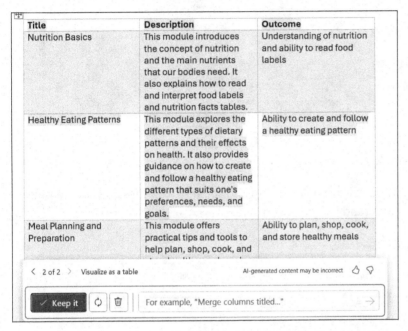

Copilot makes the changes requested and generates new content in the table.

Visualize as a table can also be useful for content such as a travel itinerary. In this example, an itinerary is listed line by line, without any standard delineation (such as a comma or dash) between the different pieces of information in each line.

You can use the Visualize a table option to transform the formatting of rows of content such as a travel itinerary.

Copilot can transform this into a much more readable table format.

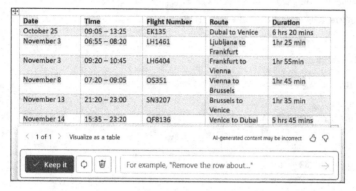

Copilot transforms the travel itinerary into a table.

You can ask Copilot to split a single column into separate columns and add new information that was not already in the document.

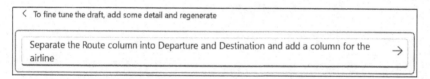

Describe the changes you want to make to the table.

Copilot will make the changes as requested. Note that it has also been able to fill in the airline name, which was not in the document content, using generative AI.

Date	Time	Flight Number	Airline	Departure	Destination	Duration
October 25	09:05 – 13:25	EK135	Emirates	Dubai	Venice	6 hrs 20 mins
November 3	06:55 – 08:20	LH1461	Lufthansa	Ljubljana	Frankfurt	1hr 25 min
November 3	09:20 – 10:45	LH6404	Lufthansa	Frankfurt	Vienna	1hr 55min
November 8	07:20 – 09:05	OS351	Austrian Airlines	Vienna	Brussels	1hr 45 min
November 13	21:20 – 23:00	SN3207	Brussels Airlines	Brussels	Venice	1hr 35 min
November 14	15:35 – 23:20	QF8136	Qantas	Venice	Dubai	5 hrs 45 mins

‹ To fine tune the draft, add some detail and regenerate

Combine the Date and Time columns →

Copilot separates the route into Departure and Destination and generates the name of the airline from the flight number.

> **TIP** You can also ask Copilot to merge columns together. In this example, you could use a prompt such as "Combine the Date and Time Columns."

Chat with Copilot

Start the chat with Copilot experience by opening an existing Word document and selecting the **Copilot** button at the right end of the Home tab of the ribbon.

Select the Copilot button on the ribbon.

This will launch the Copilot pane, which is docked to the right side of your screen, allowing you to chat with Copilot while working on your document.

Copilot pane with prompt suggestions and the prompt area.

TIP You can close the Copilot pane using the close icon, or move or resize it using the dropdown arrow.

 TIP You can also select the microphone icon to dictate your prompt.

Summarize your document

To summarize the key ideas in your document

1. Open Copilot by selecting its button on the ribbon.

2. Select the suggested prompt **Summarize this doc** or type the prompt into the prompt area to provide more information about the output of the summary—for instance, you can write a prompt such as "Summarize this document in one paragraph."

⚠ **IMPORTANT** There is a limit to the size of the document that Copilot can summarize. It can work with documents up to about 80,000 words. If you are working with a longer document, it may work only with the beginning of the document (approximately the first 80,000 words) and not any content beyond that.

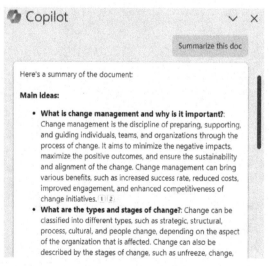

Copilot generates a summary of the document with references.

Copilot generates a summary of the main ideas in the document, providing citations to the relevant content for each point. You can hover over each citation number to see more detail.

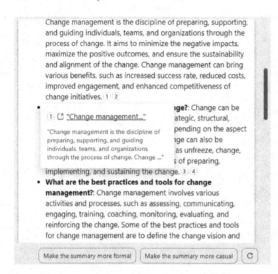

Hovering over the citation number provides detail from the document that was used to create the summary.

At the end of the summary, Copilot generates an expandable list of all the references used.

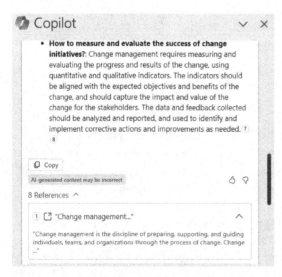

You can expand the full list of references at the end of the summary.

Finding all references in the document

You can also ask Copilot to find all references to a particular topic in the document.

Type a prompt into the pane to ask Copilot to find all references to a topic in the document.

Copilot returns a list of all the references to that content in the document, with citations that you can hover over for more details.

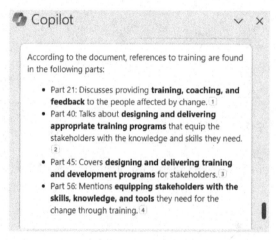

Copilot lists all the references to training in the document, with citations.

Ask Copilot questions

You can use Copilot to ask specific questions about the content of your document or the topic related to your document. This is particularly useful if you are given a long document and need to understand the content or find answers quickly or if you need to do additional research while you are reading or drafting a document.

By default, Copilot has the web plug-in enabled, which means when Copilot responds to your questions, you will get answers both from your document and from the web. You can set the toggle switch to off if you prefer to disable this option for Copilot to use the web when generating responses.

*Select the plug-in icon in the prompt area
to view the status of the web content plug-in.
It is enabled by default.*

Type your question into the prompt area and press Enter or select the **Send** icon.

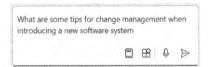

*Type your prompt into the prompt area
and press Enter.*

Copilot responds, indicating information it found in the document and information drawn from sources on the web.

When Copilot finds the answer to the question in the document content, that section of the response will start with the phrase "From your document:" and will provide citations to where that content is in your document.

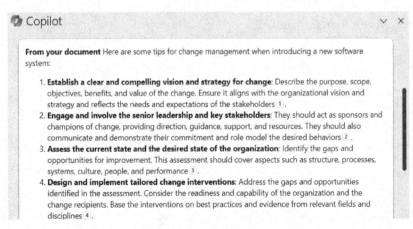

Copilot responds with information based on the document content, with citations.

When Copilot uses the web to generate the response, that section of the response will start with the phrase "From the web." Copilot will provide citations and links to the websites it has used against each part of the text.

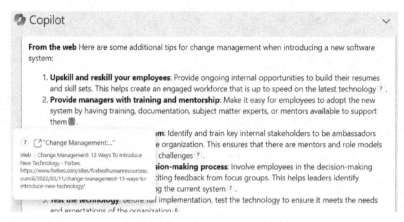

Copilot responds with information based on the web, with citations.

> ⚠️ **IMPORTANT** Always check the content generated by Copilot for accuracy, particularly when it is not based on your document content, before using it.

Using prompt suggestions and Copilot Lab

To discover more ideas for prompts you can use when chatting with Copilot in Word

1. Select the **book** icon in the prompt area.

2. Select one of the options to browse prompts arranged by type or select **View more prompts** to open Copilot Lab.

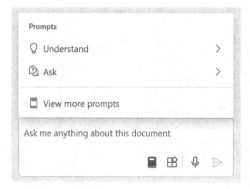

Select the book icon to open the prompt suggestions.

3. Select the **Understand** menu item to view a list of suggested prompts you can use to understand more about the content of your document. You can select any of these suggested prompts and fill in additional information in the prompt area.

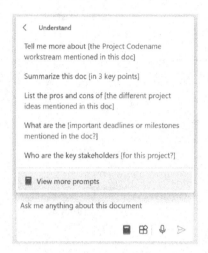

*Select the **Understand** menu option to view prompts relating to understanding the content of your document.*

4. Selecting **View more prompts** will open the Copilot Lab window to provide you with more ideas. You can browse and filter by the type of prompt and the type of job role or industry.

Select View more prompts to open Copilot Lab.

5. Understand is prefilled from our previous selection. Expand this menu to view the other options.

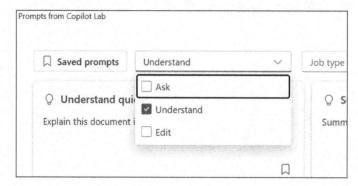

Select the filter to select the prompt type(s).

6. Expand the **Job type** menu to view a list of departments and industries that you can use to filter the suggested prompts.

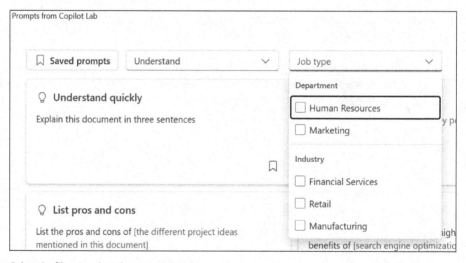

Select the filter to select the prompt type(s)

7. Select the **ribbon** icon on a prompt to save it for future reference. Click or tap a second time on the **ribbon** icon to remove the prompt from your list of saved prompts.

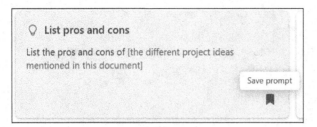

Select the ribbon icon to save the prompt.

8. Select the **Saved prompts** button to view all the prompts you have saved.

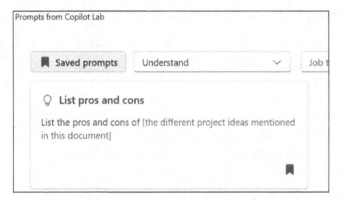

Select the Saved prompts button to view all your saved prompts.

When you have finished working through the suggested prompts in Copilot Lab, close the pop-up Copilot Lab window to return to your Word document.

Skills review

In this chapter, you learned how to:

- Draft content in a Word document using different prompting techniques, in a range of different scenarios.

- Use Copilot to draft new content based on an existing document.

- Rewrite content in an existing content using Copilot by writing prompts or using the Auto Rewrite feature.

- Transform content to visualize it as a table.

- Chat with Copilot to summarize your document, find all references to a topic, and get answers to questions.

Practice tasks

No practice files are necessary to complete the practice tasks in this chapter.

Start Copilot in Word

Start Word, and then perform the following tasks:

1. Create a new blank document.

2. Select the **Copilot** icon in the ribbon of the **Home** tab to open the Copilot pane.

3. Close the Copilot pane by selecting the **X** button at the top right of the pane.

4. Select the **Copilot** button on your document page to open the prompt area in the document.

Create a draft of your document

Continuing from where you left off in the previous step with the Copilot prompt area open in your document, perform the following tasks:

1. Type the following prompt in the Copilot prompt area, and then press the **Generate** button: Help me create a plan to improve my time management.

2. Wait until Copilot has finished generating your draft, and then review the content by scrolling through the document. Do not click away from the document.

3. Select the **Regenerate** icon to generate an alternative version of the draft. Wait for Copilot to finish generating, and then use the left and right arrows to compare the new draft with the first one.

4. Click or tap in the prompt area to refine your draft. Enter the following prompt: Add a section describing some of the most popular time management methods.

5. Select the **Keep it** button to accept the draft into your document.

Draft additional content in an existing document

Using the document you created in the first part, perform the following tasks:

1. Scroll to the end of your document, create a new paragraph, and select the **Copilot** icon.

2. Enter the following prompt: Write 5 tips suitable to share on social media.

3. Select the **Keep it** button to add these to your document.

Rewrite content

Using the document you created in the first part, perform the following tasks:

1. Highlight the paragraph in the Introduction section, select the **Copilot** icon, and then select **Auto Rewrite**. Scroll through the different versions to find the one you like best.

2. Select the **Tone** icon and choose **Casual**, and then select the **Regenerate** button.

3. Scroll through the different versions to find the one you like best and select the **Replace** button to replace the original paragraph with this new one.

Transform content into a table

Using the document you created in the first part, perform the following tasks:

1. Scroll to the section of the document where Copilot added the section on popular time management methods and highlight the bullet points in that section.

2. Select the Copilot icon, and then select **Visualize as a Table**.

3. Wait for Copilot to generate the table. Click or tap in the prompt area and refine your table by entering the following prompt: Add a column describing the challenges. When Copilot has generated the new column, select the **Keep it** button to add the table to your document.

Chat with Copilot

Using the document you created in the first part, perform the following tasks:

1. Open the Copilot side pane by selecting the **Copilot** icon on the ribbon.

2. Select the suggested prompt: **Summarize this doc.** When Copilot has generated the summary, read through it, hover over one of the citation numbers, and expand the references list at the end.

3. Ask a question in the prompt area: How can I avoid distractions?

4. Ask a question in the prompt area: Who invented the Pomodoro technique?

5. Select the book icon to view more suggested prompts. Select the **View more prompts** option to open Copilot Lab. Browse and filter through the suggested prompts and select the ribbon icon on at least two prompts you think you will use in future.

6. Close the Copilot Lab window.

7. Save your document if you wish to keep it; otherwise, close the document without saving.

Copilot in PowerPoint

Using Copilot in PowerPoint, you can type a natural language prompt to create a first draft of a presentation, complete with presentation content, images, speaker notes, and design. Copilot can help you come up with new ideas, learn more about a topic, or structure your existing content and ideas into a presentation that you can edit and make your own. It can also help you understand the content of a presentation, when you need to understand a lot of information quickly, and help you find answers to questions you have about the presentation or related content.

This chapter guides you through using Copilot for creating presentations, adding slides and images, using Copilot and Designer together, organizing your presentation into sections, understanding the key points in a presentation, summarizing information, asking questions related to the presentation and to your topic, and writing prompts to get the best results.

> 🔍 **SEE ALSO** Chapter 2, "Writing effective prompts for Copilot," covers a range of prompting ideas and techniques that you can use with Copilot in PowerPoint.

In this chapter

- Start Copilot in PowerPoint
- Create presentations
- Edit and organize presentations
- Understand presentation content

Practice files

No practice files are necessary to complete the practice tasks in this chapter.

Start Copilot in PowerPoint

There are two ways to work with Copilot in PowerPoint.

When you open a new presentation, you will see the Copilot icon at the top left corner of the blank slide in the main window. Click or tap the **Copilot** icon to start creating presentations or to ask Copilot questions. This option uses the Narrative Builder to create structured presentations, allowing you to work with a presentation outline and refine the content before generating the presentation.

Click or tap the Copilot icon at the top left of the blank slide in the main window to see options for creating presentations or asking Copilot questions.

You can also work with Copilot in PowerPoint using the chat experience in the side pane. To start the Copilot chat, open a new blank presentation and select the **Copilot** button at the right end of the **Home** tab of the ribbon.

Select the Copilot icon on the ribbon.

This will launch the Copilot pane, which is docked to the right side of your screen, allowing you to chat with Copilot while working on your presentation. This option allows you to work side-by-side with Copilot to create, edit, and structure your presentation through an iterative conversation.

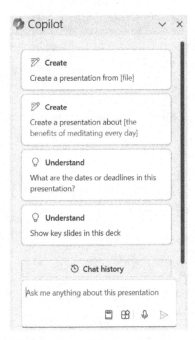

The Copilot pane shows prompt suggestions and the prompt area.

 TIP You can close the Copilot pane by using the Close icon or move or resize it using the dropdown arrow.

 TIP You can also use Copilot in PowerPoint on the web or on an iPad.

Create presentations

Copilot can create a first draft of a presentation for you based on a prompt or based on an existing document. It will create slides with content, images, and speaker notes based on what you ask. In this section, you will learn how to create presentations with Copilot using the Narrative Builder, a prompt in the chat pane, and a Word document, as well as how to write effective prompts to create presentations.

Create a presentation using the Narrative Builder

Use the Narrative Builder to create a presentation when you want to generate and work with an outline of the presentation structure and content before generating the full presentation.

To create a presentation using Narrative Builder

1. Start a new blank presentation.

2. Select the **Copilot** icon at the top left of the blank slide and select **Create a presentation about....**

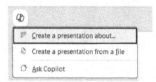

Select the Copilot icon at the top left of the blank slide and select Create a presentation about....

3. This will open a new window with a prompt area at the top and a prompt that starts with **Create a presentation about....**

4. Complete the prompt with the details of what you want your presentation to be about, using a simple phrase.

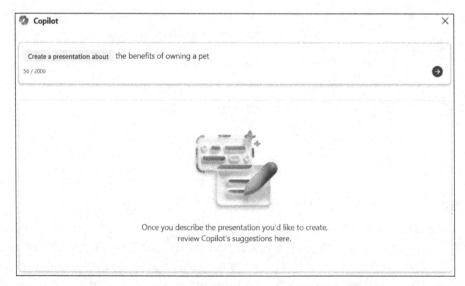

Complete the prompt in the Narrative Builder with the details of what you want your presentation to be about and then press Enter or select the Send icon in the prompt area.

5. Press **Enter** or select the Send icon in the prompt area.

You will see a series of progress messages, such as "Generating presentation topics...," "Gathering more ideas...," and "Adding more details..." as Copilot creates the presentation outline.

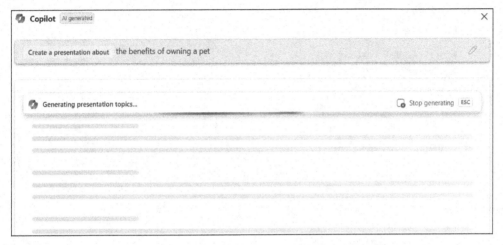

Copilot will show a series of progress messages as it generates the presentation outline.

 TIP You can select "Stop generating" or select the Esc key to stop Copilot from generating content.

When Copilot has finished generating, you will have a title and outline of the presentation based on your prompt. The outline will include sections with bullet points under each one. When you generate a presentation based on this outline, each main heading will become a section title slide, and each bullet point will become a slide with content, images, and speaker notes.

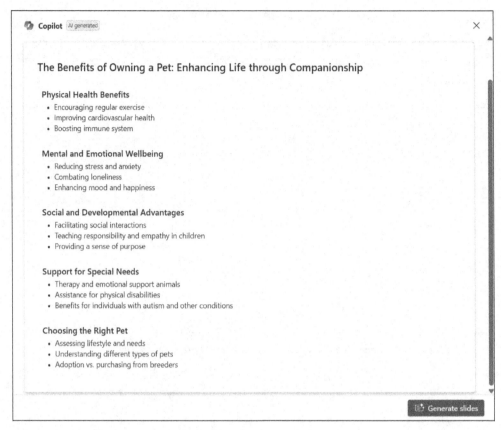

Copilot generates an outline of your presentation, with a main heading, section headings, and bullet points under each section.

You can edit the outline at this stage by reordering the content, removing content, or adding new content.

To edit the presentation outline

1. Hover over the section you want to move or delete. You will see a Grip dots icon appear to the left of the section and a Delete icon at the right end of the section.

Hover over a section to see options to move, delete, or provide feedback.

2. Select a section you want to move, and then press and hold the mouse button to drag and drop it to where you want it in the presentation.

3. Select a section you want to delete and select the **Delete** icon to delete it from the outline.

4. Repeat this process until you are satisfied with the order and content of the presentation outline.

You can use the Narrative Builder to ask Copilot to create new sections of content in the outline before generating the presentation.

To create new content using the Narrative Builder

1. Position your cursor between two sections. You will see an orange divider appear between the sections, with the option to add more content.

2. Select the plus icon (+) to open the Copilot prompt area.

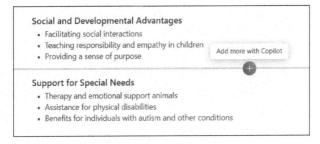

Position your cursor between sections to show the option to add more content to the presentation outline.

3. This opens a Copilot prompt area, with the beginning of a prompt to add a topic. Complete the prompt with the details of the new section you want to add.

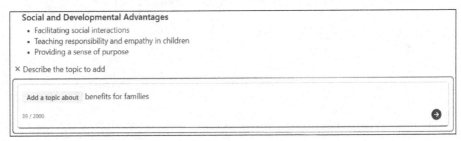

Enter the details of the new content you want to add to the presentation outline.

Copilot will show a series of progress messages as it generates the new content. When Copilot has finished generating, the content will be added to the presentation outline.

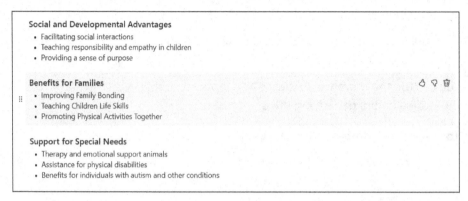

Copilot generates content about the new topic based on your prompt and adds it to the presentation outline.

4. Repeat this process to generate any additional content you want in your presentation, until you are satisfied with the outline.

5. When you have finished editing and adding new content to the outline, select the **Generate Presentation** button to ask Copilot to start generating the presentation.

Select the Generate slides button to ask Copilot to generate the presentation.

Copilot will display a series of progress messages such as "Crafting a compelling narrative" and "Adding titles to slides" as it generates your presentation. You will see the presentation generating in stages, first with headings added, and then the outline of the content.

Copilot will show a series of progress messages as it generates the presentation.

When Copilot has finished generating the presentation, it will open in Slide Sorter view. You will see that the presentation includes sections, content, and images on each slide, as well as speaker notes.

6. Select the **Keep it** button to keep the presentation or select the **Delete** icon to discard it.

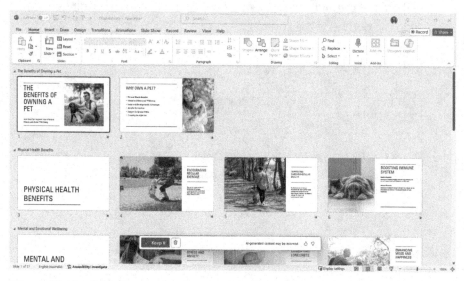

When Copilot has finished generating the presentation, select the Keep it button to keep it.

> **TIP** When you are ready to edit your presentation, switch to the normal view by going to the View menu and selecting Normal view.

> **SEE ALSO** See the section "Edit and organize presentations" later in this chapter to learn how to use Copilot in the chat pane to edit and add additional slides and images to your presentation.

Create a presentation using the Copilot chat pane

Use the Copilot chat pane to start with a blank presentation and ask Copilot to create a draft presentation by describing what you want. When you use the chat pane, Copilot will immediately create a presentation in response to your prompt.

To create a presentation from a prompt

1. Select the suggested **Create a presentation about** prompt or start typing Create a presentation about directly into the prompt area.

2. Complete your prompt by describing what you want the presentation to be about with a simple phrase.

3. Press **Enter** or select the Send icon in the prompt area.

Type your prompt into the Copilot prompt area.

 TIP You can also select the microphone icon to dictate your prompt.

You will see a series of progress messages, such as "Working on a response for you," "Looking things over," "Almost there," "Putting things together," and "Still working on it" while Copilot creates the presentation.

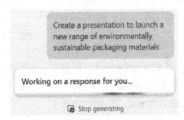

Copilot displays progress messages.

 TIP If you make a mistake or change your mind about your prompt, you can select the **Stop generating** button to stop Copilot and enter a new prompt.

When Copilot has finished, you will get a confirmation message in the Copilot pane, and you will see that it has created a presentation with multiple slides. Copilot has used AI to create content based on your prompt, added images from a Microsoft licensed stock library, and used Designer to design the layout of the presentation.

> ⚠️ **IMPORTANT** The nature of generative AI is that it is creative, so you will not always get the same results from the same prompt every time. You can get different content, images, and designs with the same prompt.

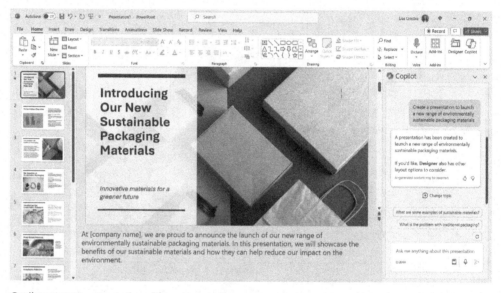

Copilot creates a presentation with content and images.

Copilot has also used AI to generate suggested speaker notes for each slide. Here is an example of the speaker notes generated for a slide about the benefits of sustainable packaging:

"Sustainable packaging materials are designed to have a minimal impact on the environment. They are made from renewable resources, such as plant-based materials, and are biodegradable or recyclable. We will discuss the benefits of sustainable packaging, including reducing waste, conserving energy, and protecting the environment."

The presentation also includes speaker notes.

Scroll through the presentation to see the variety of slides and images Copilot has created and notice the structure of the presentation. You will find a title slide, presentation overview, and conclusion slides, with content slides in between, based on your prompt.

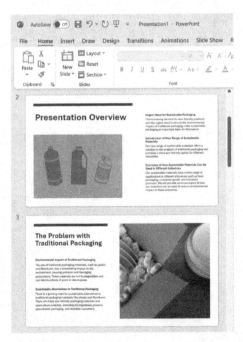

Slides created by Copilot are shown in the thumbnail pane.

8

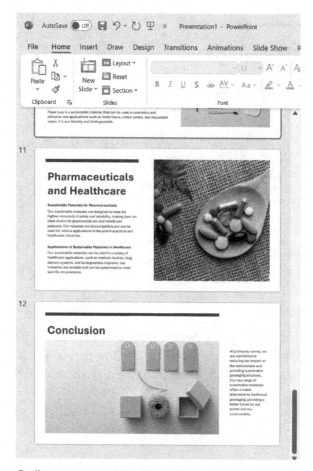

Copilot creates a conclusion slide to finish your presentation.

You can save, change, edit, or add to this presentation as you want. Treat it as a first draft to get you started or to help with ideas for the content, design, and structure of your presentation.

Create a presentation from a document

You can also use Copilot in PowerPoint to generate a draft of a presentation based on a document. Copilot will use the content of your document, including text, headings, and images, to generate the presentation.

If you use styles in Word to organize your document using heading levels, it will make it easier for Copilot to understand the structure of your document and to use that structure when creating the presentation.

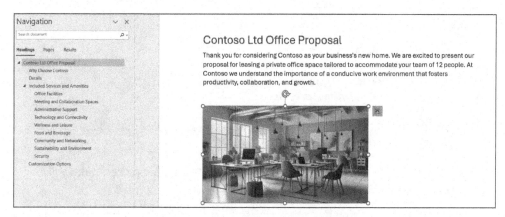

Use styles in your Word document to help Copilot understand the structure of your document. Include images in your document that you want Copilot to use in the presentation

 IMPORTANT The Word document must be saved in your personal OneDrive that goes with the Microsoft account you used to sign up for Copilot Pro.

 IMPORTANT You can create a presentation only from a Word document with Copilot Pro. To create a document from a PDF, you need a Copilot for Microsoft 365 license.

 TIP Copilot will also use stock images in the presentation if there are not enough images in your document. Make sure you check and edit the final presentation.

8

To create a presentation from a document

1. In the Copilot prompt area, select the suggested prompt **Create a presentation from [file]**, or type Create a presentation from in the prompt area and press the Spacebar.

    > **TIP** You can also select the Create a presentation from a file option from the menu when you select the Copilot icon at the top left of the slide.

    *Type **Create a presentation from** in the prompt area, and then press the Spacebar.*

2. Type the character / (forward slash) to indicate to Copilot that you are looking for a file as the source.

3. Start typing the name of the file you want to use. The file picker menu will appear, displaying suggested files that match what you type.

    > **TIP** You will see the most recent files. It will be easier to find the file you want if you have recently opened it in Word.

    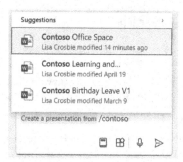

    Start typing the name of your file to search for it and select it from the file picker menu.

4. Select the name of the file you want to use as the source for your presentation. You will see the file name appear in the prompt area.

5. Select the arrow icon to send your prompt to Copilot.

6. Copilot will show a series of progress messages, including showing you the outline of the presentation it is creating.

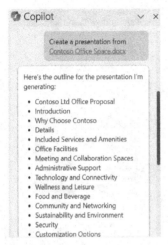

Copilot shows the outline of the presentation it is creating based on the structure of the Word document.

7. Wait for Copilot to finish generating the presentation.

The notes in the first slide of the presentation will show the file path for the document that was used to generate the presentation.

The notes on the first slide show the file path for the source document used to create the presentation.

8

The presentation will include content and images from your Word document, as well as speaker notes. Under the speaker notes on each slide, Copilot shows the original content it used to create them.

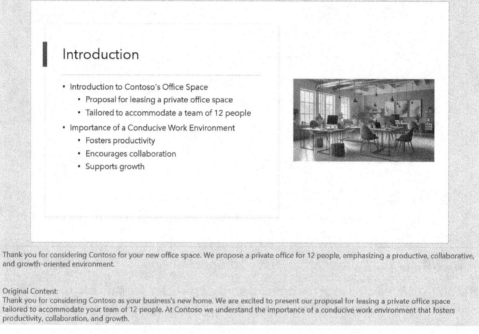

Copilot shows the original content from the Word document under the generated speaker notes.

Writing effective prompts for Copilot in PowerPoint

The way you write your prompt makes a big difference to the content of the presentation created by Copilot. This section will guide you through different ideas for writing and changing your prompt to get different results.

Remember that Copilot is using generative AI, which by nature is creative, so simply trying the same prompt again can sometimes give you a much better result—particularly if you would like a different design or different images. This approach will work best when you are creating a presentation based on a relatively broad subject. The more narrow or specific your subject, the less variety you will get with this approach.

To create a different presentation with the same prompt

1. Open a new blank presentation.

2. Open the Copilot pane by selecting the **Copilot** button on the Home ribbon.

3. Type the same prompt into the prompt area and press Enter.

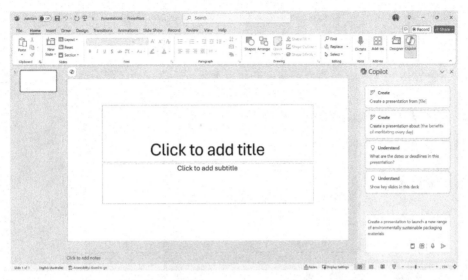

Type the same prompt into Copilot to generate a new presentation.

Review the newly created presentation. You will most likely find that Copilot has created different topics, different content, and speaker notes, and used different images and a different design.

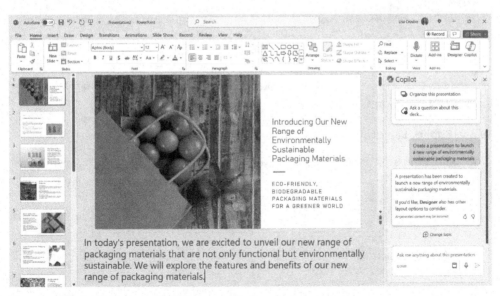

Copilot creates a different version of the presentation from your prompt.

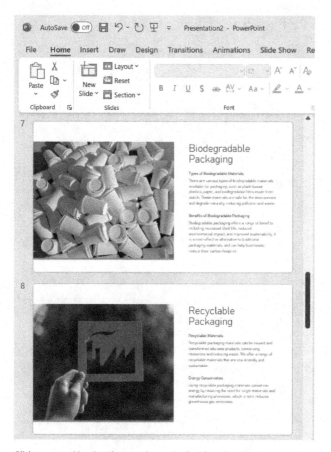

Slides created by Copilot are shown in the thumbnail pane.

Copilot Lab provides you with a list of suggested prompts and ideas to help you write more effective prompts.

To use Copilot Lab prompt suggestions

1. Select the **View Prompts** icon in the prompt area.

Select the book icon to view suggested prompts.

2. This expands a menu showing prompts by category. Select the **View more prompts** option at the bottom of this pop-up menu.

Copilot prompts are grouped into suggestions to create, understand, edit, and ask.

3. Scroll through the options to get new ideas, including prompts to add images, create vacation presentations, add agendas, and add slides.

> ⊘ **TIP** You can select the **See all prompts in Copilot Lab** link to open Copilot Lab in a web browser.

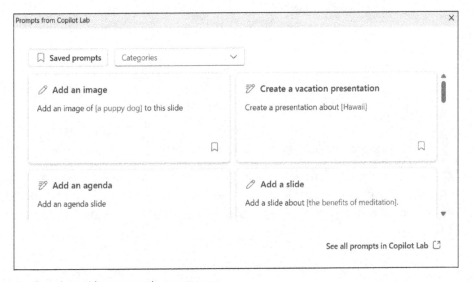

Copilot Lab provides suggested prompts to use.

4. Select the **Task** dropdown menu to select prompts by Edit, Create, Understand, Ask, Manage, or Catch-up categories.

5. Check the Create box to get more ideas for prompts to help you create presentations.

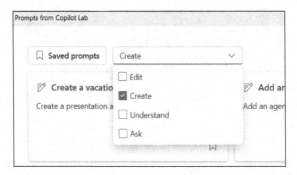

You can filter Copilot Lab prompts by category.

6. Select the ribbon icon on any prompt you want to save for later.

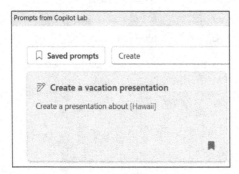

Select the ribbon icon to save a suggested prompt for later.

7. Close the Copilot Lab pop-up menu to return to your presentation.

Adding more specific information about your content, structure, context, or particular slides you want created can help Copilot create a presentation that is more aligned to what you have in mind. Here are some strategies for different kinds of prompts to try.

Write a prompt using specific information

You can expand your prompt to ask Copilot to include specific topics or themes or to emphasize things that are important to include in the presentation.

Enter a new prompt in the Copilot prompt area.

Copilot will create a presentation with content that includes the information you've requested.

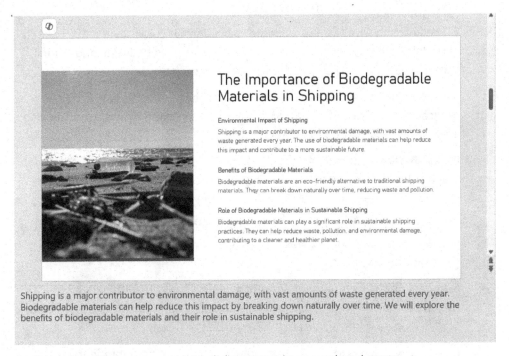

Copilot creates a slide from your prompt, including content, images, and speaker notes.

Write a very detailed and structured prompt

You can use up to 2000 characters in your prompt, which allows room for you to provide a lot of detail. If you have a specific structure or content notes already prepared, you can use these in your prompt to provide Copilot with more detailed instructions.

Here is an example of a detailed and very specific prompt that fits within the 2000-character limit:

> Create a presentation to introduce our innovative line of biodegradable packaging materials. Begin with an engaging introduction that highlights the significance of eco-friendly solutions in today's world.
>
> 1. Why Biodegradable Packaging Matters: Start with the current environmental challenges and consumer demand for sustainable products. Explain the necessity for businesses to adopt green practices.
>
> 2. The Problem with Non-Sustainable Packaging: Discuss the negative impacts of traditional packaging materials on nature, including pollution and landfill waste. Use statistics to emphasize the urgency of the issue.
>
> 3. Benefits of Biodegradable Packaging: Outline the advantages such as reduced carbon footprint, compostability, and the positive perception among environmentally conscious consumers.
>
> 4. How Biodegradable Packaging Is Made: Provide a detailed explanation of the manufacturing process, from sourcing renewable resources to the final product. Include visuals or diagrams to illustrate the process.
>
> 5. Impact on Cost: Analyze the cost implications of switching to biodegradable materials. Compare initial investment versus long-term savings and potential government incentives.
>
> 6. Impact on the Environment: Present a compelling case with data on how biodegradable packaging reduces environmental harm. Highlight success stories or case studies of companies that have made the switch.
>
> Conclude with a call to action, encouraging the adoption of biodegradable packaging as a step toward a more sustainable future. Ensure that the presentation is visually appealing, with a clear and concise layout that facilitates easy understanding and retention of the information presented.

Review the slides created this time and notice the difference between what Copilot created with this prompt compared to the more general prompts.

 TIP Select the Slide Sorter button in the View ribbon to get an overview of the full presentation.

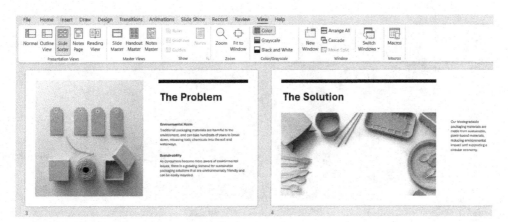

Slides created by Copilot are shown in the slide sorter view.

Write a prompt to generate ideas or learn about a topic

You can also prompt Copilot with context or background about what you are interested in, even if you don't have specific details. This prompt asks Copilot to create a presentation about a trip to Paris, where the writer is interested in food and is looking for ideas.

Enter a new prompt into the Copilot prompt area.

Copilot creates a presentation that suggests a range of food experiences and locations to try in Paris. This type of prompting can be a great starting point for learning or research on any topic.

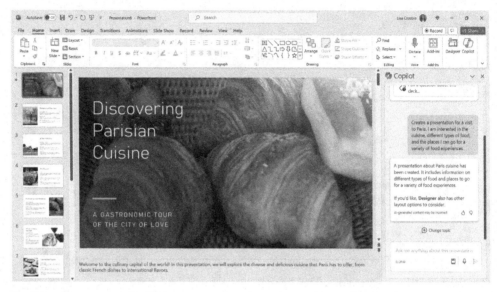

Copilot creates a presentation from your prompt.

Write a prompt with instructions about specific slides

You can ask Copilot to create specific slides as part of your prompt.

Enter a new prompt into the Copilot prompt area.

The presentation is created with the slide that you requested in the prompt. You can also create slides using a prompt after you have created your presentation. This will be covered in detail in the next section.

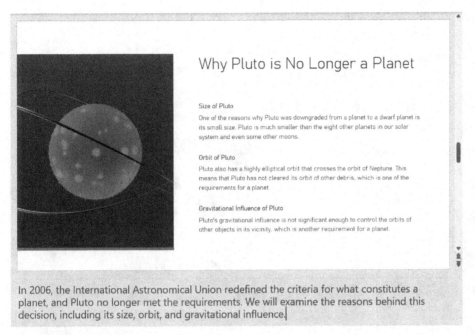

Why Pluto is No Longer a Planet

Size of Pluto

One of the reasons why Pluto was downgraded from a planet to a dwarf planet is its small size. Pluto is much smaller than the eight other planets in our solar system and even some other moons.

Orbit of Pluto

Pluto also has a highly elliptical orbit that crosses the orbit of Neptune. This means that Pluto has not cleared its orbit of other debris, which is one of the requirements for a planet.

Gravitational Influence of Pluto

Pluto's gravitational influence is not significant enough to control the orbits of other objects in its vicinity, which is another requirement for a planet.

In 2006, the International Astronomical Union redefined the criteria for what constitutes a planet, and Pluto no longer met the requirements. We will examine the reasons behind this decision, including its size, orbit, and gravitational influence.

The slide is created by Copilot from your prompt.

8

Edit and organize presentations

You can use Copilot to help you edit and organize your presentation, by adding slides, adding images, and structuring the presentation into sections. You can also use Copilot together with Designer to change the design and layout of your slides quickly and easily.

Using prompts to add slides to your presentation

In the Copilot prompt area, write a prompt to describe the slide you want to add, and press Enter. Your prompt can be very general, or very specific, using the same techniques you learned in the previous section.

Create a slide about the International Astronomical Union

Enter a prompt describing a slide you want Copilot to create.

Copilot creates the slide you've described and adds it to the deck.

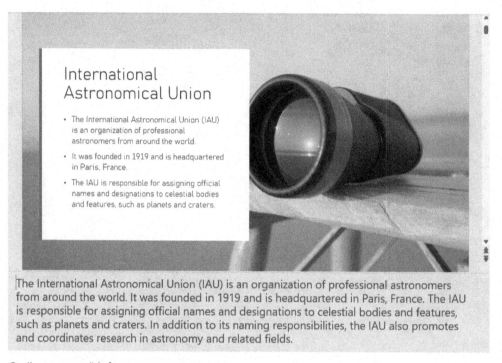

Copilot creates a slide from your prompt.

> ✅ **TIP** Copilot will put the new slide after whichever slide you currently have selected. If you want to choose the position before you ask Copilot to create the slide, select that slide position before you enter your prompt.

You can ask Copilot to create multiple slides at once in a single prompt.

Write a prompt asking Copilot to create multiple slides.

Copilot adds all the slides as described in the prompt.

Copilot creates slides from your prompt.

Using Designer to change slide designs

Copilot uses Designer to create the presentation and the slides, and you can switch back and forth to use Designer alongside Copilot to edit and change the design of your presentation.

To use Designer to edit your presentation

1. Select the Designer button on the ribbon next to the Copilot button.

Select the Designer button on the ribbon.

2. Designer now replaces Copilot in the side panel. Scroll through the suggested designs until you find one you like and select it. The design of your selected slide will be updated.

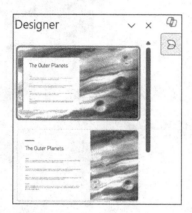

Designer suggests alternative designs for you to select.

3. Use the icons in the right rail to switch back and forth between Designer and Copilot.

Copilot and Designer icons in the right rail.

Using Copilot to add images to your slides

You can change the images in your presentation by using a prompt to describe what you want. Depending on the prompt you use, Copilot will either add images selected from a Microsoft stock image library or generate an image using DALL-E3 with Designer.

In this example, Copilot created a slide about the sun, where the image is perhaps not as clear or as representative as it could be.

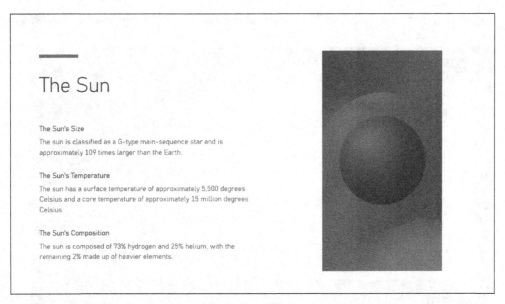

A slide created by Copilot with a suboptimal image.

To use Copilot to add a stock image to a slide

1. Select the slide where you want to add the image.

2. Delete the image you don't want.

3. Write a prompt to describe the image you want on the slide. You can write a very general prompt or something more specific and descriptive.

> **TIP** Starting your prompt with "Add an image" asks Copilot to find an image from the stock library.

Write a prompt to ask Copilot to add a different image.

> **TIP** If you want to keep the original image and add additional images, don't delete the original image. Prompting Copilot to add an image will add a new image and reformat the slide including the original image, rather than replacing it.

Copilot adds the new image and may also automatically reformat the slide using Designer.

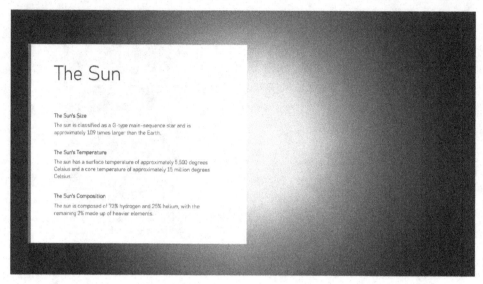

A slide is created by Copilot using the new image.

To use Copilot and Designer to generate new images for your presentation

1. Select the slide where you want to add the image.

2. Delete the image you don't want.

3. Write a prompt to describe the image you want to generate.

Write a prompt to ask Copilot to generate an image for your presentation.

 TIP Starting your prompt with "Create an image" asks Copilot to use Designer to generate an image.

 SEE ALSO Chapter 2 includes tips on how to write effective prompts for image generation that you can use here.

4. Designer will generate four images based on your prompt and display them in the Copilot chat pane.

Designer generates four images based on your prompt.

> ⚠ **IMPORTANT** Generating images in PowerPoint consumes the image generation boosts available for the day with your Copilot Pro subscription. You will see the number of boosts remaining each time you prompt Copilot to generate an image.

5. Select the image you want to use and then select the **Insert** button to add the image to your slide.

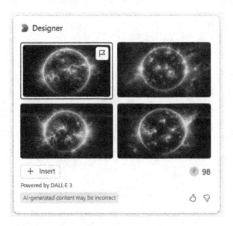

Select the image you want to use and then select the Insert button to add it to your slide.

IMPORTANT When you select an image, a flag icon appears at the top right of the image. Use this to report the image if there is anything concerning about it.

 TIP Use the Designer options to help redesign the slide with the new image.

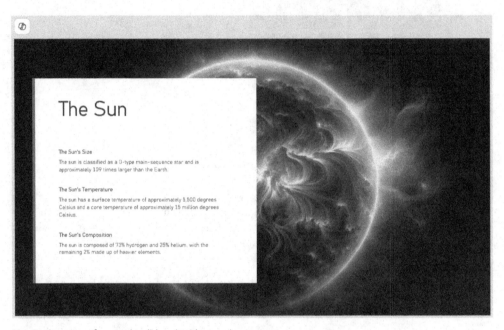

Use Designer to reformat the slide using the new image.

Using Copilot to organize your presentation

Copilot can organize your presentation, adding an agenda slide (if you haven't already created one), and structuring it into sections by grouping slides with similar content together and creating a section header slide for each group.

To ask Copilot to do this, type Organize this presentation into the prompt area.

Type "Organize this presentation" into the prompt area.

Copilot responds with a summary of a suggested structure for your presentation and makes the changes it describes.

 TIP You can always use Ctrl+Z to undo anything Copilot does that you don't like.

8

Copilot describes how it has organized the presentation.

Copilot will create an agenda slide, listing the sections it has created.

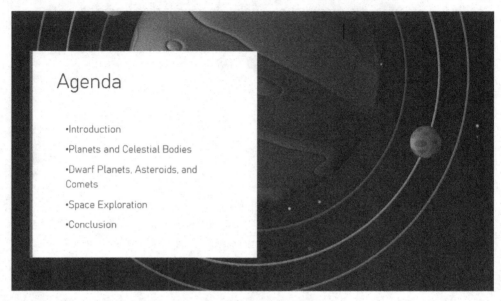

Copilot will create an agenda slide when it organizes the presentation.

It has also grouped your presentation content into those sections and created a header slide for each section.

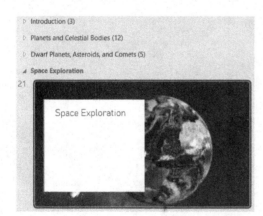

Copilot will add sections to your presentation.

> ✓ **TIP** You can use the Organize this presentation command on an existing presentation that you created, or that has been shared with you, to help structure and organize it quickly and easily.

Understand presentation content

When you are given a slide deck with a lot of information in it, Copilot can help you understand the content by summarizing it for you, by answering specific questions about the content, or by generating answers from outside the presentation content using AI. In this section, you will be guided through how to ask about and understand presentation content, using the example presentation created earlier in the chapter about environmentally sustainable packaging materials.

Using Copilot to summarize your presentation

You can scroll up to select the suggested prompt, **Understand: Summarize this presentation** or type Summarize this presentation into the prompt area.

Ask Copilot to Summarize this presentation.

 TIP When requesting a summary or asking questions for which Copilot responds with a lot of information, resize Copilot to make it wider on the screen so that it is easier to read.

8

You can move or resize Copilot.

Copilot will respond with a summary of your presentation content. You will see Copilot creating and changing the summary in real time as it works through the presentation. When it finishes, you will see a full summary, including citations for each point.

You can hover over or select any of these citations to refer back to the original material to check for accuracy and context.

> **TIP** If you want a shorter summary, try a prompt such as "Summarize this presentation in 3 bullet points."

> **IMPORTANT** You should always check any Copilot-generated content for accuracy. Generative AI can sometimes get things wrong.

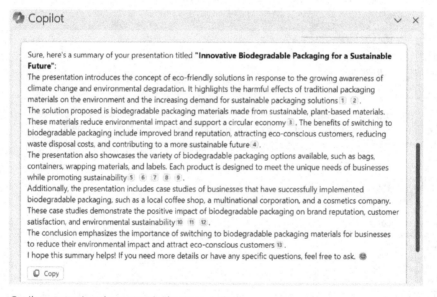

Copilot summarizes the content in the presentation.

Using Copilot to ask questions about your presentation

You can type a question into the prompt area to ask Copilot about any information in the presentation content. Copilot will respond with the information and provide a link that references the content in the presentation. Following that link will take you to the relevant slide so you can see the content side-by-side with Copilot. When Copilot finds the information in the document, the response will start with the phrase "From your document."

Copilot provides citations when it responds to questions about content.

Copilot will also prompt you with suggested questions you can ask based on the presentation content. You can select one of these to automatically fill that question in the prompt area and have Copilot find the answer.

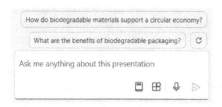

Copilot suggests other questions you can ask.

You can also ask questions about content that may not be in the presentation or when the presentation content is not enough to fully answer the question.

Ask Copilot a question about a related topic when the content isn't in the presentation.

Copilot in PowerPoint has access to web content to help answer your question via the web content plug-in. This is switched on by default. To view or change the status of the web content plug-in, select the plug-in icon in the prompt area and adjust the toggle switch.

Copilot uses the web content plug-in to draw on content from the web to answer questions.

When Copilot uses the web plug-in to answer the question, you will see a progress message that says, "Combing through web results I found…" and the answer may include web references or citations.

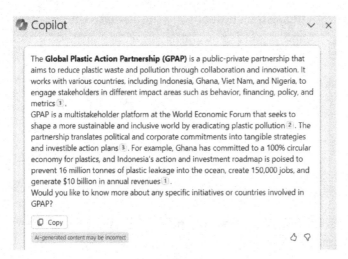

Select the Copy button to copy the response to the clipboard.

 TIP You can use the Copy button to copy any Copilot response to the clipboard to use elsewhere.

Using Copilot to find key information in your presentation

You will find other suggested prompts in the Copilot Lab that can help you get key information from your presentation content. Here are some examples:

You can use the prompt Show key slides in this deck to get a list of the most important slides and a short summary of each.

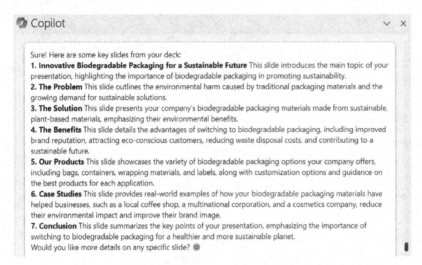

Copilot lists the key slides in your presentation with a short description of each.

You can use the prompt What are the action points to find and summarize any key action points in your deck.

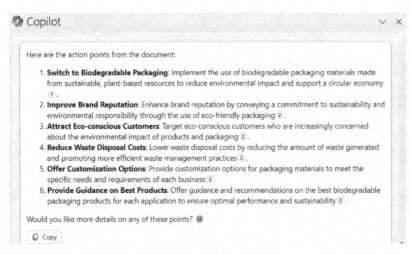

Copilot extracts the action points from your presentation.

Using Copilot to answer general questions

You can also ask Copilot for answers to general questions related to improving your presentation, becoming a better presenter, or even general questions unrelated to your presentation.

> ✅ **TIP** Copilot in PowerPoint is better at answering questions related to the presentation content or questions in the context of your work in PowerPoint and how to improve your presentation. You will get better responses to general questions by using Copilot on the web.

You can ask Copilot how to make your presentation more engaging.

I am presenting to a customer to pitch the value of biodegradable containers. How can I make my presentation more engaging?

Ask Copilot a question about how you can make your presentation more engaging.

If your question is in the context of your presentation content, Copilot will respond with suggestions based on the presentation, with citations.

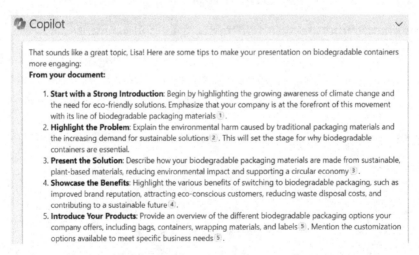

Copilot

That sounds like a great topic, Lisa! Here are some tips to make your presentation on biodegradable containers more engaging:

From your document:

1. **Start with a Strong Introduction**: Begin by highlighting the growing awareness of climate change and the need for eco-friendly solutions. Emphasize that your company is at the forefront of this movement with its line of biodegradable packaging materials [1].
2. **Highlight the Problem**: Explain the environmental harm caused by traditional packaging materials and the increasing demand for sustainable solutions [2]. This will set the stage for why biodegradable containers are essential.
3. **Present the Solution**: Describe how your biodegradable packaging materials are made from sustainable, plant-based materials, reducing environmental impact and supporting a circular economy [3].
4. **Showcase the Benefits**: Highlight the various benefits of switching to biodegradable packaging, such as improved brand reputation, attracting eco-conscious customers, reducing waste disposal costs, and contributing to a sustainable future [4].
5. **Introduce Your Products**: Provide an overview of the different biodegradable packaging options your company offers, including bags, containers, wrapping materials, and labels [5]. Mention the customization options available to meet specific business needs [5].

Copilot provides you with suggestions in response to your question.

You can also ask more general questions about presentation skills, such as:

- What are some tips for designing an effective presentation?

- What are some common mistakes to avoid when creating a presentation?

- What is the best font size for a presentation?

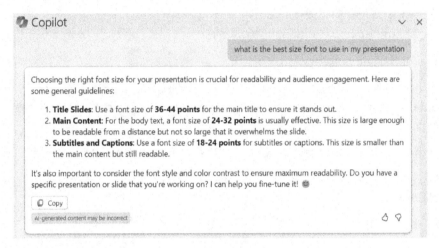

Copilot provides a response not based on the presentation content.

Copilot generates a response to these types of questions using the large language model or the web plugin, depending on the nature of the question.

Skills review

In this chapter, you learned how to:

- Create presentations using different prompting techniques.

- Edit your presentation by using prompts to add slides and images, use Copilot and Designer together to edit slide designs, and organize your presentation into sections with a simple prompt.

- Understand presentation content by asking Copilot to summarize your presentation and by prompting it with questions about the presentation and related content.

Practice tasks

No practice files are necessary to complete the practice tasks in this chapter.

Start Copilot in PowerPoint

Start PowerPoint, and then perform the following tasks:

1. Create a new blank presentation.

2. Select the Copilot icon at the top left of the blank slide and view the options available to create presentations or ask Copilot questions. Select the Copilot icon again to close this menu.

3. Select the **Copilot** button on the ribbon on the Home tab to activate Copilot.

Create presentations

Start with a blank presentation in PowerPoint and then perform the following tasks:

1. Select the Copilot icon at the top left of the blank slide, and then select **Create a presentation about....**

2. In the prompt area, complete the prompt as follows, and then press Enter:
   [Create a presentation about] how stringed instruments create notes

3. Review the presentation topics and the suggested structure of the presentation. Move one of the sections up or down in the order and delete one of the sections.

4. Select the Generate slides button and wait for Copilot to generate your presentation.

5. Select the **Keep it** button.

6. Go to the **View** menu and select **Normal** view.

7. Leave this presentation open and start a new blank presentation by going to the **File** menu and selecting **Blank Presentation**.

8. Select the Copilot icon from the Home menu to open the Copilot pane.

9. Type the same prompt into the Copilot prompt area (Create a presentation about how stringed instruments create notes) and press Enter.

10. Wait for Copilot to finish generating your presentation.

11. Review the content of your presentation, including the text on each slide, images, and speaker notes.

12. Compare the presentation with the one you generated using the Copilot chat, noticing differences in the structure, content, images, and design.

13. Continue working with this version of the presentation to complete the remaining tasks.

Edit and organize presentations

Continue working with the presentation you just generated, and then perform the following tasks:

1. Select any slide where you think the design or layout could be improved.

2. Select the **Designer** button on the ribbon on the Home tab to activate Designer.

3. Scroll through the design options, choose one you like, and select it. Your slide will now be redesigned with your selected design.

4. Select the **Copilot** button in the right rail or on the ribbon to return to Copilot.

5. Select the **Presentation Overview** slide (second slide) and remove the image.

6. In the Copilot prompt area, type the following prompt, and then press Enter: Add an image showing sheet music

7. Your slide will be updated with the new image.

8. Remove the image you just added.

9. In the Copilot prompt area, type the following prompt, and then press Enter: Create an image of a beautifully crafted stringed instrument, such as a violin or guitar, with intricate details and a polished finish. The instrument should be set against a soft, warm background that highlights its elegance

10. Your slide will be updated with the new image.

11. Scroll through the slide thumbnail pane to find a place in your presentation where it makes sense to add new slides and select the slide before where you want the new slide to be created.

12. In the Copilot prompt area, type the following prompt, and then press Enter: Create a slide comparing a guitar to a bass guitar

13. When you receive a confirmation message from Copilot, click or tap to view the new slide that was created.

14. In the Copilot prompt area, type the following prompt, and then press Enter: Organize this presentation

15. Review the changes Copilot has made to your presentation by scrolling through the slide thumbnail pane. You should now have an agenda slide, and your presentation will be divided into sections, with a section header slide for each section.

Understand presentation content

Using the presentation you created and edited in these practice tasks, perform the following tasks:

1. In the Copilot prompt area, type the following prompt, and then press Enter: Summarize this presentation

2. Read through the summary and select at least one of the citations to view where the content came from in the presentation.

3. In the Copilot prompt area, type the following prompt, and then press Enter: What are the different types of strings

4. Copilot will provide an answer based on presentation and/or web content, depending on the content of your presentation. Select at least one citation to view where the content came from in the presentation.

5. Copilot will suggest some other questions you can ask about the presentation content. Select one and review the answer.

6. In the Copilot prompt area, type the following prompt, and then press Enter: Tell me about the history of the harp

7. Review the response. Copilot will provide an answer that comes from the web, and may include website references.

8. In the Copilot prompt area, type the following prompt, and then press Enter: How can I make my presentation more interactive?

9. Review the tips provided by Copilot.

10. If you want to keep the presentation, save and close it; otherwise, close it without saving.

Copilot in OneNote

9

Copilot in OneNote can improve your notetaking by helping you draft content, come up with new ideas, and get organized. You can chat with Copilot to generate all sorts of notes, such as paragraphs or pages of new content, meeting agendas, tips, and lists of pros and cons. You can use Copilot in OneNote to help brainstorm and generate a list of ideas on a topic or get help with your planning. You can use it for personal planning, including organizing a party, planning for a holiday, or working on your fitness goals, as well as with business content including drafting training plans, marketing plans and content, ideas for new products, and more. You can use Copilot in OneNote to help you get organized by creating to-do lists for new projects or use it to automatically identify key action items from your notes and generate a to-do list.

Copilot can also help you rewrite your existing notes, automatically generating an alternative version or using a prompt to change the way your notes are written. You can make your notes longer or shorter, change the writing style or tone, or rewrite notes for different purposes.

In this chapter

- Start Copilot in OneNote
- Create new notes
- Rewrite notes
- Create to-do lists, tasks, and plans
- Chat with Copilot to understand your notes

Practice files

You will need to use the practice files provided with this chapter to complete the practice tasks.

You can also use Copilot to understand your notes by creating summaries and by asking questions to make it easier to find and analyze information when you have a lot of notes.

This chapter guides you through using Copilot to enhance your notetaking. You will learn how to generate new pages of notes, to-do lists, plans, and summaries. You will also learn how to use Copilot to rewrite and understand your notes.

 SEE ALSO You will find detailed instructions and suggestions to help you write prompts in Chapter 2, "Writing effective prompts for Copilot."

Start Copilot in OneNote

You can start Copilot in OneNote by opening your notebook and selecting the Copilot button at the right end of the Home tab of the ribbon.

Select the button on the ribbon to open the Copilot pane.

⚠ **IMPORTANT** Copilot in OneNote is available only in OneNote for Microsoft 365 on Windows. You will need a Microsoft 365 license that includes OneNote as well as your Copilot Pro license.

This will launch the Copilot pane, which is docked to the right side of your screen, allowing you to chat with Copilot while working on your notes.

The Copilot pane opens with suggested prompts to help you get started.

9

Create new notes

You can use Copilot in OneNote to generate new content for your notes, including paragraphs of text or whole pages. You use the Copilot pane to generate new content and then copy and paste it into your notebook.

Write a prompt to create new notes or pages

To create new notes using a prompt

1. Click or tap in the Copilot prompt area.

2. Describe what you'd like to create, using a simple phrase.

3. Select the **Generate** button in the prompt area or press the Enter key.

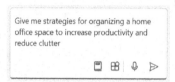

*Enter your prompt in the prompt area and press Enter
or select the arrow icon to enter the prompt.*

Copilot will display a series of progress messages, such as "Working on a response for you...," "Pulling it together...," and "Finishing up...."

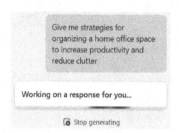

*Copilot will show a series of progress messages
while it generates a response to your prompt.*

 TIP If you make a mistake or change your mind about your prompt, you can select the Stop generating button at any time to stop Copilot and enter a new prompt.

After a moment, you will see Copilot generating a response in the chat pane. Copilot will generally produce a response that could fill a page of notes (depending on your prompt). Wait for Copilot to finish generating the notes.

 IMPORTANT The nature of generative AI is that it is creative, so you will not always get the same results from the same prompt every time.

> ⚠️ **IMPORTANT** To generate notes in Copilot, you use Copilot chat, and then you can copy and paste the generated notes into your notebook if you want to keep them. If you don't copy and paste the notes from the chat pane, you will lose them when you close OneNote.

> ✅ **TIP** You can close the Copilot pane using the close icon or move or resize it using the dropdown arrow. Copilot in OneNote generates lengthy notes in the chat, so resizing it to make it wider is often helpful so that you can view the generated notes more easily.

To keep the generated notes and add them to your notebook

1. Select the **Copy** button at the end of the generated notes in the Copilot pane.

2. Position your cursor on the page of your notebook where you want to add the notes (or create a new page).

3. Right-click or long press (tap and hold) and select **paste**.

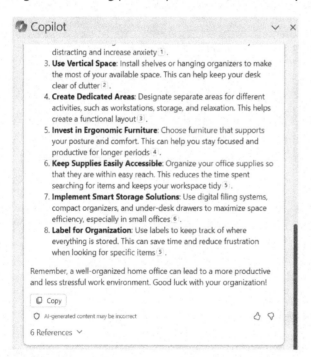

Copilot generates notes in the chat. Select the Copy button to paste the notes into your notebook to keep them.

9

Copy and paste the response into a page in your notebook.

Working with the web content plug-in

Copilot in OneNote can reference content from the web in response to your prompt, using an optional plug-in setting. This plug-in is enabled by default, but you can choose to toggle it on or off at any time depending on the type of notes you are creating and whether you want Copilot to include information from the web.

You can view the status of the web plug-in by selecting the **plug-in** icon in the Copilot prompt area. Leave this plug-in enabled for now.

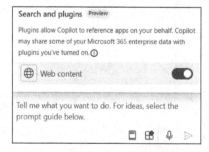

When the web content plug-in is enabled,
Copilot will reference web content in the response.

You can continue the chat with Copilot by entering another prompt on a related topic. Now that you have notes in your notebook, Copilot can reference that content, as well as content on the web. This is useful when you want to generate ideas or notes that include some web research.

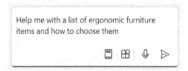

Enter your prompt in the prompt area and press Enter or select the arrow icon to enter the prompt.

Copilot generates notes based on the content already in your notebook. The response begins by telling you that the content is from your document.

Copilot responds with content from your document.

Copilot also provides notes based on the content from the web. This part of the response begins by telling you that the content is from the web.

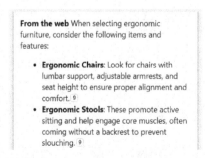

Copilot also includes content from the web in response to your prompt.

Copilot provides citations for all references, showing website titles and URLs for any content from the web. Hover over a citation number to view the details.

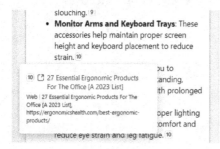

Hover over a citation reference number to get details about that reference.

Copilot provides a full list of references at the end of the response, both for content in your notes and for content on the web. You can expand this menu to view the card for each reference.

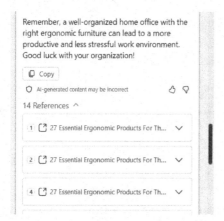

Select the arrow to open the expandable list of references at the end of the response.

Select the Copy button at the end of the response and paste the notes into your page to keep them.

> **From your document** Investing in ergonomic furniture is essential for maintaining good posture and comfort during long hours of work. Here are some key points to consider when choosing ergonomic furniture for your home office:
> - **Envision Your Goal**: Determine what you want your home office to look like and the kind of ergonomic furniture that will help you achieve that vision.
> - **Declutter**: Clear your space to make room for ergonomic furniture that supports your posture and comfort.
> - **Use Vertical Space**: Consider furniture like shelves or hanging organizers to maximize space and keep your desk area clear.
> - **Create Dedicated Areas**: Designate specific areas for workstations, storage, and relaxation, and choose furniture that fits these purposes.
> - **Invest in Ergonomic Furniture**: Look for furniture that supports your posture and comfort, such as chairs with lumbar support and adjustable features.
> - **Keep Supplies Easily Accessible**: Organize your office supplies within easy reach to minimize distractions and maintain a tidy workspace.
> - **Implement Smart Storage Solutions**: Opt for digital filing systems and compact organizers to enhance space efficiency.
> - **Label for Organization**: Use labels to keep track of where everything is stored, which can save time and reduce frustration when looking for specific items.
>
> **From the web** When selecting ergonomic furniture, consider the following items and features:
> - **Ergonomic Chairs**: Look for chairs with lumbar support, adjustable armrests, and seat height to ensure proper alignment and comfort.
> - **Ergonomic Stools**: These promote active sitting and help engage core muscles, often coming without a backrest to prevent slouching.
> - **Monitor Arms and Keyboard Trays**: These accessories help maintain proper screen height and keyboard placement to reduce strain.
> - **Standing Desks**: These allow you to alternate between sitting and standing, reducing the risks associated with prolonged sitting.
> - **Task Lights and Foot Rests**: Proper lighting and foot support can improve comfort and reduce eye strain and leg fatigue.
>
> Remember, a well-organized home office with the right ergonomic furniture can lead to a more productive and less stressful work environment. Good luck with your organization!

Copy and paste the response into a page in your notebook to keep it.

Disabling the web content plug-in

In some scenarios, you will want to generate notes using only your existing notes or the large language model without reference to web content. This example shows you the difference between the responses Copilot generates when this plug-in is enabled or disabled, and a scenario where you may prefer to disable it.

9

In this scenario, you have started a new notebook section, and you are brainstorming with Copilot for ideas about content for a new leadership development workshop program.

Enter your prompt in the prompt area and press
Enter or select the arrow icon to enter the prompt.

You don't have any content in your notebook related to this topic, so Copilot generates a response based only on web content.

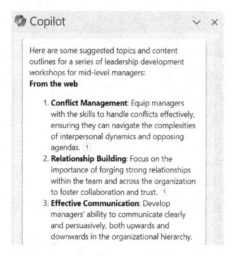

Copilot responds with suggestions from the web.

Copilot provides a list of references in the response, showing which websites the content has been derived from.

Copilot provides citations and a list of references for the content from the web.

In this scenario, you were looking to brainstorm some general workshop topic ideas, but Copilot has generated the response with reference to other leadership courses found on the web, which may be from your competitors, or which may put you in danger of copying their course content, which you don't want to do.

To force Copilot to generate an answer without referencing web content, you can disable the plug-in. Follow these steps to enable or disable the web content plug-in option at any time.

To disable the web content plug-in

1. Select the **plug-in** icon in the Copilot prompt area.

2. Toggle the **Web content** option to the off position.

3. Click or tap back in the prompt area to continue.

*Select the **plug-in** icon and toggle the **Web content** plug-in to off.*

Enter the same prompt and observe the difference in the response. This time Copilot generates a response using only the large language model, without any reference to web content. Remember that because generating content with Copilot is creative, you will also likely see differences in the response just from regenerating it, as well as from removing the web plug-in. Copy and paste the response into your notes to keep it.

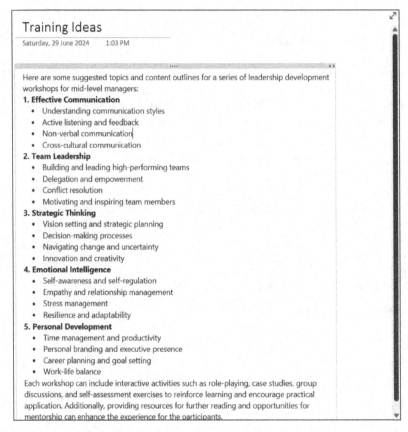

Copy and paste the content into a page in your notebook to keep it.

Continue the chat to create more notes

You can keep chatting with Copilot in the context of the conversation to generate additional notes. Now that you have generated ideas for a training plan, you can ask Copilot to help you write a proposal to help present it to potential clients.

Enter your prompt in the prompt area and press Enter or select the arrow icon to enter the prompt.

Copy and paste the response into a new page in your notebook.

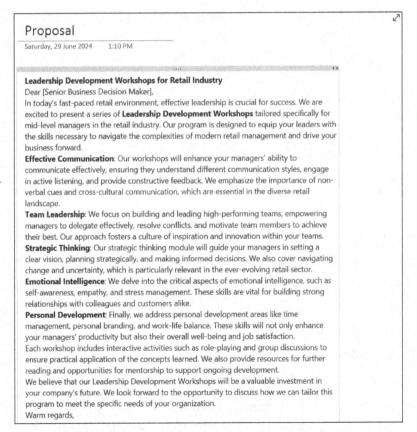

Copy and paste the response into a page in your notebook to keep it.

Change to a different topic to create new notes

When you are ready to change to a different topic, select the **Change topic** icon above the prompt area. This tells Copilot that you are switching context in the conversation so that you don't get answers related to the previous prompts and responses.

Select the Change topic icon to start a new topic in your chat with Copilot.

You will see a brief progress message and then the usual prompt pane with your "Change topic" prompt above it. Copilot is now ready to start chatting on a new topic.

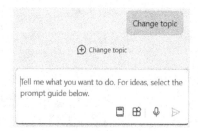

Copilot is ready to start a new conversation on a different topic.

Use suggested prompts and Copilot Lab

Copilot provides you with suggested prompts to help you understand and try new ideas for using Copilot in OneNote.

Browse and save prompts to use later

To find suggested prompts to help you with ideas

1. Select the **book** icon in the Copilot prompt area.

2. Select the **Create** menu option to expand it and view a list of suggested prompts. You can come back and select these at any time to get started with these ideas.

3. Select the **View more prompts** option.

4. The Copilot Lab window will open. Select the **Tasks** menu to see a list of prompt categories and check the **Create** option.

5. Browse the suggested prompts.

6. To save any prompt, select the **ribbon** icon.

7. Select the **ribbon** icon again to remove the prompt from the saved prompts.

Select the book icon to open a list of suggested prompts.

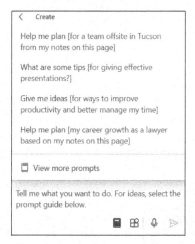

Expand the Create option to view suggested prompts that help you create notes.

9

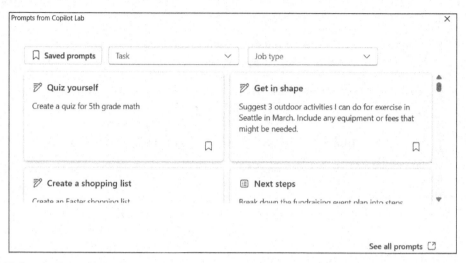

Select the View more prompts option to open the Copilot Lab.

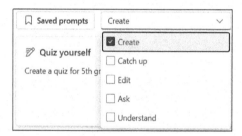

Select the Task menu to select a category of suggested prompts.

Select the ribbon icon to save a prompt.

Close the Copilot Lab window to return to your notebook.

Using a saved prompt from Copilot Lab

You can return to your saved prompts at any time to use them with Copilot.

To use a saved prompt with Copilot

1. Select the **book** icon in the Copilot prompt area.

2. Select the **View more prompts** option.

3. The Copilot Lab window will open. Select the **Saved prompts** button to see a list of your saved prompts.

4. Select the prompt you want to use.

Select the book icon in the prompt area and then select View more prompts.

Select the Saved prompts button to view your saved prompts.

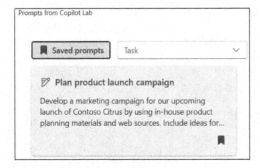

Select the saved prompt that you want to use.

This will close the Copilot Lab window, and your saved prompt will be automatically entered into the prompt area. You can edit or add to this prompt to provide additional details or make changes (in this example, change "Contoso Citrus" to something relevant to your own business). Press Enter or select the arrow icon to enter your prompt.

The saved prompt is entered into the Copilot prompt area.

Copilot provides a response to the prompt in the same way as if you had typed the prompt yourself.

Rewrite notes

Copilot can help you rewrite your notes, providing alternative wording or changing the tone, length, intended purpose, and more. You can use the automatic rewrite option in the shortcut menu to get a quick rewrite of your notes, or you can use the chat in the Copilot pane to describe how you want Copilot to rewrite the content.

Automatically rewrite your notes

The automatic rewrite feature will quickly rewrite your notes without you needing to type a prompt. This is useful when you just want to generate alternative wording for your notes without anything specific in mind that you wanted to change.

To automatically rewrite your notes

1. Select the text that you want to rewrite. This could be a paragraph, a selection of some text, or a whole page.

2. Right-click with your mouse to open the shortcut menu.

3. Expand the **Copilot** option to see the options available.

4. Select **Rewrite.**

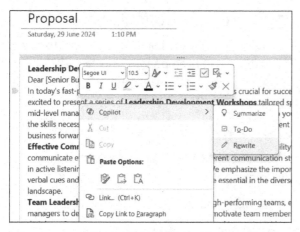

Select your text and right-click to open the Copilot shortcut menu.

5. Copilot will rewrite your content and add it to your notes above the selected text. When Copilot has finished rewriting your notes, you have the option to keep it or discard it. Select the **Keep it** button to add the notes to your page or select the **trash can** icon to discard the rewrite.

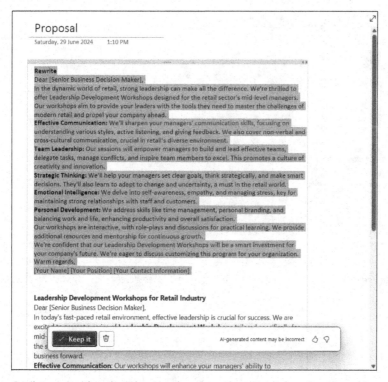

Copilot rewrites the selected text, and you have the option to keep it or discard it.

9

Rewrite your notes using a prompt with details

If you want to provide details for how you'd like the content to be rewritten, you will need to chat with Copilot in the main Copilot prompt area. You can ask Copilot to rewrite your notes to focus on specific content, to make the notes shorter or longer, or to write them with a different tone or for a different purpose.

To describe how you want Copilot to rewrite your notes

1. Select the text that you want to rewrite. This could be a paragraph, a selection of some of the text, or a whole page.

2. Type a prompt in the Copilot prompt area.

3. Press **Enter** or select the **arrow** to enter your prompt.

 TIP You can ask Copilot to respond with multiple rewrites with a prompt such as "suggest three ways I could rewrite this text to use on a website."

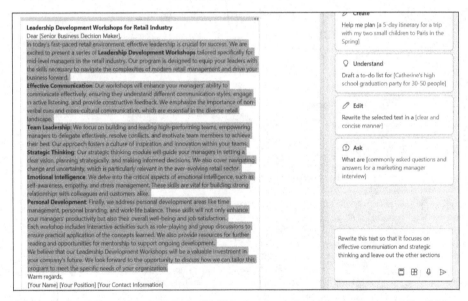

Select your text and enter a prompt in the Copilot prompt area describing how you want Copilot to rewrite it.

When you use a prompt to ask Copilot to rewrite your notes, the rewritten notes will be in the Copilot chat. To keep the rewrite, you will need to copy it from the chat and paste it into your notes.

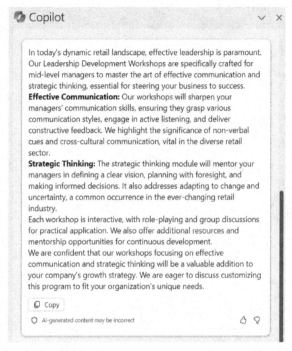

Copilot rewrites your text in the response in the Copilot pane.

Create to-do lists, tasks, and plans

Copilot can help you create to-do lists, tasks, and plans based on general prompts or your notes.

Create to-do lists and tasks

You can ask Copilot in OneNote to generate task lists or to-do lists with checkboxes. In this section, you will learn how to create to-do lists from a general prompt, as well as from your existing notes.

Create a suggested to-do list from a general prompt

Start with a blank section in your notebook and enter a prompt to ask Copilot to suggest a list of tasks for you. This is useful if you are working on a new project or organizing an event, and you don't know where to start.

Enter your prompt into the prompt area and press Enter or select the arrow icon to enter the prompt.

Copilot provides you with a suggested to-do list in the chat.

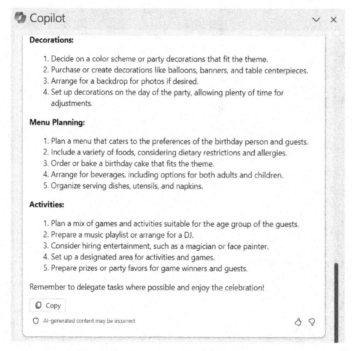

Copilot responds with a bullet point list of tasks in the chat pane.

To turn the response into a to-do list with checkboxes

1. Copy the response and paste it into your notebook.

2. Select the section of the text you want to convert to a to-do list.

3. Right-click with your mouse to open the shortcut menu.

4. Expand the **Copilot** option to see the options available.

5. Select **To-Do**.

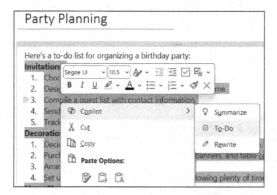

Select your text and right-click to open the Copilot shortcut menu.

9

6. Copilot adds a to-do list with checkboxes above your selected notes. Select the **Keep it** button to keep the list, or the **trash can** icon to discard it.

 TIP It can take a few seconds for Copilot to generate the full to-do list with checkboxes. You may see a simple bullet point list first while it is in progress.

Copilot generates a To-Do list with checkboxes and gives you the option to keep or discard it.

Generate a suggested task list from your notes

You can ask Copilot to generate a to-do list from your existing notes. This is useful if you have long notes or a transcript from a meeting, or other notes where you have action items in the text that haven't been identified and organized into a list.

To generate a to-do list with checkboxes from your existing notes

1. Select the section of the text you want Copilot to work with.

2. Right-click with your mouse to open the shortcut menu.

3. Expand the **Copilot** option to see the options available.

4. Select **To-Do.**

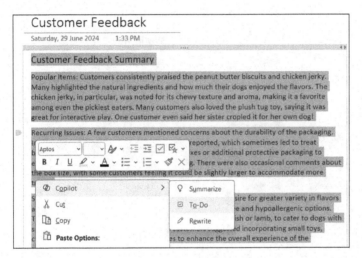

Select your text and right-click to open the Copilot shortcut menu

5. Copilot finds and extracts suggested tasks from your text and adds a to-do list with checkboxes above your selected notes. Select the **Keep it** button to keep the list, or the **trash can** icon to discard it.

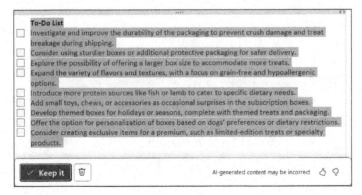

Copilot generates a To-Do list with checkboxes and gives you the option to keep or discard it.

Generate a to-do list from a section

You can also ask Copilot to identify tasks and generate a to-do list across multiple pages of notes in a section.

To generate a to-do list based on a whole section in your notebook

1. Select the section of your notebook you want to use to create the to-do list.

2. Right-click with your mouse to open the shortcut menu.

3. Expand the **Copilot** option to see the options available.

4. Select **To-Do**.

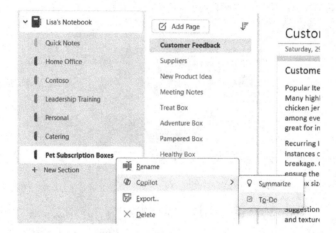

Select a section and use the shortcut menu to ask Copilot to create a to-do list from that whole section.

Copilot will add a new page to your notebook called "To-Do List" and will add the to-do list into that page.

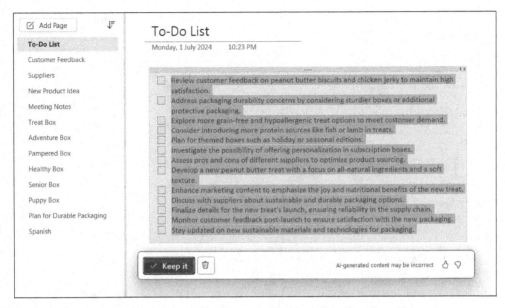

Copilot creates a new page and adds the to-do list, with the option to keep it or discard it.

9

Draft a plan

Copilot can help you draft a project plan based on your notes. This is useful if you have a lot of unstructured notes, such as meeting notes or transcripts, or customer feedback, and you need help to get started with taking action.

To generate a plan from your existing notes, reference the section you want to use in your prompt.

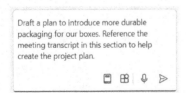

Enter your prompt into the prompt area and press Enter or select the arrow icon to enter the prompt.

Copilot generates a plan in the chat based on your notes, providing citations and references to your content. Copy and paste the response into your notebook to keep it.

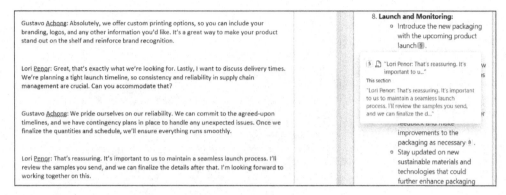

Copilot provides a response based on the selected content with citations.

Chat with Copilot to understand your notes

Copilot can help you find information in your notes and understand lengthy notebooks by summarizing content or by answering specific questions.

Summarize your notes

Copilot can help you summarize your notes in different lengths or formats, from a comprehensive summary to a short paragraph or list of bullet points. You can use the automatic summarize option in the shortcut menu to get a quick short summary of your notes, or you can use the chat in the Copilot pane to describe how you want Copilot to summarize your notes.

Generate a quick summary of your notes

You can use Copilot in OneNote to summarize the notes on a page or in a whole section of your notebook.

To automatically generate a summary of your notes

1. Select the text you want to summarize. This could be a selection of text or a whole page.

2. Right-click with your mouse to open the shortcut menu.

3. Expand the **Copilot** option to see the options available.

4. Select **Summarize.**

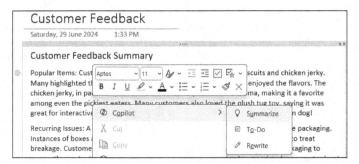

Highlight your text and right-click to open the Copilot shortcut menu.

5. Copilot summarizes your selected notes and adds the summary to the page. Select the **Keep it** button to keep the summary or select the **trash can** icon to discard it.

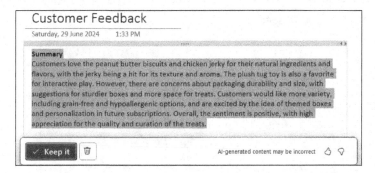

Copilot summarizes your content and gives you the option to keep or discard it.

Generate a summary of a whole section in your notebook

You can also ask Copilot to summarize notes from a whole section of your notebook, where you want a single summary of the notes from all the pages in that section.

To automatically generate a summary of a whole section

1. Select the section you want to summarize.

2. Right-click with your mouse to open the shortcut menu.

3. Expand the **Copilot** option to see the options available.

4. Select **Summarize.**

*Select a section and use the shortcut menu to ask
Copilot to summarize that whole section.*

5. Copilot creates a new page at the top of the section called "Summary" and adds a summary of all the notes in that section. Select the **Keep it** button to keep it or the **trash can** icon to discard it.

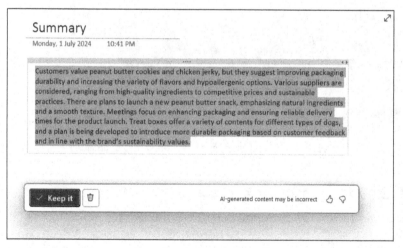

Copilot creates a new page at the top of the section for the summary.

Use a prompt to ask for a summary and describe the output

To describe how you want to summarize your notes, write a prompt in the Copilot prompt area describing the type of summary you want, the notes that Copilot should reference, and the desired output format.

 TIP You can ask for other outputs in your prompt as well as the summary, such as a list of action items.

Enter your prompt into the prompt area and press Enter or select the arrow icon to enter the prompt.

Copilot responds with the summary and output as described in your prompt. Copy and paste the summary into your notes to keep it.

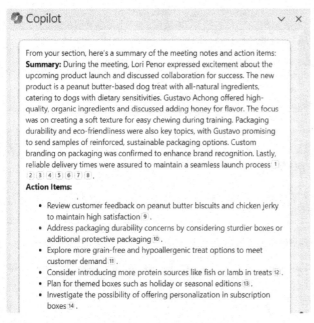

Copilot responds with a summary and a list of action items.

9

Generate a list of pros and cons

To ask Copilot to generate a list of pros and cons, write a prompt starting with the phrase "List the pros and cons of" and describe the list you want to create.

You can ask Copilot for a list of pros and cons with your prompt.

Copilot responds with a list of pros and cons from the content of your notes, and from the web if you have the web plug-in enabled.

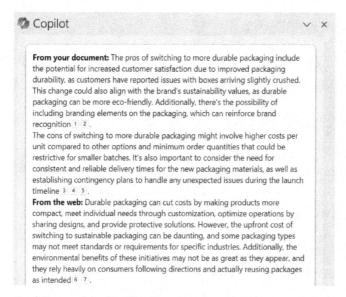

Copilot responds by describing the pros and cons based on your content.

 TIP You can also use this feature to get a general list of pros and cons when the content is not in your notes.

Chat with Copilot to answer questions about your notes

Copilot can help you find and pull together content from multiple pages in your notebook quickly and effectively. This is useful when you have a lot of notes and want to find the answer to a question without knowing where the content is. You can also ask Copilot to answer questions that require comparing information across multiple notes and pages.

In this example, the notebook has multiple pages outlining the details of different subscription boxes for pets.

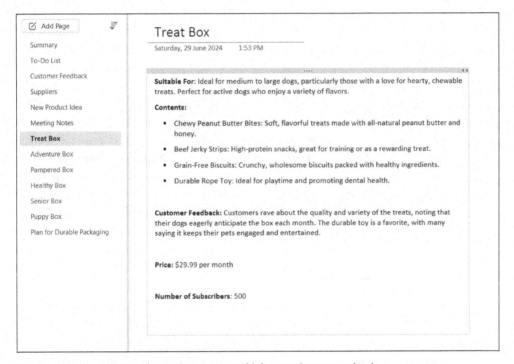

Copilot can help with research questions across multiple pages in your notebook.

You can ask Copilot a question for which it will need to search across multiple pages to find the answer. Copilot responds with the information you ask for, providing details and citations.

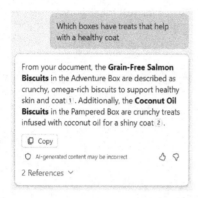

Ask Copilot questions to help you find information across multiple pages in your notes.

You can also ask Copilot to help you understand the information in your notes to work out the highest or lowest value of something, as shown in the following example.

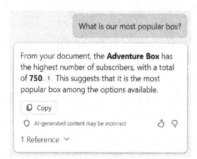

Ask Copilot questions to help you find information across multiple pages in your notes.

Skills review

In this chapter, you learned how to

- Generate new notes using suggested prompts from Copilot Lab and by writing your own prompts.

- Add generated content into your existing notebook.

- Use or disable the web content plug-in to allow or prevent Copilot from using web sources to generate notes.

- Rewrite your notes automatically or by describing the changes you want Copilot to make in a prompt.

- Create to-do lists, tasks, and plans based on general prompts or your notes.

- Summarize your notes and ask questions to understand the content of your notes.

9

Practice tasks

Before you can complete these tasks, you must copy the book's practice files to your computer. The practice files for these tasks are in the CopilotProSBS\Ch09 folder.

The introduction includes a complete list of practice files and download instructions.

Start Copilot in OneNote

Start OneNote, and then perform the following tasks:

1. Select the **Copilot** button on the ribbon on the Home tab to open Copilot.

2. Select the **View Prompts** icon in the prompt area to expand the list of suggested prompts.

3. Click or tap to expand the **Create** menu and view the suggested prompts.

4. Click or tap back into the prompt area to close the suggested prompts view.

Create new notes

Open the practice file called "Catering Notes" in OneNote and go to the Catering section. Create a new blank page, and then perform the following tasks:

1. Select the **Copilot** button on the ribbon on the Home tab to open Copilot.

2. Type the following prompt in the Copilot prompt area, and then press Enter: Give me strategies for expanding my business into a new city

3. Copy the response and paste it into your notebook.

4. Type the following prompt in the Copilot prompt area, and then press Enter: What are some ideas for a name of a corporate catering business

5. Copy the response and paste it into your notebook. Review the suggestions and keep the ones you like. Delete the other suggestions from your notes.

Rewrite notes

Select the Expansion Notes page in the Catering section of your notebook, and then perform the following tasks:

1. Click or tap in the Copilot prompt area, type the following prompt, and then press Enter: Rewrite the text in this section as a short paragraph to use as a pitch for potential investors

2. Copy and paste the response into your notes on this page.

Create to-do lists, tasks, and plans

Select the Expansion Notes page in the Catering section of your notebook, and then perform the following tasks:

1. Click or tap in the Copilot prompt area, type the following prompt, and then press Enter: Draft a plan to expand into the corporate catering market based on the notes on this page

2. Copy and paste the response into a new page in your notebook. Name the new page: Expansion Plan

3. Highlight all the text on the page and right-click with your mouse to open the shortcut menu.

4. Expand the **Copilot** option and select **To-Do**.

5. Select the **Keep it** button to add the generated to-do list to your page.

Chat with Copilot to understand your notes

Start in the Catering section of your notebook, and then perform the following tasks:

1. Select the Catering section, and right-click with your mouse to open the shortcut menu.

2. Expand the **Copilot** option and select **Summarize**.

3. Copilot will add a new page to your notebook called Summary, with a summary of the section. Select the **Keep it** button.

4. Click or tap in the Copilot prompt area, and enter the following prompt to ask a question about your notes: Which event had the most guests?

5. Ask another question: How many events have included mini quiches on the menu?

6. Ask another question: What was the feedback from the Tailspin Toys event?

Index

Plug into learning at

MicrosoftPressStore.com

The Microsoft Press Store by Pearson offers:

- Free U.S. shipping

- Buy an eBook, get multiple formats – PDF and EPUB – to use on your computer, tablet, and mobile devices

- Print & eBook Best Value Packs

- eBook Deal of the Week – Save up to 60% on featured title

- Newsletter – Be the first to hear about new releases, announcements, special offers, and more

- Register your book – Find companion files, errata, and product updates, plus receive a special coupon* to save on your next purchase

 Pearson